MARY BAKER EDDY

BY NORMAN BEASLEY

THE CROSS AND THE CROWN
The History of Christian Science

THE CONTINUING SPIRIT

THIS IS THE PROMISE

MARY BAKER EDDY

MARY BAKER EDDY

by NORMAN BEASLEY

Duell, Sloan and Pearce

New York

First edition

The writings of Mary Baker G. Eddy or literary property and material of The Christian Science Board of Directors of The Mother
Church. The First Church of Christ, Scientist, in Boston, Massachusetts, or its affiliated activities from which quotations, adaptations,
and abstracts appear herein, have been copyrighted in the United
States and other countries, either by the Trustees under the Will
of Mary Baker G. Eddy, The Christian Science Board of Directors, or
The Christian Science Publishing Society, and are used by permission whether or not the literary source is identified by notes; but
such consent carries no responsibility for the accuracy thereof.

The frontispiece is used by permission of The Christian Science
Publishing Society. Copyright, The Christian Science Publishing
Society.

The photograph appearing as the front endpaper is from *A
Banner in the Hills*, by George Ellis Moore, Appleton-Century-
Crofts, courtesy of the West Virginia Centennial Commission,
Charleston, West Virginia. The photograph appearing as the rear
endpaper is by Clemens Kalischer—dpi.

Affiliate of
MEREDITH PRESS
Des Moines & New York

Library of Congress Catalogue Card Number: 62-15467

MANUFACTURED IN THE UNITED STATES OF AMERICA FOR MEREDITH PRESS

VAN REES PRESS • NEW YORK

Contents

Introduction

Once, all there was of Christianity was an infant in a manger in Bethlehem. In 1866, all there was of Christian Science was a woman raised from a sickbed in Swampscott, Massachusetts.

Now, because the woman who was healed turned the lock in a door that had not been opened in more than fifteen hundred years, multitudes have found a whole new world.

By her act, Mary Baker Eddy turned a thousand other locks in a thousand other doors, behind which were teachings that have extended so far that they have more listeners now than they had only a moment ago.

MARY BAKER EDDY

CHAPTER ONE

The House by the Merrimack

THE New England into which Mary Morse Baker was born was a land still under the spell of the sermons of Jonathan Edwards that depicted God as a vengeful deity holding sinners over "the pit of hell . . . worthy of nothing else, but to be cast into the fire."

The date of her birth was July 16, 1821. The place was Bow, New Hampshire. Her father was Mark Baker. A stern, assertive, puritanical man, Mark Baker was the son of Joseph Baker and Marion Moor, whose father was Lieutenant William Moor. Her mother was Abigail Barnard Ambrose, daughter of Deacon Nathaniel Ambrose and Phoebe Lovejoy. A woman of earnest thoughtfulness, Abigail Baker was known throughout the countryside for her gentleness, her kindness, and the hospitality of her home.

The home was a frame, two-story dwelling, built on a hill overlooking a farm of about five hundred acres and the Merrimack River, which, joining with the Pemigewassett and Winnipesaukee rivers at Franklin, comes winding down from the White Mountains, flowing south and east to empty into the Atlantic Ocean at Newburyport, one hundred and ten miles from its source.

In the home were six children, of whom the youngest was Mary. The others were: Samuel Dow Baker, born July 8, 1808; Albert Baker, born February 5, 1810; George Sullivan

Baker, born August 7, 1812; Abigail Barnard Baker, born January 15, 1816; and Martha Smith Baker, born January 19, 1819.

In 1821, at the time Mary Morse Baker was born, the physical surroundings were not greatly changed from days in 1774 when the New Hampshire militia seized Fort William Henry, at Portsmouth, approximately forty miles to the east of Bow, and captured one hundred barrels of powder, fifteen light cannon, and a quantity of small arms, some of which were used by the patriot army at Bunker Hill in 1775. In the years of the War of Independence, as well as in the years before, every able-bodied man in New Hampshire was a trained soldier.

Between the years 1675 and 1762 the people of the province were engaged in six wars against the French and Indians. There were a few years of uncertain peace between the close of the French-Indian wars and the start of the War of Independence. In 1783 the country was at peace, but not for long. In 1812 war came again—and rendering distinguished service in all the conflicts were members of the families of Mark and Abigail Baker.

These two, Mark and Abigail, were married in 1807, so that by 1814, when peace returned, there were three children, all boys, in the house that was built on a hill in the village of Bow. It was a strict household.

A devout Congregationalist, Mark Baker held morning and evening devotions consisting of Bible reading and prayer. They were devotions that were sincere and never perfunctory. He asked a blessing and gave thanks before and after every meal. Sunday was observed as the Sabbath. It was a day of church attendance, rest, and prayer. In its observance of Sunday, and in its daily prayers, the Baker home was not greatly different from other New Hampshire households. Yet there was one difference.

It was a home where the clergy often gathered. The ministers enjoyed the warmth of Abigail Baker's welcome; they also enjoyed tilting doctrinal points with Mark Baker.

It has been said of New Hampshire, as well as of Massachusetts, that each was "a plantation of religion, and not of trade," although representatives of commercial houses in England were the first colonists in New Hampshire. In each colony, following the construction of family shelters, meetinghouses for church services and schoolhouses for education were built.

In numbers, at the close of the eighteenth century, the Congregationalists were well ahead of the Presbyterians and Baptists. Episcopalians came early but did not attain the numerical strength of the Methodists. There were Unitarians, Universalists, Quakers and other sects as well, so that at the close of the War of 1812 there were a score or more of Christian denominations.

Increasing numbers brought sectarian animosities that discolored the politics of almost all communities. By 1815 the animosities reached the state legislature, and four years later, in 1819, the so-called Toleration Act became law. By its passage, New Hampshire placed itself among the first of the states, if not the first, to implement Article One of the Constitution of the United States, with its guarantee of religious freedom.

It was not until after the union of New Hampshire with Massachusetts in 1641 (thus placing New Hampshire under Massachusetts school laws) that schooling was placed on a formal basis in New Hampshire. Suspecting Satan of always striving to prevent reading of the Scriptures, the Puritans enacted a law in 1647 which read, in part:

"It being one chiefe project of that old deluder, Sathan, to keep men from a knowledge of the Scriptures, as in former times, keeping them in an unknown tongue, so that at least, the time since and the meaning of the originall might be clouded with the false glosses of saint seeming deceivers; and that learning may not be buried in the grave of our forefathers in church and commonwealth, the Lord assisting our endeavors:

"It is therefore ordered by this Courte and the authority thereof, that every townshipp within this jurisdiction, after the Lord hath increased to the number of fifty howsholders, shall then forthwith appointe one within their towne, to teach all such children as shall resort to him, to write and read . . ."

In 1693, a year after New Hampshire and Massachusetts were separated and made two provinces by order of the Crown, the following law was passed in New Hampshire:

"It is enacted and ordained that for the building and repairing of meetinghouses, minister's houses, schoolhouses, and allowing a salary to a schoolmaster in each town within this Province, the selectmen, in the respective towns, shall raise money by an equal rate and assessment upon the inhabitants—and every town within the Province shall from and after the publication hereof, provide a school master for the supply of the town, on penalty of ten pounds; and for neglect thereof, to be paid, one half to their Majesties [William and Mary] and the other half to the poor of the town."

In the years that followed progress was continuous, so that when the children of Mark and Abigail Baker were coming of school age there were common schools everywhere in the state. There were a score of academies, the best known of which was Phillips Academy, at Exeter, which was founded in 1781. There was Dartmouth College, founded in 1769. There were more than 150 library associations. Of the states, New Hampshire was one of the leaders in education.

In 1830 a school building often consisted of one room, with facilities for twenty or more pupils. Older pupils sat on the rear benches, and each class took turns, coming from the seats to the open floor, standing in line and reciting. There was a wide range of subjects studied. Individual help from the teacher was not possible; at the same time, there were advantages for the brighter students. Daily they listened to instruction in subjects all the way from spelling to Latin grammar.

Corporal punishment was regarded as a necessary part of a child's schooling, and some teachers gained reputations as disciplinarians. A common instrument of correction was a black leather strap about a foot long, made of two strips of leather with a thin sheet of lead stitched between to give authority. When laid on outstretched hands, it was effective. Birch canes of a length sufficient to reach almost any pupil in the room were popular. There were milder forms of punishment such as sitting on nothing, stooping and holding a nail in the floor, sitting with the girls (for a boy), and standing in a corner; on rare occasions, a girl was punished by being made to sit with the boys.

More than one town planted enough wheat or rye to pay the teacher's salary, which was from four to six dollars a month, with families taking turns at boarding the teacher. Good grain could always be traded for whatever was needed, for specie usually was scarce, and paper money often was worthless.

Essentially, New Hampshire was an agricultural state when Mary Morse Baker was born. The forests had been pushed back; the soil was fertile; fields of grain were grown with great success; fruits were in abundance—apples, cherries, peaches, grapes; pasturage was lush. Cabins had given way to two-story frame dwellings, in the center of which were big chimneys to carry off the wood smoke from the fireplaces and stoves.

The great event of early spring was reducing maple sap to maple syrup and maple sugar; each fall beef and pork were salted and put down in the cellar, along with lamb and poultry to add to the winter's supply. Wool still was carded and spun and made into clothing; butter was churned; wild honey was gathered; wild strawberries, wild raspberries, and wild plums were gathered and preserved; wood ashes from the stoves and fireplaces were saved and used in making soft soap. Stones and rocks peppered the land; they were gathered and converted into fences.

These were a sturdy people. They worked hard, but each day was a day of thanks, and not of complaint. They were proud of their faith in God. To be sure, they differed on points of religion, but they looked upon life as a gift of divine favor. They tried to be worthy of the gift.

As the farms developed, industry began to appear. Tanneries, blacksmith shops, cobblers, clockmakers, carriage shops, gristmills, sawmills sprang up. Dams were thrown across streams to develop power; bridges were built; roads began to crisscross the state. Already in 1807 Concord, a few miles to the north of Bow, was an important community, and being named as state capital in that same year added to its importance. Spinning jennys were at work in New Ipswich; a few more years and a spinning mill at Amoskeag Falls, Manchester, was furnishing employment. In 1819 the power loom was introduced. It added to employment.

Yankee ingenuity was beginning to make itself felt. It was ingenuity that was born on the farms of New England where a boy learned to use the tools of a carpenter, a stonemason, a painter, a leatherworker, or a blacksmith—and became expert with that tool which was always within hand reach, his jackknife. The day when almost everyone was his own manufacturer was ending.

In 1825 three boys and three girls were growing up in the Baker family. Samuel was seventeen years old; Albert was fifteen; George was thirteen; Abigail was nine; Martha was seven; and Mary was four. Even at four Mary was a stranger to her father, but not to her mother; a stranger to her other brothers and sisters, but not to Albert.

Her father never forgot the morning at family devotions when, after the Bible reading, all eight members of the family were on their knees listening to his extemporaneous prayer. On this particular morning he became so immersed in words that his prayer was longer than a little girl's patience.

In possession of a shawl pin from a cushion on the table, she crawled along the floor to a point directly behind her exhorting parent and applied the pin to the nearest spot in his anatomy. In the immediate confusion, she made her escape.

Fair like her mother, to her mother she was a precious child who often went to sleep cradled in protecting arms while a gentle voice whispered in song:

> "How can I sleep while angels sing,
>   And hover o'er my bed;
>   And clap their wings in joy to Him
>   Who is their glorious Head."

Next to her mother, Albert was deepest in her love. Openly, she reached out to Albert to be the guardian of her confidences. With his chores and schoolwork over for the day, it was Albert who carried her over places when winter

snows lay heavy, who introduced her to the mystery of
flowers in spring, who showed her the canal boats being
drawn up the Merrimack on their way to Concord.

Abigail Ambrose Baker spent a great deal of time with
her youngest daughter. Early she recognized the presence
of an unusual child, and she often spoke of this conviction
to a neighbor, Mrs. Sarah Gault, saying: "I know these are
sinful thoughts for me to entertain, but I cannot shake
them off." Nor was Abigail Baker alone in this conviction.
On a good many occasions Mark Baker sought to break
down the child's sensitiveness to the sufferings of others.

As brothers often do, her brothers quarreled among themselves, sometimes to the extent of using their fists. Always
she came running, going from one brother to the other,
pleading with them to settle their differences without fighting and without ill will. Sometimes she was able to stop
the fighting; always she was able to prevent rancor.

Once her eldest brother, Sam, received a severe gash on
one of his legs when the axe slipped while he was chopping
cordwood. The wound did not heal. One night Mark Baker
picked up his youngest daughter—she was perhaps three
years old—and carried her to where Sam was lying, lifted
up the bedcovers, and placed Mary's hand upon the wound.
The leg healed, but for several days the frightened little
girl was also in bed, suffering from a high fever.

At the age of not more than eight years one of her favorite
Bible stories was of Daniel and how with "his window open
in his chamber toward Jerusalem, he kneeled three times a
day, and prayed, and gave thanks before his God." Emulat-
ing Daniel, the little girl left the house, went into the
woodshed where she could be alone, and there prayed not
three times daily but seven times. To make sure of the number of her visits, she put a chalk mark on the side of the
shed.

The family dog was named Ben, and, of evenings, it liked to be with the family in the sitting room. Especially was this true of winter evenings when a wood fire was blazing in the fireplace. On these evenings the dog was not always content to lie under the table, as trained, but preferred to sit with the family before the fire. To keep Ben out of trouble, Mary would order Ben, mentally, to "get under the table, and lie down." The dog would obey.[1]

The little girl was trying to be worthy of God. It was a quest she never neglected.

The Baker home was an orderly household. Each member of the family had his, or her, work to do, as Mark Baker did his. In addition to his work on the farm and his duties as a member of the Congregational Church, Mark Baker was clerk of the church, its delegate to church conferences, and quartermaster sergeant major in the New Hampshire militia. He was a strong admirer of Thomas Jefferson, an equally strong supporter of James Madison in his campaigns for the Presidency of the United States in 1808 and 1812 and of James Monroe for the same office in 1816.

This was a time when, as bringers of goods and information, the railroad, the telephone, and the telegraph were still dreams; news from Europe was two months on the ocean; news from Washington was from five to ten days on the road; news from Boston, about seventy miles distant over turnpikes, was nine hours by the fastest means of travel, the four-horse stagecoach.

As were other houses in Bow, the Baker home was lighted

[1] These two or three glimpses of her childhood were told by Mrs. Eddy to Adam Dickey, at different times at Chestnut Hill, in Boston, when Dickey was a member of her household. After Dickey's passing, in 1925, his recollections were copyrighted in 1927 by Lillian S. Dickey and renewed in 1955 by The Christian Science Board of Directors.

by candles. Unless one was going a distance, travel was on foot. Families walked as much as five miles to attend church services. Peddlers, on foot or on horseback, made regular calls, having in their packs everything that could be easily carried—cottons, silks, needles, pins, handkerchiefs, thread, and stockings being among the staples. The peddlers were always welcomed, and not only because of their wares. Frequently they were the only sources of news.

There was a Concord newspaper, and frequently, in the Baker home, there was a Boston newspaper. Treasured were newspapers of other days, one of which contained a full account of the death and funeral of George Washington. The papers belonged to Grandmother Marion Moor, whose husband, Joseph Baker, was among the first settlers of Bow. He had been a soldier in the War of Independence. Joseph Baker's mother was Hannah Lovewell, only daughter of Captain John Lovewell, famous in New England history as an Indian fighter.[2] And in the Baker home, of course, there were books, all well thumbed, including one that was read oftener than all the others. This one was the Bible.

It was this Bible that Mark Baker used in morning and evening prayers, the same Book that was at his side when the preachers gathered to argue over doctrine. Thus, from early childhood, the little girl was a listener as men talked of events which had to do with love and faith and fruition.

As the years followed each other, Albert Baker finished his common schooling in Bow, then entered Pembroke Academy in Pembroke, across the Merrimack River from Bow. As they grew older, Albert acquainted his sister with his own reading, so that at an early age she was sharing his love for literature. Her natural curiosity was such that her father became worried and persuaded himself into the be-

[2] See Appendix I for account of Captain Lovewell's last expedition.

lief that her brain was too large for her body, therefore going to school every day was not good for her.[3]

Abigail Baker and her youngest daughter read together
frequently. Among the family books often open between
them were Lindley Murray's *English Grammar* and the
Westminister Catechism for Young People.

Murray's *Grammar* was a book of three hundred pages
"adapted," as was said on the title page, "to different classes
of learners, with an Appendix containing rules and observations for assisting the more advanced students to write
with perspicuity and accuracy." The book was printed for
Longman and Rees, London, England. The *Westminister
Catechism,* a much smaller book, was printed in Philadelphia for the Presbyterian Board of Publication.

At the age of ten years, Mary was as familiar with the
three hundred pages in the *Grammar* as she was with the
Westminister Catechism, from which she had to recite each
Sunday. They were not easy steps to an education. Particularly was this true of the *Grammar.* The contents of
this book were divided into several parts: Orthography,
Etymology, Syntax, Prosody, and Punctuation; in addition,
there was an Appendix containing two parts, one part being
of three chapters and another part of four chapters.

As one result of the proximity of schools, all six of the
Baker children were introduced to books, each at an early
age. Of the six, Albert and Mary found the same interests.
Albert was twenty-one and a student at Dartmouth when
Mary was ten. Each was a learner. Each had the power of
application. Neither trifled with what each believed was
right. Each believed truth to be all one fabric. Each put
the test of truth to what was written or said.

[3] See page 10, *Retrospection and Introspection,* by Mary Baker Eddy.
Published by the Trustees Under the Will of Mary Baker Eddy. Copyright,
1891, 1892, copyright renewed 1919, 1920.

To pay for the cost of his education at Dartmouth Albert taught school and tutored. In his freshman year at college he joined the United Fraternity, a group having as its purpose "literary and forensic improvement." He was an excellent student and, as his instructors soon learned, he was not given to accepting, without discussion, their conclusions. He was not stubborn and not given to argument, but he was unyielding in what he believed to be right.

After four years he graduated from Dartmouth in 1834 with an A. B. degree and "the reputation of being one of the finest students who had ever attended that institution." [4] In his senior year he was elected to Phi Beta Kappa. In commencement exercises, he delivered the salutatory address. Upon graduation he continued his studies in the law offices of Franklin Pierce, in Hillsborough (now Hillsboro), New Hampshire.

In the Biography of Franklin Pierce,[5] there is this paragraph:

"Albert Baker was the son of Mark Baker, an old friend of the general's [Benjamin Pierce, father of Franklin], and while he was at Dartmouth the Pierces had become interested in the boy and had helped him. They invited him, when he graduated in 1834, to live at the homestead and study law with Franklin, the general paying his expenses during his novitiate."

Benjamin Pierce was Governor of New Hampshire in 1827–29, a veteran of the War of Independence, and had interests in common with Mark Baker. One interest was politics. Each was an active supporter of the Presidential ambitions of Andrew Jackson; each had supported Madison and Monroe. Each saw in Albert Baker a resemblance to Andrew Jackson. Particularly was Benjamin Pierce at-

---

[4] Browne's *History of Hillsborough*, Vol. 1.
[5] Ray Franklin Nichols, copyright, 1931.

tracted by the incisiveness of Albert Baker's mind; confi-
dently, he expected great things of the young Dartmouth
graduate.

Writing of those days in the history of the American Bar
in New Hampshire, Hosea W. Parker, after identifying
Daniel Webster, John S. Wells, Franklin Pierce, Charles G.
Atherton, John Sullivan, and James Wilson as being among
the outstanding names in New Hampshire law, went on
to say:

"Atherton and Pierce were often engaged in the trial
of the same cases, and the courtroom would be crowded
when these great lawyers met, and crowds listened to their
eloquence with breathless attention. It is said that Atherton
excelled in the trial of causes, and has few equals in this
department . . . In Franklin Pierce he had a formidable antagonist. He was a model advocate and had all the graces
of an orator. Attractive in his personality, with a clear, musical voice, cultivated in all the arts of public speaking, he
carried the juries along with him." [6]

Albert Baker was not long associated with Franklin Pierce
before the two were strong friends. Six years older and a
graduate of Bowdoin College, in Brunswick, Maine, Pierce,
while still in his twenties, had served two terms in the New
Hampshire legislature and was now a member of the Congress of the United States. Like his father, he saw in Albert
Baker not only a lawyer of unusual ability but a public
official of equal ability.

Being interested in the law, as well as in public life, it
was natural that Albert Baker should spend a great deal of
time asking questions of and listening to a man who would
be elected to the United States Senate before he was thirty-

[6] *State Builders,* copyright, 1903, by George Franklyn Willey. Heintze-
mann Press, Boston, Massachusetts.

five years old and to the Presidency of the United States before he was fifty years old.

The four years at Dartmouth, and the two years in the
law offices of Franklin Pierce, did not separate brother and
sister. There were vacations. During them the two were
together a great deal. During his vacations Albert studied
Hebrew, and he not only imparted to his sister a knowledge
of Hebrew but gave her lessons in Latin and Greek as well.
She listened eagerly to his discourses on the classical languages; he listened sympathetically to her emerging spiritual thoughts and her disagreement with harsh church doctrines that were offered as truth.

Together, they came to know the wonder of the New
England seasons and watched them change, as generations
of their Puritan ancestors also had watched.

Spring: The impatience of a brook coming down from
the hills . . . the willows offering catkins but holding back
their slender leaves . . . frogs calling from the swamps . . .
a robin greeting the sunrise, an oriole's nest swinging from
the outstretched fingers of an elm tree . . . a sudden south
wind bringing down a shower of apple blossoms . . .

The world alive, teeming with life and sound in summer
. . . wild roses along the stone fences in the back fields, fra-
grance and simple beauty . . . swallows lining up in military
precision along the eaves of the barn; hummingbirds dart-
ing in and out; dragonflies hovering . . . long afternoons;
the high song of the locust; night birds swooping and feed-
ing on the wind; dusk sprinkled with fireflies . . .

All of a sudden glistening green leaves are dull green;
overnight, it seems, they become brilliant with every color
and every hue caught in a flaming display that spreads over
the hills and across the valleys. Nature had opened its doors
to autumn . . . wild asters crowd the roads and beckon from
the fields; pumpkins yellow on the vines, the milkweed's

silken floss riding the winds ... squirrels and chipmunks gathering and storing nuts and seeds; crickets finding shelter ... overhead, the chatter of wild geese, flying south ...

Snow fell, and the world was new. White and clean and beautiful it covered the land, reshaping the hills and silhouetting leafless trees where gathered a company of crows gossiping the early arrival of winter ... ice thickening on the ponds; frost biting deep ... snug in its cocoon, a butterfly sleeping ... January thaw, winter again; February winds and deep snows ... the vernal equinox; warmth coming into the sun; big, clinging, wet snowflakes sifting down; sap pails hanging from the spiles in the bush maples ...

The miracle of bud and seed never went unnoticed by succeeding generations of the descendants of the Puritans; nor did Thanksgiving, Christmas, and Easter lose their flavor. Thanksgiving remained a day set aside for national examination to make certain that spiritual growth had kept pace with the harvest; Christmas remained a day when prophecy shone on the uplifted faces of mankind; Easter remained a day when troubled questions found sure answers in the reflected rays of a glorious morning.

After spending two years with Franklin Pierce in Hillsborough, Albert Baker transferred to the law offices of Richard Fletcher (afterwards a justice of the Supreme Judicial Court of Massachusetts) in Boston; and, after spending twenty-nine years of their married lives on the farm in Bow, Mark and Abigail Baker moved to a newly acquired farm near Sanbornton Bridge, twenty-odd miles north of Bow, but on the other side of the Merrimack River. The year was 1836. Mary Morse Baker was fifteen years old. Never strong physically, it may be assumed she was not unhappy in the new surroundings.

As a candidate for church membership in the Congrega-

tional Church (of which denomination her parents were
members for half a century), Mary would be asked if she
would accept John Calvin's doctrine of predestination,
under which sinners and nonbelievers were doomed to
everlasting punishment in the fires of hell.

This request would bring back another day, when her
father, seeking to save her from being guilty of the crime
of heresy, sought to force her by vehement argument into
embracement of the doctrine. Instead of yielding, she protested that vengeance could not be in the nature of God,
and she became so upset that her parents summoned a
doctor. He found her suffering from a fever.

Her mother bathed her hot forehead, and comforted her
by asking her to do what she often had done—go to God
in prayer, asking His guidance. Deeply, earnestly, and forgetting all else, she prayed. With her prayer in Another's
keeping, all doubt as to what her answer would be when
asked to accept Calvin's doctrine as a condition of church
membership was gone. Gone, too, was the fever, causing
the doctor to speak of the event as a miracle.

In 1838 (she was then seventeen years old), with the congregation listening, the minister did ask the expected question. She replied, maintaining, as she later wrote, that she
"was willing to trust God, and take my chance of spiritual
safety with my brothers and sisters,—not one of whom had
then made any profession of religion,—even if my creedal
doubts left me outside the doors." [7]

Instead of condemning, the minister sought explanation
and finding not willfulness, but resolute conviction, admitted her to partake of communion and membership in the
Congregational Church.

In Sanbornton Bridge, Mark Baker found himself in dis-

[7] *Retrospection and Introspection,* p. 14.

agreement with another daughter, this one being his eldest daughter, Abigail. Upon moving from Bow, Baker used a farm wagon as a means of transportation for his family. The day was not long delayed when the twenty-year-old Abigail informed her father that she had taken her last ride in the wagon.

There were differences in opinions between Mark Baker and all six of his children. As they grew older the three boys made their own ways; the three girls married and went into their own homes.

Mark Baker was not a penurious man, nor always intolerant; but he was frugal, and he was highly respected. While still living in Bow he represented the town in a dispute with the community of Louden. Representing Louden was Franklin Pierce. Baker won. In Sanbornton Bridge, he was superintendent of the Sunday School of the Congregational Church and a trustee of the Sanbornton Academy.

In Boston, Albert Baker was continuing his law studies in the office of Richard Fletcher. To meet expenses he was forced to sell his classical books and to borrow money. These problems he kept to himself as he continued to correspond with his younger brother and his youngest sister. In his book, *Historical Sketches,*[8] Clifford P. Smith refers to one of these letters. Under date of March 27, 1837, Albert wrote:

"My dear Sister,
"I have an opportunity of sending a letter by a friend of mine, Mr. Harrison Andrews, who is going to Sandbornton with the intention of attending the academy. I take great pleasure in introducing him to your acquaintance. You will find him a sterling fellow, a little enthusiastick, but none of Sol Wilson about him. What is that poor devil doing? I

[8] Copyright, 1934, 1936, 1941. The Christian Science Publishing Society.

hope you treat him as he deserves, with entire neglect. Abi will recollect Andrews' sister, a particular friend of hers. He is a very close student, and is as much given to *discursive talking* as yourself, though he has not quite so much poetry at his command. . . .

"Your affect. br.

"A. Baker"

The "Sol" Wilson referred to was Solomon Wilson, an instructor in the Sanbornton Academy; the "Abi" was their sister, Abigail.

On November 23, 1837, in a letter to George, his younger brother, Albert gave this advice:

"My rule is *to do the best I can,* and whatever happens, if it cannot be avoided, to submit cheerfully. Is not this true philosophy? Now apply this rule. Have you done all you could do? If so, be content with the event; if not, learn by the past how to regulate the future."

In 1837, Albert was twenty-seven years old; George was twenty-five; Mary was sixteen and, when her health permitted, was attending Sanbornton Academy. George was away from home, living in Connecticut.

CHAPTER TWO

A Promise Is Made

IN Boston, Mary Baker's favorite brother, Albert, was completing his year of apprenticeship in the law offices of Richard Fletcher and was debating, within himself, his own future. He could remain in Massachusetts and practice law; he could go west and practice law in the Territory of Wisconsin; or he could return to New Hampshire and practice law.

Having been admitted to the practice of law in Massachusetts, Albert's future was bright. That was Fletcher's opinion, and, considering the standing of the testifier in the legal profession, it was an opinion that could not be put aside easily. At Dartmouth, Albert had been friendly with a fellow student named James W. Grimes. For Grimes, no place in the United States offered the opportunities that existed in the town of Burlington, which was in the District of Iowa, which, in turn, was in the Territory of Wisconsin.

After graduation, writing to Albert from Burlington, Grimes pressed his case, saying Iowa soon would be a territory, then a state.[1] Burlington, he said, would be its capital, and he urged Albert not to delay his participation in the huge expansion that was sure to come. The call of

[1] Iowa became a territory in 1838, and a state in 1846. Burlington was the first capital. Among Iowa's early governors was James W. Grimes; among its early United States senators was the same James W. Grimes, who tried so hard to persuade Albert Baker to migrate.

pioneering was strong; but, strong as it was, from New
Hampshire he heard a stronger call.

Concord was the capital of New Hampshire, as Washington was the capital of the United States. As a member of the
United States Senate, Franklin Pierce was spending so much
time in the two cities that he was finding it necessary to
move his law office from Hillsborough to Concord. To
do that, he had to have someone to look after continuing
business affairs in Hillsborough, but, more importantly, he
needed someone he could trust to watch over and supply
the needs of his aging parents, whose home was in Hillsborough.

Communicating with Baker, Pierce explained the situation and made the request. Mindful of the friendship
between his own father and General Pierce; mindful, too,
of the help the Pierces had given him, it was a request Albert Baker could not refuse, although sickness would cause
a delay in his departure from Boston. On April 23, 1837,
he wrote his brother George, saying he had done no work
since the first day of March, had been in a hospital, but now
was preparing to go to Hillsborough.

He was not long in Hillsborough before he was representing property owners along the right of way of a railroad
that was being built to link up Concord with Manchester
and Boston. Begun in 1835, it was the first railroad in the
state. At about the same time he was employed to represent
a number of stagecoach companies in litigation defining the
responsibilities of such companies as carriers of passengers.

These important clients were an asset to his fast-growing
law practice. Nor was he long in Hillsborough before he
was being importuned to represent the district in the New
Hampshire legislature.

Judging by the frequent letters that passed between the
two men, it was solicitation that had the full support of

Franklin Pierce, as well as the backing of Charles G. Atherton, congressman from the surrounding area.

In 1839, when twenty-nine years old, Albert was elected to the first of two successive terms in the state legislature. As a member, he was particularly interested in legislation affecting individual freedom. He concerned himself with legislation involving New Hampshire with southern states; he supported legislation prohibiting imprisonment for debt as well as that which concerned the protection of bank accounts and the limiting of powers conferred on corporations. Not overlooked was his insistence upon economy in the administration of government.

By mail, he discussed certain legal matters concerning slavery with John C. Calhoun, who resigned the vice-presidency of the United States to become a United States senator from South Carolina; he corresponded with Franklin Pierce on a multitude of subjects; among the most frequent recipients of his thoughts and his views were his mother, his sister, and his brother George. He was in demand for speeches, and his work in the New Hampshire legislature was of such a caliber that he was being pressed by Pierce, by Atherton, and by other state leaders to accept promotion to the Congress of the United States.

When he could, he visited Sanbornton Bridge. For two people, brother and sister, they were visits that always were too short, always over too soon. In these exchanges not only did Albert see his sister as their cousin, D. Russell Ambrose, pictured her—"a frail, fair young maiden with transparent skin and brilliant blue eyes, cheerful, hopeful, enthusiastic" —but he saw more. He saw an emerging quality that increased his interest, already strong. The quality was the independence of her thought.

The difference in their ages—eleven years—was not evident in their conversations. He respected her sincerity by extending his own. He must have thought many times of her refusal to accept the doctrine of predestination as a condition of membership in the Congregational Church. As a boy he was present at the family devotions and with his parents, his sisters, and his brothers was a regular attendant at church services. Away from home at Dartmouth, in Boston, and in Hillsborough, he was not so constant.

This was not because of an absence of interest. Rather, it was due to dissatisfaction with the Christianity that was being preached. Ten years had passed since he was living at home (he was thirty years old; the year was 1840) and he was always eager to read, and discuss with his sister, her writing efforts, especially the poems, in which she was disclosing a deep religious feeling. From the time she was seven years old (she was now nineteen) they had shared a secret. When she was seven she confided in him that some day she would write a book, and just as seriously he promised to help her.

The desire to write had grown. At Sanbornton Academy, where she was a student at sixteen, two of her teachers singled her out for encouragement. The teachers were Sarah J. Bodwell, principal of the Academy, and Dyer H. Sanborn, author of Sanborn's *Grammar*. Whatever her activity, whether it took the form of a trip to Boston, a wedding at which she was a bridesmaid, or letters that she wrote to her brothers, Albert and George, she made it a vehicle of communication for her thoughts.

During Albert's visits, the probabilities are that talks between them were mainly of writing and religion. Her facility with words, and her ability to weave them into patterns of prose or poetry, pleased him. When he criticized he did not fail to sprinkle his words with encouragement. It was tutoring for which she was grateful.

She listened as carefully to his opinions about writing as

he listened to her thoughts about religion. Already she was referring to God as "the Source of all good"; was saying "there is one who has promised to be a 'father to the fatherless,' and if we go to him, we shall indeed find consolation"; and in a number of poems [2] had disclosed a strong awareness of God. In Albert was this same awareness.

Shadowing the happiness each felt in the other's presence was the concern of each for the health of the other. Three years before, Albert had written his brother George, saying that when he came to Hillsborough after graduating from Dartmouth he "never expected to see" Mary again; and, in the same year, in another letter to his brother, he commented upon his own health as being "unusually good." Like his sister, Albert was not strong physically.

Returning to Hillsborough from his last visit, he plunged into his duties as a legislator and the work of his office. To these responsibilities he added another. He agreed to become a candidate for the Congress of the United States. On October 17, of the same year, at the age of thirty-one, he was dead—from overwork, some said.

His place in the heart of his youngest sister was permanent. In the years that awaited her she often spoke of him, and in *Retrospection and Introspection* she preserved one of the tributes that marked his passing:

"Albert Baker was a young man of uncommon promise. Gifted with the highest order of intellectual powers, he trained and schooled them by intense and almost incessant study throughout his short life. He was fond of investigating abstruse and metaphysical principles, and he never forsook them until he had explored their every nook and corner, however hidden and remote. Had life and health been spared to him, he would have made himself one of the most distinguished men in the country. As a lawyer he was able

[2] *Poems,* pp. 18, 32, 58, 60, 62.

and learned, and in the successful practice of a very large business. He was noted for his boldness and firmness, and for his powerful advocacy of the side he deemed right. His death will be deplored, with the most poignant grief, by a large number of friends, who expected no more than they realized from his talents and acquirements. This sad event will not soon be forgotten. It blights too many hopes; it carries with it too much of sorrow and loss. It is a public calamity." [3]

In 1832, Samuel Dow Baker, eldest of Mark Baker's six children, was married to Eliza Ann Glover, sister of George Washington Glover, a contractor and builder of Charleston, South Carolina. With Samuel Baker, Glover had learned the building trade in Boston. At the wedding he was attracted by Mary Baker, fair-haired and luminous-eyed sister of the groom. She was eleven years old. At one point in their conversation Glover pulled her to his knee, asking "How old are you?" She told him. Banteringly he said he would be back in five years and would make her his wife. In embarrassed confusion and to his delight, she jumped off his knee, ran into another room, and hid herself.

Five years later he did come back, this time to be a guest at the wedding of Abigail Baker to Alexander Tilton. Apparently, Glover had forgotten the teasing interlude because it was not repeated. Seven more years passed. This time, on a street in Tilton, New Hampshire, Mary saw a man walking in the same direction she was going. Hurrying her steps, she overtook the man she thought was her brother, and, slapping him on the back, she said, laughing, "You're all dressed up!" The man was not her brother. It was George Washington Glover.

After the moment of confusion that followed recognition,

[3] *New Hampshire Patriot and State Gazette,* Oct. 21, 1841.

Glover saw not a little girl of ten, nor a maiden of fifteen, but an attractive woman; from that moment, almost, there was understanding between them. They were married on December 10, 1843. As they were leaving on their honeymoon, Abigail Baker gave to Glover a letter which he was to open when the ship on which they were traveling from Boston to Charleston was "midway on [the] journey south." In the letter were two verses composed by Lydia H. Sigourney, at the time a popular American poet:

> Deal gently, thou, when, far away,
>   'Mid stranger scenes her feet shall rove,
> Nor let thy tender cares decay—
>   The soul of woman lives on love;
> And should'st thou, wondering, mark a tear
>   Unconscious from her eyelid break,
> Be pitiful, and soothe the fear
>   That man's strong heart can ne'er partake.
>
> A mother yields her gem to thee,
>   On the true breast to sparkle rare—
> She places 'neath thy household tree,
>   The idol of her fondest care;
> And by trust to be forgiven,
>   When judgment wakes in terror wild,
> By all thy treasured hopes of heaven,
>   Deal gently with my darling child.

In Charleston, the young bride quickly objected to the use of slaves and sought to persuade her husband to give them their freedom. This was not possible, he explained, without approval by the state legislature in the form of special legislation. It was legislative action that was slow and not easy to obtain. Besides, as he also explained, the slaves represented property values he could not afford to lose.

In February, Glover was called to Wilmington, North Carolina, on business. Four months later he was dead, a victim of yellow fever. Mary Baker Glover was told that months, and perhaps years, would be needed to close up the affairs of her husband's estate. She stayed on in Wilmington for several weeks and then decided to return to her parents' home. But before doing so, she freed the slaves and, as best she could, completed some of the details remaining from her husband's business.

The return trip to New Hampshire was lonely; and, a dozen years afterwards, she wrote of this loneliness without her husband:

> Ye scenes my heart still loves to own,
> Ye scenes which thrill deep notes of woe,
> Departed joys, blest friendships flown,
> Sad in the south wind murmur low.

> Yet stay! Ah! whither wouldst thou roam,
> Gay, restless essence bounding free?
> Bliss to my bosom were the boon,
> Of wings, to wander back with thee.[4]

Two and a half months after returning to New Hampshire, the widow gave birth to a son. In changing degrees of fair and poor health, she provided for her son, whom she named George Washington Glover, after his father, by teaching school and writing for New Hampshire newspapers.

[4] Original copyright 1911, The Curtis Publishing Company, Philadelphia, Pa. The poem contains ten verses and is entitled *Wind of the South*. This poem, along with letters, all written by Mary Baker Glover, was found in an old leather trunk in the attic of George Baker's home in Tilton, New Hampshire, after his passing.

On November 21, 1849, Abigail Ambrose Baker, whose love was her daughter's most tender possession, was gone. Flooded by grief, Mary wrote to her brother George under date of November 22:

> My Dear Bro': This morning looks on us bereft of a Mother! Yes, that angel on earth is now in Heaven! I have prayed for support to write this letter, but I find it impossible to tell you particulars at this time. She failed rapidly from the time you saw her, but her last struggles were most severe; her physician spoke of it as owing to so strong a constitution. Oh! George, what is left of earth to *me!* But oh, my Mother! She has *suffered long with me;* let me then be willing she should now *rejoice,* and I bear on till I follow her. I cannot write more. My grief overpowers me. Write to me.
>
> Your affec' Sister,
Mary.
>
> Died last night at half-past seven o'clock; will be buried next Saturday. I wish you could be here.

With her son, Mrs. Glover continued to live in her father's house for another year, after which he married again. The new arrangements made it necessary for her to move to the nearby house of her sister Abigail, who was now married to Alexander Hamilton Tilton. But Mrs. Tilton was unwilling to take in Mary's child, a strong, sturdy lad of six.

Without funds, she finally yielded to the demand that she agree to arrangements that had been made to provide for the care of her son elsewhere.

Mahala Sanborn, a woman who had served as a helper in

Mark and Abigail Baker's home in her childhood, was now the wife of Russell Cheney. The couple lived near North Groton, in the foothills of the White Mountains some forty miles distant. Not only was Mrs. Cheney willing, but she was anxious to co-operate with the wishes of the Baker family. The widow was promised that when, physically, she was able to care for her son he would be returned.

Writing of a parting that was not easy, she said:

> The night before my child was taken from me, I knelt by his side throughout the dark hours, hoping for a vision of relief from this trial. The following lines are taken from my poem, "Mother's Darling," written after this separation:—
>
> Thy smile through tears, as sunshine o'er the sea,
>   Awoke new beauty in the surge's roll!
> Oh, life is dead, bereft of all, with thee,—
>   Star of my earthly hope, babe of my soul.[5]

Some of the tension in Mark Baker's home disappeared when Abigail Tilton offered her sister a home. Alexander Hamilton Tilton was owner of several woolen mills, and it was after his family that the town of Tilton was named. For a time after moving in with the Tiltons, Mary Baker Glover's condition showed little improvement. Daily, Abigail took her on carriage rides; after a few months she was able to walk unaided, and then became strong enough to care for her own needs.

In his book, *Historical Sketches*, Clifford P. Smith referred to this period, saying: ". . . in 1850–1853, her circumstances included lack of dependable health, limited earnings, living in a home as a dependent, widowhood, separation from her child, and attentions from several apparently de-

---

[5] *Retrospection and Introspection*, p. 20.

sirable suitors who might or might not fulfill the obligations of a husband and a stepfather."

Among the suitors was Dr. Daniel Patterson, a dentist, and a relative of her father's second wife. Well regarded in the community, Dr. Patterson was sympathetic with Mrs. Glover's repeated assertion to the effect that "if I am to marry again, the compelling reason will be to get back my child so he will have a home of his own." Pressing his suit, Dr. Patterson talked with Mark Baker. A blunt-speaking man, Baker probably told the dentist that, from childhood, his daughter had been "sickly." Having studied homoeopathy, along with dentistry, Patterson held out hope that in homoeopathy he might find a way to establish Mary's health.

At the time the widow was described as being "very pretty, her cheeks very red, her hair was brown curls, she had beautiful eyes . . . her bonnet was white straw and had a pink rose in each side, with her curls she was just lovely."

Patterson continued his attentions. They married in 1853 and made their home in Franklin, a few miles distant, where the dentist had an office. She was not long married before she realized that her husband's frequent excuses for not taking her to North Groton to recover her son were caused, at least in part, by the fact that his income from his practice was scarcely sufficient to support two people; and, instead of increasing, his was an income that was shrinking because his practice was declining.

For two years they lived in a pinched financial atmosphere. Then the dentist borrowed enough money to buy a house, one hundred acres of land, and a sawmill in North Groton. In the new surroundings, Dr. Patterson operated the sawmill and practiced dentistry on the side. The former maid allowed the mother to see her son, but the visits were few because permission was infrequent. After a year of infrequent visits Mrs. Patterson lost sight of her son. Taking the boy with them, the Cheneys had moved to Minnesota.

Under the strain of the disappearance of her son into a remote territory, and the added weight of burdensome debt, the woman's health (that is, whatever measure of health she had) collapsed.

Altogether, the Pattersons lived in North Groton five years, and it was in this period that a blind girl came to the house asking for employment. Unable to send the girl away, Mrs. Patterson, who at the time was confined to her bed, told the stranger to stay. The housekeeper quit. The blind girl made her home with the Pattersons for some time.

In 1860, the dentist's creditors took over the sawmill, the land, the house, and everything in the house, including books, a gold watch, and furniture, which Mrs. Patterson had pledged as security for her husband's borrowings.

The ensuing six years found the Pattersons living in a number of towns in New Hampshire and Massachusetts. There was some improvement in her health, but no improvement in family finances. These years saw the couple nearing final separation, with the dentist abandoning his wife on at least two occasions, only to return asking forgiveness. Trying to make the marriage a success, she accepted his explanations although she knew they were not true.

In the periods of separation, Mrs. Patterson resumed writing for New Hampshire newspapers, and what she wrote found an immediate market. During all these years Mrs. Patterson wrote many letters to her son. She later learned that her letters were kept from the boy and that finally the boy had been told that his mother was dead. About this time she received word from her sister Abigail that the boy had run away from his foster-parents' home, and had enlisted in the Northern Army in the War Between the States. Soon after that the mother and son corresponded.

Along with her writing, she undertook the study of homoeopathy. In the early years of her marriage to Dr. Patterson she had familiarized herself with the contents of whatever books and literature he had on the subject. It was an interest that began in her girlhood. When she was about eighteen years old, she was sick. In Concord lived a doctor named Morrill, a homoeopath who had been successful in treating cases in which followers of allopathy encountered difficulties. With some misgivings, Mark Baker sent for him, although, as Mrs. Patterson remembered, her father, while thinking of Morrill as "a fine fellow," felt that "he must have gone mad to take up homoeopathy." At the time, homoeopathy was a fairly new theory in medicine. However, the girl responded to Morrill's treatment.

Remembering her studies, and strongly suspecting homoeopaths were on the right track in their limited use of drugs, Mrs. Patterson accepted as a patient a woman who was suffering from dropsy. The attending physician regarded the case as "hopeless." Instead of continuing the usual doses, she began administering a high attenuation of the drug the medical doctor had prescribed.

The patient began showing signs of recovery. Then came a relapse. Instead of continuing the drug, Mrs. Patterson substituted a high attenuation of common table salt. There followed a complete turnaround in the patient's condition. Taking away the salt, she substituted a sugar pellet. The patient continued to gain. Then the patient was told she needed no more "medicine." She went without it for three days, then told Mrs. Patterson, "I feel some of the old symptoms." More sugar pellets were administered. The patient recovered.

Mrs. Patterson sent samples of the salt attenuation to Dr. Charles T. Jackson, in Boston, for analysis. A chemist, Dr. Jackson reported: "I cannot find a particle of salt in it."

This experience, Mary Baker Eddy recalled in 1907, "was a falling apple to me—it made plain to me that mind governed the whole question of . . . recovery." [6]

To find the answer to the question of "What mind?" she began serious investigations into spiritualism, hypnotism, and mesmerism. In them she found no answers, only deception.

Again in need of healing because of her recurring sickness, this time the result of the continuing derelictions of her husband, she turned again to the Scriptures—Jeremiah's prayer, "Heal me, O Lord, and I shall be healed"; the exhortation of the Psalmist to God "who forgiveth all thine iniquities; who healeth all thy diseases"—and told her sister Abigail of the experience that was "a falling apple" to her.

Still searching for the mind that governed the recovery of the woman suffering from dropsy, she suggested to her sister that this mind was God. Generous but strong-willed, Abigail scoffed at the suggestion and urged her sister to go to Hill, New Hampshire, and see Dr. W. T. Vail, who operated what was called the Granite State Water Cure. Mrs. Patterson said she preferred going to Portland, Maine, where a magnetic healer named Quimby gave no medicine.

Angrily, Abigail characterized Quimby as a faker, not a healer but a hypnotist who had traveled New England as a sideshow attraction at county fairs. This was partly true. Quimby had started out as an avowed mesmerist and had traveled New England as such. Abigail's youngest sister agreed to place herself in the care of Dr. Vail. Grateful for the generosity that supplied ample funds for a protracted stay, if necessary, Mrs. Patterson went to Hill. She was not there long before she lost whatever confidence she may have had in water treatments and, with several other patients, went to Portland, Maine.

[6] Testimony before a Board of Masters in Concord, New Hampshire.

In Phineas P. Quimby she met a man who helped her and, keenly interested, she talked with him, convinced that his healings had nothing to do with the manipulation of the head he practiced but that God was the power behind them. They discussed his "theory," which she later came to understand and repudiate as mental suggestion but which at that point she tried to link up with her own thoughts of God and with the many Scriptural passages which identified God as the healer.

Quimby was in his own way a religious man. He asked many questions, and they exchanged many views about God. For the first time, probably, since the passing of her mother, the sick woman had a sympathetic listener to thoughts that, however incomplete, were so foreign to popular theology as to bring instant dispute.

The woman and the healer had many talks. Quimby disclosed, and gave to her, written notes of his own observations, his theory, his belief in God, and asked her to put them in better shape. She did so, returned the manuscripts, and explained her changes.

After a stay in Portland, much improved in health, Mrs. Patterson returned to her sister's home in Tilton. There were several more visits to Quimby, one of them lasting several months, and various lengthy visits to friends. In 1864 she went to Lynn, Massachusetts, to make an effort to repair her marriage. It was beyond repair. Patterson met her with apologies, and with more explanations. She was to learn that his promises were worthless.

The dentist's disappearance on one occasion had been caused by his elopement with a patient who was the wife of a prominent citizen of the community. Enraged, the husband threatened to swear out a warrant for Dr. Patterson's arrest but was dissuaded from taking the action by the abandoned wife. She asked the aggrieved husband to forgive and to become reconciled with his wife. This was done. In the years of her marriage to the dentist, Mrs. Patterson had a number of similar experiences. The day of final separation was inevitable.[7]

[7] She obtained a divorce in 1873, charging desertion in preference to the more serious charge of adultery. In her possession were affidavits of her husband's guilt. She chose the lesser charge, feeling it was less damaging to Dr. Patterson's professional standing.

CHAPTER THREE

The Year of Discovery

I N the forty-fifth year of a life bounded by lowly ways, Mrs. Mary Patterson came to her appointed task. The day was Sunday, February 4, 1866. Three days previously she had fallen on an icy sidewalk, sustaining injuries to her spine and back. A doctor was called. The injuries were such that he described her condition as critical. Now the woman was lying in an upstairs bedroom in a frame dwelling in Swampscott, reading her Bible.

Open before her was the ninth chapter of the Book of St. Matthew and the story of the "man sick of the palsy, lying on a bed: and Jesus seeing their faith said unto the sick of the palsy; Son, be of good cheer; thy sins be forgiven thee."

> And, behold, certain of the scribes said within themselves, This man blasphemeth.
>
> And Jesus knowing their thoughts said, Wherefore think ye evil in your hearts?
>
> For whether is easier, to say, Thy sins be forgiven thee; or to say, Arise, and walk?
>
> But that ye may know that the Son of man hath power on earth to forgive sins, (then saith he to the sick of the palsy,) Arise, take up thy bed, and go unto thine house.
>
> And he arose, and departed to his house.

Returning to the verses, her eyes lingered on one verse:

> For whether is easier, to say, Thy sins be for-
> given thee; or to say, Arise, and walk?

She perceived that the same Principle healed both sin and sickness; and, in so perceiving, she saw in the words of the Master the golden thread that forever holds man in the image of his Maker. Humbly, reverently, she felt the presence of God. She rose from her bed, healed.

Clinging to the moment of Truth that brought healing, she sought to understand that she might take it to others so they might be healed.

In that year, Abigail offered to build her sister a home and promised to settle upon her enough money to make her independent so she could devote all her time to writing—if she would give up what, to Abigail, was an insane delusion that prayer could heal the sick.

To give up her search for the Source of all healing was something Abigail's youngest sister refused to do.

To her appointed task the woman who became Mary Baker Eddy brought no money, no deed of note, no acclaim, no position in society—but she did bring humility, and she did bring unselfishness. Perhaps, in the larger sense, those two things are one and the same thing; but, whether two things or one, what she brought was enough—although three years were to pass before she found the way to enable others to do what was done for her.

She found the way by going, in prayer, to the same Source to which Jesus went.

She went to God.

Of those three years, she afterwards wrote:

> The search was sweet, calm, and buoyant with
> hope, not selfish nor depressing. I knew the Prin-
> ciple of all harmonious Mind-action to be God,

and that cures were produced in primitive Christian healing by holy, uplifting faith; but I must know the Science of this healing, and I won my way to absolute conclusions through divine revelation, reason, and demonstration. The revelation of Truth in the understanding came to me gradually and apparently through divine power.[1]

Doubtless, to the woman's inspired sense, "the search was sweet, calm, and buoyant with hope," but, in a human sense, it was a period in which, disowned by her sisters and brothers, she supported herself on an income of less than twenty dollars a month, lived in boardinghouses, made and mended her own clothes, spent most of her time in a single room reading and studying the Scriptures, and was shunned and gossiped about as only a small town in New England, in the mid-eighteen-hundreds, could shun, and gossip about, a woman who was living alone, separated from her husband.

On Sunday, she attended services in the Congregational Church and, of evenings, took occasional walks to Red Rock, a picturesque formation jutting into the Atlantic Ocean, a distance of two or three miles from her boardinghouse. Around the supper table she talked, sometimes, of her Bible studies, and gossip had it that she was rewriting the sacred pages. The town was small, and her words were not long reaching the ears of the clergy, who called on her in protest.

It was not easy to put into words what this woman was experiencing, but somewhere on the hidden shore where light disputes darkness, a victory was being won. She spent no time trying to rectify the past. That would but delay her work. She knew that what was right would remain and what was wrong would vanish. She sharply disagreed with much of what was being preached and practiced as Christianity,

[1] *Science and Health,* p. 109.

but she held in honored respect sincere workers of all faiths who, struggling in great cities or in the lonely places of the earth, sought to bring comfort to the afflicted.

At the same time this acknowledgment did not prevent her from realizing that the preaching from Christian pulpits was little changed from other centuries or not changed at all, except, perhaps, for a greater emphasis on pageantry and ritual and dogma. To her, this was not the way that leads into the presence of God.

In searching for the way into the future every Christian knows to be the only possible future, she was mindful of the words spoken at the well of Jacob:

> The hour cometh, and now is, when the true worshippers shall worship the Father in spirit and in truth: for the Father seeketh such to worship him.
> God is a Spirit: and they that worship him must worship him in spirit and in truth.

Unnoticed but by the very few, a woman, forty-five years old, was setting out to reclaim for Christian teachings long-neglected spiritual values, and to obey the command of the Teacher: "Heal the sick, cleanse the lepers, raise the dead, cast out devils: freely ye have received, freely give."

Through the centuries many denominations were formed, all identifying themselves with Christianity, but none included in its tenets obedience to the command or acknowledgment of its imperativeness. She was sure the words of Christ Jesus were the words of God; she was sure Jesus was able to heal because he knew more about God than did other men.

She knew that for almost three centuries after the Ascension healing was an integral part of Christian doctrine; she knew, too, that healing was lost after Emperor Constantine gave Christianity political status in Rome.

Believing it was the Truth Jesus represented that restored the man sick with the palsy and herself as well, although more than eighteen hundred years separated the events, she began her search into what she believed was God's law, spiritual law.

In spiritual law she perceived law that heals; law that is changeless, everlasting good; law that shelters all who obey it; law that is not affected by praise, by pageantry, by ritual, or by burnt offerings; law that knows no intermediaries; law that imposes no penalties for violation, but law that requires of each individual that he cleanse himself before he can partake of its fullness.

In setting out to prove the supremacy of spiritual law, she had her counterpart in the physical scientist, so called, who spends his days and nights, if need be, in a research laboratory studying the laws of matter.

Surrounded by test tubes and acids and equipment quite as complex to the average human mind as the subjects studied, physical scientists have a long list of accomplishments. Each day they are accumulating new knowledge by the use of instruments such as the electron microscope which measures to 40-*billionth* of an inch, or the electron microprobe, by which investigators often are able to determine the thermal history of a piece of metal by comparing two similar spots on the metal, each spot being 40-*millionth* of an inch in diameter, separated by 100-*millionth* of an inch.

As Edison's first incandescent lamp merely hinted at what was yet to be in artificial lighting, so it is with all physical research. Instructed in laws of matter, physical scientists are in the world, yet not wholly of it, because the world they are building is yet to come.

The world is a different place than it was when Edison

began his experiments in lighting. The airplane overhead, the ship that sails the seas, the submarine beneath the sea; the air-conditioned train that crosses the continent; the automobile that takes men to their work and back to their homes; the telephone that permits friends to talk with each other although oceans separate them; the screen that brings a President into a ranch house in Texas at the moment of his inauguration in Washington; the capsule in which man rides in outer space—these and countless other changes have come as the result of the restless quest of physical scientists into the nature of matter.

But, important as the work of physical scientists is to the world, this woman was setting out to search into laws vastly more important than the laws of matter. She was setting out to search into life itself. Life is the law of God. No test tubes, no acids, and no complex equipment awaited her. Prayer was her instructor; the Bible was her laboratory.

The world also is a different place, although in quite a different way, than it was when Mary Baker Eddy was setting out in her search. She looked not for new things to add to the world's stockpile of knowledge about itself but searched into the nature of God.

Very early she began to perceive what afterwards became so clear—that all life reflects the Giver of life, God. In life, she found only those things that are spiritual, hence eternal. Matter was not among them.

In 1862 she was questioning the validity of matter. Behind her questioning was the conviction that the ways of matter are not the ways of spirit, nor the way into the spiritual. In the first year following her healing, doubt had vanished. Taking the place of doubt was the certainty that man is not material, but spiritual, in accordance with the twenty-seventh verse in Chapter One of the Book of Genesis: "So God created man in his own image, in the image of God created he him; male and female created he them"—and, since man was created in the image of God, life, for man, is eternal.

She was not to speak out on these things until she knew and not to testify until she proved.

In her preparation she was not unlike David, who, because he had not proved it, rejected the armor of Saul and went forth with his sling and five stones in his shepherd's bag to meet Goliath. She tested every word by one word—truth. Knowing that the truths which guided her had eternity for their unfoldment, she was not dismayed by the nature of the obstacles.

Believing the keys of faith and prayer were opening the gate to the understanding of eternal life, she never forgot to listen to the inner voice that always speaks in moments of great decision. Believing, too, that no gate should be opened that bars evil, the woman who became known to the world as Mary Baker Eddy found in her prayers the peace that lies deep and offers no opportunity for the intrusion of fear.

It was on the night of the feast of the Passover that Jesus said to the eleven who were with him: "Let not your heart be troubled: ye believe in God, believe also in me"; and emphasized his instruction: "Peace I leave with you, my peace I give unto you: not as the world giveth, give I unto you. Let not your heart be troubled, neither let it be afraid."

In those words, imperishable then, even as now, the woman found a guarantee on which was written, *no one needs to be afraid.*

She was not alone in her uneasiness over what was being preached from the pulpits as Christianity. Her New England contemporary, Ralph Waldo Emerson, also was uneasy; and, although she did not know it, he was saying:

"The religion which is to guide and fulfil the present and

coming ages, whatever else it must be, must be intellectual. The scientific mind must have a faith that is science. 'There are two things,' said Mahomet, 'which I abhor, the learned in his infidelities, and the fool in his devotions.' Our times are impatient of both; and especially the last. Let us have nothing now which is not its own evidence. There is surely enough for the heart and imagination in the religion itself. Let us not be pestered with assertions and half-truths. . . .

"There will be a new church founded on moral science, at first cold and naked, a babe in the manger again, the algebra and mathematics of ethical law, the church of men to come, without shawms, or psaltry, or sackbut; but it will have heaven and earth for its beams and rafters; science for symbol and illustration; it will fast enough gather beauty, music, picture, poetry. . . ." [2]

In searching for eternal verities, Mrs. Eddy was looking only for those things which carry proof of their divine origin. To her, life was not a casual word; nor was it a casual word on the lips of the great Teacher, Christ Jesus.

There was his meeting with a woman of Samaria, and her question:

> How is it that thou, being a Jew, askest drink of me, which am a woman of Samaria? for the Jews have no dealings with the Samaritans.
>
> Jesus answered and said unto her, If thou knewest the gift of God, and who it is that saith to thee, Give me to drink; thou wouldest have asked of him, and he would have given thee living water.
>
> The woman saith unto him, Sir, thou hast nothing to draw with, and the well is deep: from whence then hast thou that living water? Art thou greater than our father Jacob, which gave us the well, and

[2] *Essays,* Ralph Waldo Emerson.

drank thereof himself, and his children and his cattle?

Jesus answered and said unto her, Whosoever drinketh of this water shall thirst again: But whosoever drinketh of the water that I shall give him shall never thirst; but the water that I shall give him shall be in him a well of water springing up into everlasting life.

When he arrived in Bethany he said to Martha, sister of Lazarus who had been dead four days: "I am the resurrection, and the life: he that believeth in me, though he were dead, yet shall he live: And whosoever liveth and believeth in me shall never die ... And he that was dead came forth, bound hand and foot with graveclothes: and his face was bound about with a napkin. Jesus said unto them, Loose him, and let him go."

There was his resurrection of the daughter of Jairus; and his resurrection of the son of the widow of Nain; there was his own resurrection.

There was the day in the temple in Jerusalem when Jesus was talking to the Pharisees not of life in the flesh, but of eternal life, or spirit; and they said to him: "Thou art not yet fifty years old, and hast thou seen Abraham? Jesus said unto them, Verily, verily, I say unto you, Before Abraham was, I am. Then took they up stones to cast at him."

There were his words to his disciples on the night of Gethsemane: "This is life eternal, that they might know thee the only true God, and Jesus Christ, whom thou hast sent."

There were a few who believed him. Peter believed him— "and all the widows stood by him weeping, and shewing the coats and garments which Dorcas made, while she was with them. But Peter put them all forth, and kneeled down, and prayed; and turning him to the body said, Tabitha, arise. And she opened her eyes: and when she saw Peter, she sat up."

Paul believed him: "And there sat in a window a certain young man named Eutychus, being fallen into a deep sleep: and as Paul was long preaching, he sunk down with sleep, and fell down from the third loft, and was taken up dead. And Paul went down, and fell on him, and embracing him said, Trouble not yourselves; for his life is in him. . . . And they brought the young man alive, and were not a little comforted."

That Jesus was born of Mary to bring to the world confirmation of the immortality of the spiritual was the testimony of the prophet, John the Baptist: "For he whom God hath sent speaketh the words of God: for God giveth not the Spirit by measure unto him. The Father loveth the Son, and hath given him all things into his hand. He that believeth on the Son hath everlasting life."

She who became Mary Baker Eddy believed, continued to believe; and later wrote: "Life is eternal. We should find this out, and begin the demonstration thereof." [3]

But this she first had to understand before she could uphold that for which she stood. In the years she spent searching the Scriptures that she might find the way to do for others what was done for her, she grew in the patience that waits on God and came to know that when the individual is able to understand he will hear what he needs to hear.

Now open before her was the same Book she was reading when she herself was healed. This time she was reading in chapter 16 of the Book of St. Matthew:

> When Jesus came into the coasts of Caesarea Philippi, he asked his disciples, saying, Whom do men say that I the Son of man am?

[3] *Science and Health*, p. 246.

And they said, Some say that thou art John the Baptist: some, Elias; and others, Jeremias, or one of the prophets.

He saith unto them, But whom say ye that I am?

And Simon Peter answered and said, Thou art the Christ, the Son of the living God.

And Jesus answered and said unto him, Blessed art thou, Simon Bar-jona: for flesh and blood hath not revealed it unto thee, but my Father which is in heaven.

There were other statements which, also, she gave long and prayerful attention: "Verily, verily, I say unto you, The Son can do nothing of himself, but what he seeth the Father do: for what things soever he doeth, these also doeth the Son likewise" . . . "The Father that dwelleth in me, he doeth the works" . . . "My Father is greater than I" . . . "I and my Father are one" . . . "Believe me that I am in the Father, and the Father in me: or else believe me for the very works' sake". . .

There are many similar statements in the New Testament, all speaking of the inseparable nature of the relationship between the Father and the Son—and, in pondering all the testimony, Mary Baker Eddy found the way Jesus healed.

"Thou art the Christ, the Son of the living God"—this statement by Peter forever separated the Master from all men. The human Jesus was the offspring of the human Mary; the Christ was the Son of God. *"The Father that dwelleth in me, he doeth the works"*—it was the Christ that healed.

The search was over.

Mary Baker Eddy beheld God as she believed Jesus beheld Him. She beheld God as the Creator of all that is eternal and of nothing that is temporal. In the work and words of Jesus she perceived scientific proof of the nature and power of that which is always available, and always responsive, to the prayer of understanding.

That which is always available, and always responsive, to the prayer of understanding is God's law, and so perceiving she was able to bring spiritual healing and did.

Something important had only begun.

CHAPTER FOUR

Written on the Heart

THE search was over, but there remained for Mary Baker Eddy the task of finding and choosing men and women to do what she was able to do. How to heal the sick was something that could not be taught to the nonreceptive mind.

The way could be shown on a blackboard or on a piece of paper. It could be memorized and repeated a thousand times. These things could be done, over and over and over. There would be no healing.

Healing would come only as it came to Mary Baker Eddy —*when the words are written on the heart.*

On page 123 of *Science and Health,* Mrs. Eddy said:

The term CHRISTIAN SCIENCE was introduced by the author to designate the scientific system of divine healing.

The revelation consists of two parts:

1. The discovery of this divine Science of Mind-healing, through a spiritual sense of the Scriptures and through the teachings of the Comforter, as promised by the Master.

2. The proof, by present demonstration, that the so-called miracles of Jesus did not specially belong to a dispensation now ended, but that they illus-

trated an ever-operative divine Principle. The operation of this Principle indicates the eternality of
the scientific order and continuity of being.

As was her custom, she waited on prayer for guidance before choosing others to take up the work. In these, the beginning years of her revelation, she wrote the first of her
copyrighted manuscripts. Entitled *The Science of Man* and
copyrighted in 1870, the printed manuscript was in the form
of a pamphlet containing twenty-four pages. In *Historical
Sketches,* Clifford P. Smith quoted Mrs. Eddy as saying she
spent "two and a half years [of] incessant labor, seven days
a week," in preparing the first edition of *Science and Health.*

In the summer of 1866 she was boarding with Mr. and
Mrs. George D. Clark in Lynn, but she spent much of her
time, whenever she had time to spare, in the home of Mr.
and Mrs. Thomas Phillips. A manufacturer of shoe findings,
Phillips probably was the first of her sympathetic listeners.
He never embraced her teachings, although in one of her
short visits she healed his son, Dorr, of a felon on one of his
fingers.

In the boardinghouse, she sat at the head of the dining-
room table while Clark and his wife sat opposite each other
in the center of the table. There were fourteen places, most
of which were occupied by men employed in the local shoe
factories. Among them were Hiram S. Crafts, and his wife,
both of whom were spiritualists. Crafts sat beside Mrs.
Eddy and often, after the dishes had been removed from
the table, continued to sit and ask questions about her Biblical studies.

Before long Crafts was so interested and asked so many
questions that Mrs. Eddy put some of her thoughts on paper
and gave the paper to Crafts for study. Eagerly he sought
further information until he pressed her to accompany his

wife and himself to East Stoughton, Massachusetts, where he lived when he was not temporarily employed in Lynn. She agreed. After several months of tutelage, Crafts expressed the desire to make healing his life's work. Receiving encouragement, he moved to Taunton, Massachusetts, with his wife and his teacher. In Taunton he opened an office and was able to bring about a number of healings when, with his wife persuading him, he closed his office.

In spite of this disappointment, there was gain in Taunton. Returning to Lynn, Mrs. Eddy was sure she could show others the way into the Source of all healing. In Lynn she sought the help of friends, Charles Winslow and his wife, in finding a quiet home in which she could continue her writing with a minimum of distraction. The Winslows were friends of the Phillipses as well. Abbie Winslow had been the occupant of an invalid's chair for sixteen years. Told that his wife could be healed, Charles Winslow said he would give a thousand dollars "to see Abbie walk again." Mrs. Eddy shook her head, saying the healing itself was sufficient reward.

The woman did walk again and took long walks, unaided, along the ocean shore, as well as in the neighborhood of her home and in her own gardens. After a period of freedom, she returned to her invalid's chair. Despite her own experience, she could not believe prayer could bring healing, nor could her husband. Separately and together, they had prayed many times without response.

It was not Mrs. Eddy's first encounter with disbelief. When she was in Taunton with the Craftses she received a message that her sister Martha's daughter, Ellen, was dying. Mrs. Eddy went and was taken into a bedroom where the girl was suffering from what was called enteritis, following an attack of typhoid fever.

Requesting Martha to leave the room, Mrs. Eddy talked

to her niece, and after a few minutes she told Ellen to get out of bed and walk around the room. The following day the girl dressed herself, and three days later she boarded a train to accompany her aunt to Taunton, a hundred miles distant. On the day before Mrs. Eddy's arrival, and through several preceding days, she had to be carried on a sheet when moved from one bed to another.

While Ellen was with her aunt in Taunton, Abigail was trying to belittle the healing, afterwards Ellen denied the whole experience.

These were happenings that must have been reminders to Mrs. Eddy of the experience of Jesus when he came into "his own country, and among his own kin, and in his own house. And he could there do no mighty work . . . and he marvelled because of their unbelief."

However, the unbelief did not lessen the friendship between the Winslows and herself. Charles Winslow did try to persuade her to discontinue her efforts to prove the efficacy of spiritual healing, predicting, in all kindness, only trouble if she persisted. Finally convinced of her determination to continue, the Winslows recommended the home of a friend in Amesbury, Massachusetts.

Located in an upper corner of Massachusetts on the border of New Hampshire, Amesbury was about forty miles almost due north from Boston. It was a Quaker community with tree-shaded streets, on one of which lived the poet John Greenleaf Whittier. The river that ran by the town was the same Merrimack River that ran close to her parents' home in Bow. The ocean into which the river emptied was eight or nine miles distant to the east.

Mrs. Eddy went to Amesbury, but instead of calling on the friends recommended by the Winslows, she was attracted to the home of Mrs. Nathaniel Webster. Containing fifteen rooms, it was a three-story dwelling overlooking the river. Webster, a retired sea captain, was superintendent in a cotton mill in Manchester, New Hampshire, and was home only occasionally.

The woman lived alone, with the exception of a few boarders, so that when Mrs. Eddy called she was happy with the opportunity to supply board and room to this stranger who explained her need for quiet surroundings in order to complete the writing of a manuscript. Mrs. Eddy gave no hint as to the nature of the work and was pleased with a large corner room on the second floor from which there was an open view of the Merrimack.

She was not long in learning that the captain's wife was a believer in spiritualism. The two women, when they were together, spent much of the time discussing what each believed. Mrs. Eddy did not believe in spiritualism; Mrs. Webster did not grasp what Mrs. Eddy was calling the Science of Mind.[1] Nor was she interested, even when spiritualist friends who came to see her were healed of their sicknesses.

Mrs. Eddy resided in Amesbury until the autumn of 1868, when she returned to Stoughton, taking with her a manuscript nearing completion. In Stoughton, in the home of Mrs. Sally Wentworth, she completed her first contribution to Christian Science literature, *The Science of Man*. In Amesbury she left multiplying gossip of things she said over the dining room table to the captain's wife, such as: "There is no life in matter." [2]

[1] The word *Science* was not new in Mrs. Eddy's vocabulary. In 1843, after the passing of her brother, Albert Baker, she wrote in the *New Hampshire Patriot and State Gazette:*

> Then wherefore this anguish! lone mourner why here?
> In tones of enquiry arose from the bier,
> Wouldst call back the spirit from yon bright abode,
> The pathway of science, the smiles of a God?

[2] At the time she had dropped the name of Patterson and was known as Mrs. Mary Baker Glover. She began using the name Eddy following her

Years after she first said "there is no life in matter," physical scientists were saying and writing the same thing, as did Dr. Donald H. Andrew, of Johns Hopkins University, in the May, 1955, issue of *Main Currents in Modern Thought*:

"If I could put your body in an imaginary atomic press and squeeze those atom holes out of it, just as the holes are squeezed out of a sponge, you would get smaller and smaller until, finally, when the last hole was gone, your body would be smaller than the smallest speck of dust. . . .

"Thus, the first lesson we learn from our new science (exploring the atom) is that seeing is not believing. Your hands look solid, and feel solid, but they are more full of holes than a wire fence . . . if, materially, you don't amount to much, what are you?"

Mrs. Eddy's reasoning was different. Believing God to be spiritual, she saw man, as created in God's image, to be spiritual, not material—not matter, no matter at all.

Openly, in Amesbury and elsewhere, she was speaking of her search into the eternal verities as a Science. She was insistent in her views that, in reality, there is but one supreme universal law, and that is God's law. This was in her mind when she was in Portland, Maine, in 1862, when she told Phineas P. Quimby that "back of his magnetic treatment and manipulation of patients, there was a science, and it was the science of mind, which had nothing to do with matter, electricity, or physics." [3]

Sixty-eight years later a world-renowned American physicist would take a long step along the same road. In his book *Science and the New Civilization*, Robert A. Millikan wrote about universal law, and he said:

marriage to Asa Gilbert Eddy on New Year's Day, in 1877. It is the name that will always be identified with Christian Science.

[3] *Miscellany*, p. 307.

"The idea that God, or Nature, or the Universe, whatever term you prefer, is not a being of caprice and whim . . . but is, instead, a God who rules through law, or a nature capable of being depended upon, or a universe of consistency, of orderliness and of the beauty that goes with order—that idea has *made* modern science, and it is unquestionably the foundation of modern civilization.

"It is because of this discovery, or because of the introduction of this idea into human thinking, and because of the *faith* of the scientist in it, that he has been able to harness the forces of nature and to make them do the work that enslaved human beings were forced to do in all preceding civilizations. . . .

"The new God is the God of law and order, the new duty to know that order and to get into harmony with it; to learn to make the world a better place for mankind to live in, not merely how to save your individual soul. However, once destroy our confidence in the principle of uniformity, our belief in the rule of law, and our effectiveness immediately disappears, our method ceases to be dependable, and our laboratories become deserted." [4]

Dr. Millikan did not doubt the presence of God. Referring to this belief a short time before his passing in 1953, he expressed his conviction in words something like these:

"One of the most amazing facts about the universe is its orderliness. It is orderliness that cannot be the result of chance. In the face of all the existing confirming evidence, only a fool could be an atheist."

The views of the eminent physicist would have interested Mrs. Eddy, although her work was not concerned with investigations into the phenomena of the physical world. The science that occupied all her thought was an absolute Science. In this Science she was beginning to perceive that there

[4] Copyright, 1930, Charles Scribner's Sons, New York.

is no conflict with the so-called natural sciences to which Dr. Millikan contributed much. Nor could there be. The natural sciences deal wholly with the affairs of matter; the other science deals wholly with the affairs of Spirit. There is no conflict between the two. They never meet—on the drawing board or in the laboratory.

So it was that the years 1866–1870 were devoted almost entirely to searching the Bible, to prayer, and to putting on paper the thoughts that came to her. One of Mrs. Eddy's poems, entitled *Alone,* carries the date of August 13, 1867. The poem has five verses—the first three disclose the loneliness of other years while the closing two verses reveal the poet's determination to look beyond human desires for happiness and to look within herself, in growing realization of the nature of her search. The poem had newspaper publication. The fourth and fifth stanzas follow:

> Yet not alone, for oft I see
> Bright forms that look in love on me.
> To thee, thou lost ones, and my own
> I call—O leave me not alone!
> When answering tones this music pour:
> Thy God is with thee evermore.
> 　　O better bliss, that knows no sigh!
> 　　O love divine, so full, so nigh!
>
> And o'er the harp-strings of the soul
> Sweet sounds this trembling echo roll:
> Thy love can live in Truth, and be
> A joy and immortality;
> To bless mankind with word and deed,
> Thy life a great and noble creed.
> 　　O glorious hope, my faith renew!
> 　　O mortal joys, adieu! adieu! [5]

[5] Originally, the poem was copyrighted in 1911 by The Curtis Publishing Company, Philadelphia, Pa.

In these, the beginning years of her journey toward the Light, she encountered, with increasing frequency, the furies of the entrenched forces of materialism.

Returning to Amesbury early in 1870, Mrs. Eddy went to the home of Miss Sarah Bagley, with whom she had lived for several months in a previous stay. In Miss Bagley she found one who shared her interest in spiritual subjects, as well as in the poetry of John Greenleaf Whittier. It was through Miss Bagley that Mrs. Eddy met the poet.[6]

On one occasion during her earlier visit—it was in July, 1868—the two women called and found Whittier bundled up and sitting in front of a grate fire. His cheeks were flushed, and he talked with difficulty because of nearly continuous coughing, almost until time of their leave-taking. At that time he came toward Mrs. Eddy, and taking both her hands in his, thanked her for coming, and said, "Your visit has done me much good," and added, "Come again." The flush had left his cheeks. He had stopped coughing.

In Amesbury, Mrs. Eddy renewed her acquaintance with Richard Kennedy, whom she had met as another boarder in the Webster home. Kennedy, the owner of a small box factory in Amesbury, became interested in her teachings, so interested that he became her student. A personable young man, he made such good progress that he suggested a partnership, he to do the healing under her guidance, thus leaving her more or less free to teach. After long thought and much questioning, she agreed.

They went to Lynn, where Kennedy found a three-story building at South Common and Shepard streets that seemed to meet requirements. The building was not in the shopping district, but was convenient to it. The first floor was used as a private school for girls, while the third floor was used as

[6] Nine of Whittier's poems have been set to music and are published in the *Christian Science Hymnal*.

living quarters for the owner of the building, who managed the school. Together, Mrs. Eddy and Kennedy talked with the owner and rented the second floor.

Setting aside part of the floor for her own use as an apartment and as a classroom, Mrs. Eddy turned over the rest of the floor to Kennedy for use as an office. After furnishing the rooms in the plainest manner possible and fastening a small sign announcing instructions and healing in Science beside the entrance downstairs, they were ready for students and patients.

It was a small sign but it attracted attention in this city of twenty-eight thousand people. The sick came in search of healing and, finding it, came back to learn how to heal others. The question that troubled Mrs. Eddy most was the question of what to charge for instruction. How could there be a proper payment in money for instruction that pertained only to the spiritual? The answer awaited even while she was asking the question—there could be no financial equivalent.

Yet, and as Jesus instructed his disciples when he sent them out to heal the sick, "the workman is worthy of his meat." After much thought, she decided to charge a hundred dollars for ten lessons. In a period when a dollar was a day's wage (eggs were eight cents a dozen), one hundred dollars was a substantial sum. She knew that few would be able to pay, but the sum itself would keep out the frivolous-minded. Soon she actually raised the charge to three hundred dollars. As a result, some were taught free; some she accepted on a participation basis (10 per cent of their income if they took up the practice of healing).

In these early classes the teaching was from *The Science of Man,* in question-and-answer form which the students were required to study thoroughly out of class. An argumentative student in the first lesson was told that he was there to learn, not to teach. Persisting further, he was dismissed. If, however, one was honestly seeking enlightenment, the teacher's patience was inexhaustible. In addition to teaching, there were times when she demonstrated what she taught. As, afterwards, she wrote to a student: *"Demonstration* is the whole of Christian Science, nothing else proves it, nothing else will save it and continue it with us." [7]

One morning she felt impelled to call at the home of a family named Green. She rang the doorbell. Mrs. Green answered. When Mrs. Eddy asked if she was wanted, Mrs. Green replied that she was going to send for her but had been told she was out of town. Continuing, the woman said her daughter was sick with brain fever, and her case had been pronounced hopeless by the doctors.

Going into the room where the child was, Mrs. Eddy sat by the bed for a few minutes, then called for the child's clothes. After being dressed, the little girl and Mrs. Eddy left the house, walked a few blocks in the rain, and returned. Not until the following morning did the parents realize there had been a complete healing.

On another occasion, a student was having a difficult time treating a patient afflicted with dumbness. Mrs. Eddy was asked to help. She responded. Walking up to the dumb girl who was in the student's office, Mrs. Eddy said, "God did not send this upon you. You can speak. In the name of Jesus Christ of Nazareth, I command you to speak!"

Shrinking back against the wall, the girl cried out, "I can't, and I won't!" and fled from the room. She was healed. She continued to speak.

It was demonstrations such as these that aroused the medical profession and the Christian clergy into denouncing her teachings. In a sense, it was opposition that was understand-

[7] Copyright, 1936, by the Trustees under the Will of Mary Baker Eddy.

able. Since the time of Hippocrates, long centuries before, the medical profession had staked out a custodian's claim to the bodies of men just as, also for long centuries, the clergy had posted its claims to the souls of men.

Although she was giving no pills and prescribing no drugs, the medical profession accused her of practicing medicine without a license, while from the pulpit was flung the charge of heresy.

For centuries, the Christian clergy had used fear as a weapon to enforce its decrees. It preached that God visited punishment upon His children in the form of war, famine, pestilence, and death for wrongdoing; that for some of His children, including unbaptized babies, He ordained eternal damnation; that He was watching, every minute, and marking down every transgression in a book of records for one purpose—vengeance.

The God Mary Baker Eddy worshipped was not a God of hate, or a God of vengeance, but a God of love. Hate, vengeance, fear—these words were not in her vocabulary. Nor were they in the vocabulary of the One she followed, although they were in the archives of ecclesiasticism. On the night of his betrayal Jesus instructed the eleven who remained faithful:

> A new commandment I give unto you, That ye love one another; as I have loved you, that ye also love one another . . .
>
> Yet a little while, and the world seeth me no more; but ye see me: because I live, ye shall live also . . .
>
> He that hath my commandments, and keepeth them, he it is that loveth me: and he that loveth me shall be loved of my Father, and I will love him, and will manifest myself to him.

From the time of her first talks with her first student, and before, Mrs. Eddy insisted that "to fear God is not right; we must love God, not fear Him." One day while she was emphasizing the importance of "love" in their lives as Christian Scientists, a student inquired, "Do you mean love of person?"

"No, I mean love of good."

"How shall we know whether our love is personal or impersonal?" Her reply in substance:

"When your love requires an object to call it forth, you will know it is personal; when it flows freely to all, you will know it is impersonal." [8]

To Mary Baker Eddy the bond that joins one man to all men is the same bond that joins all men to the one God. That bond is love.

The partnership with Kennedy lasted two years. At the end of this period, Mrs. Eddy had six thousand dollars in the bank; for the first time in years she was free of the pincers of poverty. Under her direction Kennedy was a successful practitioner; but when she issued orders in 1872 that no student of hers should any longer manipulate the head of a patient while giving a treatment, he refused to give up this practice, which was an outmoded remnant of the Quimbyism she had left far behind. As a result, the partnership was terminated.[9]

But, notwithstanding her release from poverty, the two years with Kennedy began one of the most trying periods of her evangelistic career.

For a time after her discovery she was confident the Christian clergy would welcome what she offered. She knew, and so did the clergy, that the presence of the healing element was responsible for the rapid growth of Christianity

[8] *We Knew Mary Baker Eddy* (First Series). Copyright, 1943, by The Christian Science Publishing Society.

[9] Kennedy did not continue in the teachings. In later years he lived in Boston and was a vestryman in St. Paul's Episcopal Church.

in the early centuries of the Christian era. Instead of accepting her proof, the clergy refused it and ridiculed her claims,
so that by the summer of 1872 she realized if her findings
were to be useful to the world she would have to have a
church of her own.

On this particular summer night in 1872 she was walking
home from the railroad station in Lynn with George Clark,
son of the owners of the boardinghouse to which she had
returned after dissolving the partnership with Kennedy.
With Clark she had gone to Boston that morning to see the
same publisher. Each had a book to sell. Clark sold his. It
was a story of the sea. Hers was rejected. It was an outline
of a book she had started to write. She was told that such a
book had no sales possibilities, and she was advised to drop
the idea.

The book was published three years later. Its title was
Science and Health.

On the way from the railroad station to the Clark residence in Lynn she suddenly stopped, put a detaining hand
on the arm of her companion, and broke a silence that had
engulfed her almost from the moment she had boarded the
train in Boston.

"George," she said, pointing to a church, "some day I
shall have a church of my own."

Rumors again began to be circulated that Mrs. Eddy was
rewriting the Bible. They gained wide circulation. One of
her disloyal students began writing letters to the newspapers, charging her with practicing mesmerism.

In the spring of 1875 she finally had a home of her own.
The address was 8 Broad Street, in Lynn. Shadowed by an
elm tree, the house was a frame structure of two and one-
half stories, containing seven rooms. There was a bay window in the parlor on the first floor, small balconies in back
on the first and second floors, and on the top floor a room

lighted by a skylight which could be opened for ventilation.

Of the seven rooms, she reserved two for herself. One was the small room in the attic which would serve as a bedroom and for writing. The other, the parlor, was to serve as a classroom. It was her plan to rent the other rooms to students. The property cost $5,650. The outlay almost exhausted her savings. The transaction was completed on March 31. Less than two months previously, on February 9, $500 had been paid to W. F. Brown and Company, printers, 50 Bromfield Street, Boston, as a down payment for the printing of a book that was nearing completion.

She began writing the book in February, 1872, while still in partnership with Richard Kennedy, and completed it in the small room under the skylight at 8 Broad Street. As the writing progressed she changed her mind about the first title she had in mind, this being *The Science of Life;* and after weeks of prayer the answer came to her in the night. That title was *Science and Health*.[10]

On August 14, 1875, there was a second payment of two hundred dollars to the Boston printer, making a total of seven hundred dollars, which was more than half of an estimated cost of one thousand dollars for printing and binding and delivering a thousand copies. She had completed her manuscript, except for a part of one chapter, when she heard that work on the printing of the book had been stopped.

After repeated attempts to persuade the printer to complete what he had promised to complete, she "yielded," as she wrote in *Retrospection and Introspection*,[11] "to a con-

[10] Six months after the book was published Miss Dorcas Rawson, one of her students, called Mrs. Eddy's attention to John Wyclif's use of the same words in his translation of the New Testament. It was Mrs. Eddy's first knowledge of their prior use.

[11] Copyright, 1891, 1892, by Mary Baker Eddy. Copyright renewed 1918, 1922. Published by the Trustees under the Will of Mary Baker Eddy, Boston, Mass.

stant conviction that I must insert in my last chapter a partial history of what I had already observed of mental malpractice."

Accordingly, I set to work, contrary to my inclination, to fulfil this painful task, and finished my copy for the book. As it afterwards appeared, although I had not thought of such a result, my printer resumed his work at the same time, finished printing the copy he had on hand, and then started for Lynn to see me. The afternoon that he left Boston for Lynn, I started for Boston with my finished copy. We met at the Eastern depot in Lynn, and were both surprised,—I to learn that he had printed all the copy on hand, and had come to tell me he wanted more,—he to find me *en route* for Boston, to give him the closing chapter of my first edition of Science and Health. Not a word had passed between us, audibly or mentally, while this went on. I had grown disgusted with my printer, and become silent. He had come to a standstill through motives and circumstances unknown to me.

Not until after the book was published did Mrs. Eddy learn what, probably, had caused the printer to stop the work. Instead of an estimated total cost of $1,000 for 1,000 copies, the cost was certain to be in excess of $2,000 for 1,000 books. Frequent changes and corrections in the copy had resulted in greatly increased charges for setting and plating the type. In all, the final cost for producing 1,000 copies was $2,285.35.

Somehow, and he was not able to explain it, the printer's fear of not being paid for his work vanished at the same time Mrs. Eddy began completing the final chapter.

Bound in a pale green cover, and selling at three dollars a copy, the first edition of *Science and Health* contained 456 pages. There were eight chapters and a Preface. The chapter headings were: "Natural Science," "Imposition and Demonstration," "Spirit and Matter," "Creation," "Prayer and Atonement," "Marriage," "Physiology," and "Healing the Sick." The words "Christian science" made their first printed appearance in her writings thusly: "The great Teacher of Christian science knew that a good tree sendeth not forth evil fruit." Although Mrs. Eddy continued to revise and clarify the book almost to the day of her passing, the first edition of *Science and Health* contained the basic teachings of her revelation.

Twenty months were needed to dispose of the first edition of *Science and Health*. From November 1, 1875, to May 1, 1876, sales totaled 235 copies. During the following eight months sales totaled 424 copies, the peak month for sales being December, 1876, when 88 copies were sold. On July 2, 1877, the remaining unsold copies (about 230) were disposed of, Mrs. Eddy having sold 86 copies in January and February, 1877.

Thousands of circulars were printed and distributed; among those getting free copies were the *Church Advocate,* the Palmer *Journal,* the Needham *Chronicle,* the State Normal School at Bridgewater, and the Andover Theological Seminary, all in Massachusetts. Additional copies were sent to individuals as well, mostly in Massachusetts; more than $500 was spent for newspaper advertising.

It was a disappointing beginning, but Mrs. Eddy was looking forward hopefully to the issuance of a second edition, although she had little money with which to pay for it.

Unfortunately, there were so many typographical errors in the first edition as to greatly obscure the meaning of her words. Seeking to cause strife among her followers, enemies began referring to this edition as "the pure teachings" causing Mrs. Eddy to write [12] to First Church of Christ, Scientist, Concord, New Hampshire: ". . . The first edition was spoiled by my publisher." She closed her letter by requesting the return of "that edition, and not give it out to be read."

In this book Mary Baker Eddy was saying there is no death, no such thing as everlasting punishment, no such place as hell, and no such person as the devil—and to these denials she was adding another. She was saying the miracles of Jesus were not miracles at all but the natural operation of God's law—and, were it not for their lack of spiritual understanding, all men could do as Jesus did.

[12] Letter written from Pleasant View, in 1904.

CHAPTER FIVE

A Place of Memories

I N terminating her association with Kennedy, Mrs. Eddy took a step that was much more than a simple act of dissociating herself from a student who violated her teachings. It was a much larger step because what she was doing was repudiating a counterfeit.

Everything genuine has its counterfeit, whether in art, a nation's money, or in Christianity. A work of art or a nation's money is counterfeited in the hope that the unwary will pay for that which of itself is worthless. In Christianity and in Mrs. Eddy's teachings the counterfeit of God or Spirit is the flesh.

The apostle Paul wrote about this counterfeit in his Epistle to the Galatians: "This I say then, Walk in the Spirit, and ye shall not fulfil the lust of the flesh. For the flesh lusteth against the Spirit, and the Spirit against the flesh: and these are contrary the one to the other: so that ye cannot do the things that ye would."

Continuing, Paul wrote:

> Now the works of the flesh are manifest, which are *these;* Adultery, fornication, uncleanness, lasciviousness, Idolatry, witchcraft, hatred, variance, emulations, wrath, strife, seditions, heresies, Envyings, murders, drunkenness, revellings, and such

like: of the which I tell you before, as I have also told you in time past, that they which do such things shall not inherit the kingdom of God. . . .

If we live in the Spirit, let us also walk in the Spirit.

A few verses later, Paul warned: "He that soweth to his flesh shall of the flesh reap corruption; but he that soweth to the Spirit shall of the Spirit reap life everlasting."

The things of the flesh about which Paul spoke were grouped by Mrs. Eddy, and she called them "animal magnetism." She knew, as did Paul, that in his teachings Jesus made no concessions to ritual and permitted no genuflections to matter or to the flesh. She knew that such concessions and such genuflections obscured the truth of man's relationship with his Maker, just as she knew that Kennedy's manipulation of the head and neck muscles obscured the spiritual nature of the prayer through which comes healing.

She also knew if counterfeits were permitted to enter her teachings the purpose would be not to help but to destroy. Their entrance would be infiltration by an enemy who subtly agrees with all the expressed ideals and never offers the semblance of resistance—but who does offer a short-cut to the same high goal. Finding acceptance or, if not acceptance, no resistance, it is an enemy that insinuates into the teachings what seem to be innocent additions but which, in actuality, are deceptions that draw the followers away from the precepts of the teachings, drain off their vitality, and shatter their foundations.

She knew that the best defense against any worthless thing is to know more about the genuine. She was aware that the counterfeit does not announce its presence, and that mankind does not willingly trade good money for bad;

she also knew that in the vaster areas of the spiritual mankind is not so observant. It was because she knew these
things that she could not, and did not, tolerate any dilution
of her teachings.

As she afterwards wrote, she did not immediately recognize the character of the forces that were opposing her
efforts to restore primitive Christianity and its lost element
of healing. In *Miscellaneous Writings* (pp. 222–23) she
wrote:

> I shall not forget the cost of investigating,
> for this age, the methods and power of error.
> While the ways, means, and potency of Truth had
> flowed into my consciousness as easily as dawns
> the morning light and shadows flee, the metaphys-
> ical mystery of error—its hidden paths, purpose,
> and fruits—at first defied me.

A disaffected student, Daniel H. Spofford, was a defendant in a lawsuit which charged "injuries of an irreparable
nature" to a woman who said she was not able to "escape
from [Spofford's] control and influence." In May, 1878,
Spofford was acquitted. The trial, known as the "Ipswich
Witchcraft Case," attracted wide attention. It was attention
that brought a great deal of unfavorable comment.

On New Year's Day, 1877, the Discoverer and Founder
of Christian Science married Asa Gilbert Eddy. On October 29, 1878, the *Boston Herald* carried front-page headlines
telling of the arrest of Eddy and another student on a charge
of conspiracy to murder Daniel H. Spofford.

Evidence was quickly gathered that Eddy was addressing
a group of Christian Scientists in a community miles distant
from the place where he was supposed to have met and paid
a sum of money to James L. Sargeant, a former convict, to
kill Spofford. Furthermore, an accomplice of Sargeant's soon

confessed that he had lied in saying that he had seen Eddy and Sargeant conferring.

There was never an opportunity to present this evidence before the Court, for the District Attorney entered a *nol. pros.* before trial and the case was dismissed. The mystery was not solved then nor has it been solved since. Not the least mysterious feature of the case is the fact that Spofford, having allegedly been apprised by Sargeant that he had been hired to murder him, should then have taken refuge for two weeks in the home of the hired assassin.

Later, another student published Mrs. Eddy's writings as his own, forcing her to bring court action to protect her copyright. The District Court of the United States upheld her, compelled the student to destroy his copies, and levied damages, which he had to pay.

Nor was the clergy silent through these months and years. Hearing that Mrs. Eddy actually engaged in the healing work, that she was teaching others how to heal, and that she was rewriting the Bible, it began a bitter denunciation of her and of her work. Joining in the clamor was the medical profession.

All this was but a portion of the hostility that harassed her efforts to speak of her discovery. But she did speak, and she did prove, and she kept on teaching and healing and proving and writing.

Mary Baker Eddy was not the first seeker of Truth to encounter the deceit of error. Nor was the one whose teachings she sought to follow, Jesus the Christ; nor was Daniel, nor Elisha, nor Elijah, nor Moses, nor Abraham. Nor were the tens of thousands of Christians whose persecution and martyrdom is the Book of Remembrance in the library of Christianity. There were the twelve disciples, each of whom but one met violent death; there was Stephen and there was Paul, both of whom were executed.

Tertullian, who was born a pagan but became a Christian, said in the late years of the second century in his Address to Scapula:

"To what ... does a Christian devote himself, save the affairs of his own community, which during all the long period of its existence no one has ever proved guilty of the incest, or the cruelty charged against it? It is for freedom from crime so singular, for a probity so great, for righteousness, for faithfulness, for Truth, for the living God, that we are consigned to the flames; for this is a punishment you are not wont to inflict either on the sacrilegious, or on undoubted public enemies, or on the treason-tainted, of whom you have so many."

Through long, early years Mrs. Eddy gave a good deal of thought and much prayer to the subject of animal magnetism, and she finally defined it in these explicit terms:

> Animal magnetism has no scientific foundation, for God governs all that is real, harmonious, and eternal, and His power is neither animal nor human. Its basis being a belief and this belief animal, in Science animal magnetism, mesmerism, or hypnotism is a mere negation, possessing neither intelligence, power, nor reality, and in sense it is an unreal concept of the so-called mortal mind.[1]

In 1878, three years after publishing the first edition of *Science and Health,* Mrs. Eddy brought out the second printing of the book. In some ways, it was a greater disappointment than was its predecessor. The book was written to be published in two volumes, but Volume I was never re-

[1] *Science and Health,* p. 102.

leased because of the many typographical mistakes and the liberties taken by proofreaders with Mrs. Eddy's interpretations. However, enough was salvaged from the two volumes to print five hundred copies of Volume II. The price on each copy was two dollars.

In Volume II are 167 pages, comprising five chapters: "Imposition and Demonstration," "Physiology," "Mesmerism," "Metaphysics," and "Reply to a Clergyman." Called "the Ark edition" because of the presence on the cover of a drawing of Noah's Ark, in its pages is the first indication that Mrs. Eddy was thinking in terms of a newspaper. She wrote:

> We have not a newspaper at our command through which to right the wrongs and answer the untruths, we have not a pulpit from which to explain how Christianity heals the sick, but if we had either of these, the slanderer and the physician would have less to do, and we should have more.

Mrs. Eddy seemed never to think along the lines of momentary advantage but always in terms of continuing and widening usefulness. She seemed always willing to dispense with popularity if she could effect the future good. What she was asking in this printing of *Science and Health,* as well as in the first printing, was that blame for sin and sickness and death be placed where it belongs—not upon God, but upon human beings themselves. She was willing to grant that to blame the individual for such things might be unpopular doctrine, but she was not willing to acknowledge that it need be.

In her teachings, from their inception, she insisted that, having been created in the image of his Maker, man possessed all the qualities she claimed for him but, over the ages, had allowed these same qualities to gather rust. In her teachings she was asking mankind to claim its heritage. Whether in the first, or the second, or the final printing of *Science and Health,* that is all she would ever ask.

Taking along copies of the first and second printings of her textbook, Mrs. Eddy and her husband went to Boston on January 31, 1881, to see John Wilson, one of the owners of the University Press. Mrs. Eddy, with her husband, had called on Wilson in 1878 to show him galley proofs of the second printing of *Science and Health.* They were seeking advice on how best to save something out of a mess of proof which was saturated with typographical mistakes.

A craftsman, Wilson was indignant over the poor example of printing, but managed to save approximately 170 pages, some of which were used in "the Ark edition."

In the early spring of 1880, Asa Gilbert Eddy wrote to Wilson requesting an estimate on the cost of printing a book of four hundred pages, which would be the third printing of *Science and Health.* Replying on April 3, Wilson requested details such as the number of new pages that would be needed and the quality of paper to be used, saying he would be glad to furnish an estimate as to cost but would require payment of "one-half of the amount before commencing the work." Having received no reply, the printer must have been somewhat surprised when, in the early afternoon of January 31, 1881, he was told that Mrs. Eddy and her husband were waiting to see him.

They spent the afternoon together, during which time Wilson inspected the two books through a craftsman's eyes and with a craftsman's words sought to restore Mrs. Eddy's lost confidence in printers. Near the end of the afternoon she told him she had learned that the printers of the second edition had not saved the plates so it would be necessary to reset and recast all of the book. To that she added that she would not be able to make a down payment of one-half the cost of manufacturing, but could pay "a few hundred dollars"; and she would not be able to pay the total bill on delivery of the books but was sure she could sell enough so he would not lose any money.

Brushing aside her frank explanation of her inability to meet his terms, Wilson expressed his personal interest in her proposed book and asked when she expected to complete her manuscript. Opening her handbag, Mrs. Eddy reached in and took out the completed manuscript. Astonished, Wilson took the manuscript and asked, his voice teeming with incredulity, "You brought this on the chance of my accepting it?"

Smiling, she shook her head, saying, "I never doubted."

Prayer was assuring Mrs. Eddy that her manuscript would be accepted; assuring Wilson that he would be paid was his confidence in the author.

In his volume, *Mary Baker Eddy and Her Books,*[2] William Dana Orcutt told of this experience, and wrote further:

"Mr. Wilson never explained, even to himself, his reaction to Mrs. Eddy's appeal. From a business standpoint there was every reason to decline the whole proposition. 'Yet,' he would say, after frankly admitting the situation, 'there wasn't a moment's hesitation in my acceptance of that order. I *knew* that the bill would be paid, and I found myself actually eager to undertake the manufacture.' "

In several ways the third printing is one of the most notable of all the hundreds of editions of *Science and Health.* Replacing the drawing of the Ark on the front cover are the Cross and the Crown, with the Crown circling the Cross but with the Crown free, all of it surrounded by a circle

[2] Copyright, 1950, The Christian Science Publishing Society, Boston, Mass.

containing the instruction of Jesus to his disciples: "Heal the sick, raise the dead, cleanse the lepers, cast out demons." This seal now identifies, and gives trademark protection in perpetuity, to Mrs. Eddy's writings. At the time of publication Mrs. Eddy was greatly concerned with copyright laws. The use of a trademark today provides further protection for her teachings. The third printing was in two volumes (as were several subsequent editions) and they set the editorial form for later printings.

The "Scientific Statement of Being," now so well known to Christian Scientists, makes its first appearance in the third printing. In its final form, it is a Statement which, with the correlative passages from I John, chapter 3, verses 1, 2, and 3, now is read at the conclusion of all Sunday services in Christian Science churches throughout the world.

In its original form, it read:

> There is no Life, substance, or intelligence in matter; all is Mind, there is no matter. Spirit is immortal Truth, matter is mortal error. Spirit is the real and eternal, matter the unreal and temporal. Spirit is God, and man is His image and likeness; hence, man is spiritual and not material.

In its final form, the Scientific Statement of Being reads:

> There is no life, truth, intelligence, nor substance in matter. All is infinite Mind and its infinite manifestation, for God is All-in-all. Spirit is immortal Truth; matter is mortal error. Spirit is the real and eternal; matter is the unreal and temporal. Spirit is God, and man is His image and likeness. Therefore, man is not material; he is spiritual.[3]

3 *Science and Health*, p. 468.

The correlative passages from I John are:

> Behold, what manner of love the Father hath bestowed upon us, that we should be called the sons of God: therefore the world knoweth us not, because it knew him not.
>
> Beloved, now are we the sons of God, and it doth not yet appear what we shall be: but we know that, when he shall appear, we shall be like him; for we shall see him as he is.
>
> And every man that hath this hope in him purifieth himself, even as he is pure.

In the third printing are twelve chapters: "Science of Being," "Footsteps of Truth," "Physiology," "Recapitulation," "Healing the Sick," "Demonology," "Imposition and Demonstration," "Creation," "Marriage," "Prayer and Atonement," "Platform of Christian Scientists," and "Reply to a Clergyman."

Preceding the Preface, which was written by Mrs. Eddy, are several pages addressed "To the Public." Signed by Dr. Asa G. Eddy, they echo Mrs. Eddy's concern over the evil of plagiarism. After presenting a number of illustrations of thievery from Mrs. Eddy's writings, Dr. Eddy observed that "copyrighting books is a farce," and declared: "[Plagiarism] may be convenient for an ignoramus or a villain, but a real expounder of 'The Understanding of Christianity or God,' would scarcely be caught at it."

Following Dr. Eddy's protest is another, this one being signed by thirty-one students. It, too, is addressed To the Public. In part, it reads:

"The undersigned, in justice to ourselves, hereby publicly state that we believe the abuses denominated mesmerism and malpractice are carried on by some claiming to be metaphysicians; but while our knowledge of meta-physics enables us to defend ourselves and others from their attacks, we are by no means committing their crimes, for our power lies not in mesmerism, but Truth; it is not animal magnetism, but moral and spiritual strength.

"And we are fully convinced that no one can reach the height in metaphysics that our teacher, the author of 'Science and Health,' has reached, and progress as she is pro-gressing, and be a moral or mental malpractitioner.

"If the malpractitioner is causing others to believe that we are venturing on his forbidden ground, it is only to screen himself, and to hide the results of his wrong-doing, that take away his ability to heal. . . ."

As Mrs. Eddy was sure would happen, the third printing was an immediate success, so much of a success that the print order had to be repeated and repeated again. Three printings of one thousand books each were exhausted by the time she was ready with new material.

Although Mary Baker Eddy did not quickly reach her final definition of animal magnetism, she did see clearly, as early as February, 1882, how to meet and rise above all the hostility that, in varying degrees, seems to attend the birth of all religious movements.

With her husband, she spent the early months of 1882 in Washington, D. C. She had a number of reasons for going to Washington. She wanted to study the copyright laws; she wanted to meet with possible students of her teachings; she wanted to get away from the antagonism that was pressing down upon her in Lynn. Her whereabouts, after leaving Lynn, were known to but two students.

In a letter to one of these students—the letter carries the date of February 28, 1882—she referred to falsehood, the ancient antagonist of Truth, saying: "I am above it all, my words go over the fury of the storm, with their peace, be still."

Peace, be still—the three words, and the circumstances under which they were first said, were familiar to her: "And he arose, and rebuked the wind, and said unto the sea, Peace, be still. And the wind ceased, and there was a great calm. And he said unto them, Why are ye so fearful? how is it that ye have no faith?" [4]

Peace, be still—in these words, as Jesus gave them voice, was the command of authority. Even while Mrs. Eddy was pondering the instant obedience of wind and sea, she knew that what the disciples witnessed was the operation of the same law that healed the sick and raised the dead. The law was God's law.

Throughout her long career, Mary Baker Eddy watched the departure of those who came to her door in search of healing but left because they were unwilling to listen and, by listening, come to believe:

> The physical healing of Christian Science results now, as in Jesus' time, from the operation of divine Principle, before which sin and disease lose their reality in human consciousness and disappear as naturally and as necessarily as darkness gives place to light and sin to reformation. Now, as then, these mighty works are not supernatural, but supremely natural. They are the sign of Immanuel, or "God with us . . ." [5]

They did not take into account the years of prayer that led to her own perception; failing, they did not hear these words:

[4] Mark, chapter 4, verses 39, 40.
[5] *Science and Health,* p. xi.

Is a musician made by his teacher? He makes himself a musician by practising what he was taught. The conscientious are successful. They follow faithfully; through evil or through good report, they work on to the achievement of good; by patience, they inherit the promise. . . .[6]

While in Washington Mrs. Eddy spent a good many evenings lecturing before small gatherings of interested men and women. With her husband, she returned to Boston in 1882, having decided before the Washington visit to move from Lynn to Boston. In Boston was a growing interest in the teachings, largely the result of Mrs. Eddy's lectures; in Boston was John Wilson and the facilities of the University Press; in Boston were the advantages of a community that was regarded as the great cultural, industrial, and mercantile center of New England.

The twelve years in Lynn were extremely eventful ones for Mrs. Eddy. Here, in the frame house at 8 Broad Street, with its wooden fence in front, memories were born. *Science and Health* was completed here, in the room in the attic, with its bureau, its table, and on the table a Bible, its rocker, its straight-backed chair, the framed inscription "Thou Shalt Have No Other Gods Before Me" hanging on the wall, the skylight that gave light and ventilation, and the carpet strewn with sheets of paper over which her pencil had raced in keeping pace with the illumined thoughts that flooded her consciousness.

In this house in 1876 was formed the Christian Scientist Association, which, for several years, was Mrs. Eddy's pastoral staff in directing the affairs of the young Movement. From this house in 1879 was formed the church now known

[6] *Miscellaneous Writings,* p. 340.

to the world as the Church of Christ, Scientist. In this house was formed the Massachusetts Metaphysical College, which was chartered by the state in 1881 "for medical purposes, to give instruction in scientific methods of mental healing on a purely practical basis, to impart a thorough understanding of metaphysics, to restore health, hope, and harmony to man."

The church was a natural development of Sunday services that began in Good Templars Hall on Market Street, in Lynn, in 1875, just as the services in Good Templars Hall grew out of Sunday meetings with a few students in the classroom at Shepard and South Common streets in 1872, at which Mrs. Eddy explained the Scriptures. However, in Good Templars Hall hymns were sung, there was a prayer, Mrs. Eddy preached a sermon, Mrs. Samuel P. Bancroft played the melodeon, a collection was taken. In the spring of 1875 eight students [7] had pledged to contribute ten dollars weekly to Mrs. Eddy "to preach to us, or direct our meetings on the Sabbath of each week [in the] moral science called the Science of Life."

The first services in Good Templars Hall on June 6, 1875, were attended by some twenty persons. The name of Church of Christ, Scientist, was not chosen then. It was first suggested by Mrs. Eddy at a meeting in the home of Mrs. Margaret Dunshee in Charlestown, Massachusetts, on April 12, 1879. Attending this meeting were twenty-six members of the Christian Scientist Association. It was a meeting that had been called by Mrs. Eddy for the purpose of forming "a church without creeds, to be called the 'CHURCH OF CHRIST, SCIENTIST.' " [8]

---

[7] Elizabeth M. Newhall, Daniel H. Spofford, George H. Allen, Dorcas B. Rawson, Asa T. N. MacDonald, George W. Barry, S. P. Bancroft, Miranda R. Rice.

[8] *Manual of the Mother Church*, p. 17.

Among the twenty-six persons present were a number who were in agreement with the proposal to form a church but who were not in agreement with their teacher's suggestion for a name. Mrs. Eddy did not press her suggestion, but she did insist that all members give careful thought, in prayer, to a name. A week later there was another meeting. There was no decision in the matter of naming the church, but the members did continue the work of forming a church "designed to commemorate the word and works of our Master, which should reinstate primitive Christianity and its lost element of healing." [9]

At this meeting Mrs. Eddy recommended, and the membership was in unanimous agreement, that the first Sabbath services of the church, whatever its chosen name, be held in Salem, Massachusetts, on the first Sunday in May, 1879, and be continued each Sunday thereafter at places to be designated. Since 1875 there had been Sunday services, of course, although they had moved out of Good Templars Hall and into the homes of students in Lynn and in Boston, thus saving a few dollars in rent.

On May 10, 1879, which was the Saturday following the first Sunday services in Salem, the members of the Association met again, disapproved use of the word "Scientist," but left "Church of Christ," "unless," as stated in the minutes of the meeting, "there be one already by that name."

Again, Mrs. Eddy reminded her students of the need to identify her church with her teachings—and, although she had proved to them and they had proved for themselves that the Science she taught was a demonstrable Science, they sought to avoid the testimony by concealing the precepts of her teachings under a napkin of deceit. Again she asked them to take her suggestion to the sanctuary of their pray-

[9] *Manual of the Mother Church*, p. 17.

ers. Soon afterwards the name "Church of Christ, Scientist" was approved unanimously. In August, 1879, a charter was obtained.

Thinking of her teachings in terms of permanency, Mrs. Eddy saw the need for class instruction and the importance of "thorough preparation of the student for practice" (*Miscellany*, p. 245). In 1867–1870, as in the cases of Crafts and Kennedy, she taught individual students over indefinite periods. From 1870 until 1881, she taught classes of varying sizes, satisfied herself that *class instruction* was the better way, and now, having organized her church, she began studying the laws of Massachusetts to see what they offered in the way of permitting her to establish a school in which classes of selected students could be taught systematically and scientifically.

In examining the state statutes she learned of the passage in 1874 of a law which permitted her to organize a college in which to teach scientific metaphysics. She applied for a charter. It was granted in 1881. She opened the Massachusetts Metaphysical College. It was the first and only such charter in the United States, and the only such charter ever granted in the state of Massachusetts.

In this house at 8 Broad Street in Lynn there had been seen for the first time a small sign on which was this name: "Dr. A. G. Eddy," and under the name were the words "Christian Scientist." He was the first Christian Science practitioner to so identify himself. It was in the downstairs parlor of this house that he first met the woman who became his wife.

Born in Londonderry, Vermont, Eddy learned the trade of a spinner in the cotton mills in Proctorsville, Vermont. He was acting as an agent for a sewing machine company in Boston. Eddy had suffered a general physical breakdown.

Through his friends, the Godfreys of Chelsea, he learned of Mrs. Godfrey's healing of blood poisoning.

Immediately interested, he asked so many questions that Mrs. Godfrey suggested he go to Lynn and get the answers there. A few days later Eddy went to Lynn. He became a student. On New Year's Day, 1877, he and Mary B. Glover were married by a Unitarian minister.

Rather stocky, with a countryman's wide shoulders, a countryman's steady stride, and slow, thoughtful speech, the spinner from Vermont was a sincere man who was genuinely interested in the teachings. Quite the opposite of his teacher in quickness and depth of thought, but her companion in thoroughness of application, he kept pressing her acceptance of his proposal of marriage, saying there were details he could do quite as well as could she, thus leaving her free to do what only she could do. She believed him and found him as sincere in the offer as she was in its acceptance.

Their last meeting in the Lynn house was the night before the house was to be rented, but not sold. Mrs. Eddy had provided for continuing possession by writing a student: "Let the house stand for the good it has done. Maybe, in future years, you will love to come and look upon it." Tonight, with a few students, all sitting on packing cases in the otherwise empty parlor, she closed her stay in Lynn with a church meeting.

Twelve years had gone since Mrs. Eddy returned to Lynn from Amesbury. In these years hope that the Christian clergy would embrace her discovery had vanished. Nor was she dismayed. She now knew as it was given to her to discover, so was it given to her to protect. From Lynn she had looked out toward Boston, toward her native New Hampshire, toward all New England and beyond, preparing for the day when the emerging revelation would cross the oceans.

Daily, three times daily, she withdrew from the presence of other tasks and secluded herself in the small room in the attic, there to seek in prayer the guidance so greatly desired.

Lost for more than one thousand five hundred years, the element of healing that was so important a part in Jesus' teachings must not be lost again. Patiently she awaited words of direction. They did not come quickly—but she knew that when she was ready to hear them, she would know them.

CHAPTER SIX

"I Have Come to Comfort You"

In the spring of 1882 Mrs. Eddy established her first real residence in Boston at 569 Columbus Avenue but not until, with her husband, she had changed addresses three different times. First they rented two rooms in a house on Newton Street, near Tremont Street; from here they moved to 233 Newton Street and then to a five-room flat on Hammond Street, where they lived with one of her students. In no one place was their stay very long.

The building at 569 Columbus Avenue had three floors, an attic, and a basement. Leading up to the front door from the street was a stoop with six steps. The building was of stone with bay windows in front on all floors. Several students came to live with her, and with them they brought different opinions as to furnishings. Columbus Avenue being one of the better residential streets in Boston, Mrs. Eddy rebuffed those who wanted elegance, in keeping with the neighborhood. She reminded them that "a man's life consisteth not in the abundance of things he possesseth" and kept expenditures within her means.

A piano was rented; an encyclopedia was purchased on the instalment plan; a set of ebony furniture was bought at a substantial discount. It was furniture that was delivered to the store in a defective condition but had been completely repaired. The food on the table was plain, but there was plenty of it. Occasionally Mrs. Eddy did the cooking, but usually the kitchen chores were left to the household. Punctuality at meals was a requirement.

During the evening the members of the household gathered around the piano to sing hymns, some of which Mrs. Eddy had sung in Congregational churches in Bow, in Concord, and in Sanbornton Bridge. Often in the evenings there were readings and discussions of the works of different authors, but especially Whittier, Emerson, A. Bronson Alcott, Longfellow, and Shakespeare. Of them, Mrs. Eddy felt closest to Whittier and was particularly grateful to Alcott.

Early in 1876, after reading a gift copy of *Science and Health,* A. Bronson Alcott had written Mrs. Eddy:

"The sacred truths which you announce sustained by facts of Immortal Life, give to your work the seal of inspiration. ... In times like ours so sunk in sensualism, I hail with joy any voice speaking an assured word for God and Immortality. And my joy is heightened the more when I find the blessed words are of woman's divinings."

Later Alcott visited her and introduced himself. After referring to the harsh criticism that greeted the publication of the first edition of *Science and Health,* he said, "I have come to comfort you."

The founder of the Concord School of Philosophy was welcomed then and on one or two other occasions. Mrs. Eddy never forgot his encouragement at a time when she was sorely pressed.

Emerson she did not know, nor did she read any of his writings prior to publication of the first edition of *Science and Health.* She accepted as true, as did Emerson, the Psalmist's assurance that God "healeth all thy diseases." However, unlike Emerson, who was content to affirm the supremacy of spiritual law and go no further than affirmation,

Mary Baker Eddy insisted on proving the immediate availability of the law which frees mankind of all its diseases.

She admired Longfellow's poetry and, in her childhood,
in Bow, made her acquaintance with Shakespeare by listening to family conversations with visiting clergymen and
through talks with her brother Albert.

On Thursday evenings the Eddy home was open to the
public. On these evenings hymns were sung, there were
talks by Mrs. Eddy, and there were testimonies of healings.
On one of the evenings one of the testifiers was Julia S.
Bartlett, then, as well as later, a member of Mrs. Eddy's
household.

Confined to her bed in her home in Hartford, Connecticut, and told by attending physicians that hers would be a
life of invalidism, Miss Bartlett, in April, 1880, received a
letter from a friend. Attached to the letter was a circular
written by Mrs. Eddy containing an account of the forming of the first Christian Science church in Lynn in the
previous year. In the circular it was stated: "This Church is
designed to perpetuate the teachings of Jesus, to reinstate
its primitive Christianity, and to restore the lost element of
healing."

Miss Bartlett acknowledged receipt of the letter by asking her friend to recommend a Christian Science practitioner. At the same time she wrote to Mrs. Eddy requesting
a copy of *Science and Health*. The friend also sought the
advice of Mrs. Eddy, who recommended the selection of
Asa G. Eddy as practitioner to Miss Bartlett. The invalid
was quickly healed, after seven years of sickness. On September 30, 1880, she became the third member of a class of
three that was instructed by Mrs. Eddy in the Massachusetts
Metaphysical College. The second member was the friend
who had written the letter containing the circular.

As at 8 Broad Street in Lynn, the downstairs parlor at

569 Columbus Avenue was used as a classroom for the College. In teaching, Mrs. Eddy never permitted the taking of notes by students. She learned early that words of instruction could not become careless words. Inasmuch as she was teaching a science, an exactness in language was a requirement.

There are many recorded remembrances of Mrs. Eddy's physical appearance in those days. One of these, written by Mrs. Caroline D. Noyes of Chicago, was included in Clifford P. Smith's book, *Historical Sketches:*

"In 1883," wrote Mrs. Noyes, "I attended a lecture by Mrs. Eddy at her home in Boston. Her subject was 'Belief, Faith, and Understanding.' She was beautiful in face and figure; her grace, dignity, and freedom of expression were very remarkable. Her perfect ease and her choice of language were very striking. Her exquisite taste in dress and her immaculate neatness in appearance were also very noticeable. Her fine, expressive, dark eyes, violet I should call them, beamed with kindness and intelligence. Altogether, she was most attractive and engaging. From so fine and ladylike an individual, one would hardly expect the strong and forceful way she displayed at times, both in conversation and in her lessons. She had an affectionate and endearing manner, but her strong ways also created an unfailing confidence in her ability to establish the great work she did. When I first knew her [which was prior to 1883], she was nearly sixty years of age but appeared not over thirty-five or forty."

Holding a Bible in her left hand, using her right hand and her voice for emphasis, and slowly walking back and forth in front of her class, Mrs. Eddy never closed an instruction period until every question was answered correctly. To make sure the student understood, no matter how long it took, she called the roll and repeated the questions, one by one, until she was satisfied with all the answers.

Recalling those days, another early student, Samuel Putnam Bancroft, said, "Mrs. Eddy had apparently but one purpose in life, and that was to benefit mankind ... At all times she seemed conscious of a wisdom beyond her own." [1]

In these months in Boston, Asa Gilbert Eddy continued his helpful work. In addition to his duties as a Christian Science practitioner, and his work as publisher of *Science and Health,* he taught in the Massachusetts Metaphysical College. Then suddenly, in the night of June 3, 1882, he was gone. It was a loss Mrs. Eddy felt deeply.

Following Asa Gilbert Eddy's passing, Mrs. Eddy left her household in the care of Miss Bartlett and Mrs. Abbie Whiting and, upon invitation, went to Barton, in northern Vermont, where she occupied a house owned by Arthur True Buswell, a student. At her request, Buswell had returned to Boston from Cincinnati, Ohio, where she had sent him on church work.

In Vermont she was able to give undivided attention to the making of new plans for the reopening of her College, which she closed soon after her husband's passing. The quiet surroundings also permitted her to reorganize her household. Before leaving Boston she had called a meeting of the Christian Scientist Association at which she spoke of the need for a publication that would distribute accurate information about Christian Science, saying, "If I have to give up other work, we will have the paper."

In Barton she chose a successor to her husband as manager of her household. He was a former machine operator in a shoe factory in Lynn. His name was Calvin A. Frye. Upon completion of his course in the Massachusetts Metaphysical College in 1881, he had gone to Lawrence, Massa-

[1] *Mrs. Eddy as I Knew Her in 1870.*

chusetts, where he was a Christian Science practitioner. Thoughtful, taciturn, rather short and stocky of physique, but with a sense of humor, Frye's honesty and understanding had impressed Asa G. Eddy into recommending his employment "if a reliable person is ever needed."

Returning to Boston in the early autumn, Mrs. Eddy brought Frye with her, having telegraphed him to meet her at Plymouth, New Hampshire, and ride with her to Boston. This he did, and he found himself answering penetrating questions concerning his willingness and his ability to assume responsibilities that would be his if he was to be the co-ordinator of her household. In the nearly thirty years of his association with Mrs. Eddy, he came to occupy a position of great trust.

However, he was not equal to the opportunity she may well have had in mind for him when she telegraphed him to meet her train at Plymouth. With her husband gone, she needed a publisher's help for her textbook, a teacher's help in the Massachusetts Metaphysical College and, with the "paper" she wanted coming into focus, she needed help with it. Perhaps, in this dilemma, her thoughts went back a few years.

In 1879 or 1880, while temporarily in Boston, she heard that her son was living in Deadwood, South Dakota. She telegraphed him, asking him to come to Boston. He did and told her he was married, and was raising a family. It was a happy meeting, although, in a sense, it must have been an uncomfortable meeting for both. Now past his middle thirties in years, his memories of his mother were fragile; her memories of him were of a baby in her arms, growing into a boy of eleven. In interests, they were far apart. His concern was in prospecting for gold and silver. He had no interest at all in her work, although, while in Boston, he accepted its hospitality.

Clifford P. Smith wrote about this experience in his book *Historical Sketches:* "In 1879 or 1880, while Mrs. Eddy was living temporarily in Boston ... her realization of a spiritual fact healed her granddaughter and namesake, Mary Baker Glover, of the material belief called crossed eyes. In 1934, her granddaughter, now Mrs. Billings, related this healing as follows:

" 'During the fall and winter of 1879 and 1880, when we lived at Deadwood, South Dakota, and I was three years old, my father went to visit his mother at Boston. At that time my eyes were what is termed crossed, and during his visit he told grandmother about them. According to my father, grandmother said, "You must be mistaken, George; her eyes are all right."

" 'When he returned to our home in Deadwood, and during a conversation with my mother at my bedside while I was asleep, they awakened me and discovered that my eyes had become straightened. Mother has a picture of me taken before this incident, showing my eyes crossed. This healing was often told me by my father and mother, and is at this time verified by my mother, who is with me.' "

Whatever may have been Mrs. Eddy's hopes concerning the usefulness of her son in her work, it was well that she had in John Wilson, of the University Press, a man who was genuinely interested in helping her. John Wilson was born in England of a Scottish father and an English mother. His father was a printer who had learned his trade in Scotland and who was a close friend of Robert Burns and the Scottish poet's first publisher. The Wilson family moved to Boston, where John Wilson served his apprenticeship under his father, and, after his father's death, became the principal partner in the purchase of the University Press.

The University Press was a direct descendant of the Stephen Daye Press, the first printers in British North America. In 1840 the Stephen Daye Press published the Bay Psalm Book, and in 1663 they published the Eliot Indian Bible. Continuing in the best traditions under John Wilson, the company published the writings of Oliver Wendell Holmes, Henry Wadsworth Longfellow, John Greenleaf Whittier, Nathaniel Hawthorne, and Ralph Waldo Emerson. These New Englanders were among the distinguished authors whose names and faces were familiar to John Wilson when, in 1881, a discouraged Mary Baker Eddy sought his advice on what to do with a mass of botched proof sheets of the second edition of *Science and Health.*

A religious man, but one who favored no particular denomination, John Wilson's admiration for Mrs. Eddy's courage and his respect for her integrity were so great that her manuscripts were given a favored position in the production schedules of the University Press. Doubtless he found it refreshing that a woman should be boldly calling for the restoration, in full measure, of the teachings of the Christ at a time when the Christian clergy was counting its prerogatives and encouraging no word of disagreement.

In 1883 she was at his desk again, this time with the manuscript for the sixth edition of *Science and Health.* Added to the title were six words—"With a Key to the Scriptures"—making the new title read: *Science and Health With a Key to the Scriptures.* This was a Glossary. Mrs. Eddy agreed with Bible students "that the Scriptures have both a spiritual and literal meaning." [2] In the Glossary she sought to fill the need for a better understanding of the spiritual meaning of various Scriptural words. Following are some of the words, with her interpretation:

> Angels. God's thoughts passing to man. Spiritual intuitions pure and perfect. The inspiration of

[2] *Science and Health,* p. 320.

good, purity, and immortality, giving the lie to evil, sensuality, and mortality.

Baptism. Man purified by Spirit, submerged in Truth. "To be absent from the body and to be present with the Lord." (II Corinthians v. 8.)

Church. The superstructure of Truth and Love. Whatever rests upon and proceeds from divine Principle. That which affords proof of its utility, is found elevating the race, rousing the dormant understanding from material beliefs to the apprehension of spiritual ideas, and the demonstration of divine science, casting out devils, error, and healing the sick.

Morning. Light; symbol of Truth, revelation, and progression.

Time. Mortal measurements; limits, in which is summed up all human acts, thoughts, beliefs, opinions, knowledge. Matter, error. That which continues after what is termed death, until the erring and mortal, disappears, and spiritual perfection appears.

In their final form as revised by Mary Baker Eddy, the words have these spiritual interpretations. To be noted is the fact that in each case there is no change in basic meaning, only clarification.

Angels. God's thoughts passing to man; spiritual intuitions, pure and perfect; the inspiration of goodness, purity, and immortality, counteracting all evil, sensuality, and mortality.

Baptism. Purification by Spirit; submergence in Spirit.

We are "willing rather to be absent from the

body, and to be present with the Lord." (II Corinthians v. 8.)

Church. The structure of Truth and Love; whatever rests upon and proceeds from divine Principle.

The Church is that institution, which affords proof of its utility and is found elevating the race, rousing the dormant understanding from material beliefs to the apprehension of spiritual ideas and the demonstration of divine Science, thereby casting out devils, or error, and healing the sick.

Morning. Light; symbol of Truth; revelation and progress.

Time. Mortal measurements; limits, in which are summed up all human acts, thoughts, beliefs, opinions, knowledge; matter; error; that which begins before, and continues after, what is termed death, until the mortal disappears and spiritual perfection appears.

As with the third, fourth, and fifth printings, the sixth was in two volumes. The first volume contained five chapters under these headings: "Science of Being," "Footsteps of Truth," "Physiology," "Recapitulation," and "Healing the Sick." In the second volume were eight chapters, with these headings: "Imposition and Demonstration," "Creation," "Marriage," "Prayer and Atonement," "Platform of Christian Scientists," "Reply to a Clergyman," "Demonology," and "Key to the Scriptures." In the Preface Mrs. Eddy made reference to the theft of her teachings by former students, as well as by others.

In part, she wrote:

Throughout our publications of metaphysical healing or Christian Science, when writing or

dictating them, we have given ourselves to con-
templation wholly apart from the observation of
the material senses: to look upon a copy would
have distracted our thoughts from the subject before us. We were seldom able to copy our own
compositions, and have employed an amanuensis
for the last six years. Every work that we have had
published has been extemporaneously written; and
out of fifty lectures and sermons that we have delivered the past year, forty-four have been extemporaneous.

It was her practice to turn over copies of these unpub-
lished compositions to students for study, and frequently
she gave them permission to copy (but not to publish!) the
papers. It was a practice that had begun as far back as 1862,
born of her desire to share the discovery and the findings.
Her generosity was returning to plague her.

The response to the sixth printing was a repetition of the
response to the third, fourth, and fifth printings. They all
disclosed a widening interest in Mary Baker Eddy and in
her teachings.

On January 17, 1883, at a meeting of the Christian Scientist Association, "the subject of a publication for the
good of the Cause was introduced, and [according to the
record of the meeting] some of the many objects to be
gained by such an organ were warmly discussed." The differences in opinion disappeared and, about three months
later, or on April 14, 1883, the first issue of *The Christian
Science Journal* made its appearance. Complete in eight
pages of three columns each, it was a modest printing effort
designed to be "an independent family paper to promote
Health and Morals."

In an article on page three, entitled "A Timely Issue," Mrs. Eddy wrote:

> An organ from the Christian Scientists has become a necessity [because] after looking over the newspapers of the day, very naturally comes the reflection that it is dangerous to live, so loaded seems the very air with disease. These descriptions carry fears to many minds, to be depicted in some future time upon the body. This error we shall be able in a great measure to counteract, for at the price we issue our paper we shall be able to reach many homes. . . .

The publication was a bimonthly, with the date of issue being the first Saturday of alternate months. The cost of subscription was one dollar a year. Single copies were sold at seventeen cents. Advertising was confined to the professional cards of the Massachusetts Metaphysical College and those of practitioners in Boston, Lawrence, Lowell, Manchester, East Cambridge, and West Medford, perhaps a dozen in all. Advertising rates were: "One square, first time, $1; subsequently, each time, 25¢; one square, yearly basis, $2; reading notices, per line, 15¢." Each square was one column wide and slightly less than one inch in depth.

In the first issue was an announcement stating that an address on Christian Science was given by Mrs. Eddy on each Sunday at 3:00 P.M., and every Thursday evening at 7:30 P.M. another lecture was given, "followed by discussion, and practical explanation of Christian Science." Occasionally, the Thursday evening lecture was given by Mrs. Eddy; usually, it was given by a student. (Later in 1883 the Thursday evening meeting was changed to Friday evening.)

The first issue of *The Christian Science Journal* was almost wholly a product of Mrs. Eddy's efforts, including the work of editing and publishing. On page 6, she commented on "Slander," addressing sharp words to some she had befriended but who now were trying to destroy both her teachings and her person.

"But Heaven defend us," she wrote, "from the spurious imitation [virtuous people], such as make a parade of 'charities,' to be seen of men, going about to do good—and *evil* too!—and with pious accent and devotion's visage get through lying about a friend in time to say their prayers."

Mary Baker Eddy was beginning to realize, as she came to realize so well, that the world does not easily surrender its prejudices.

On October 21, 1881, while she was living in Lynn, eight students publicly withdrew their support from the Christian Scientist Association. Among the eight were two who had signed the compact that provided for Sabbath Day services in Good Templars Hall. In withdrawing their support they expressed sorrow for Mrs. Eddy's "departure from the straight and narrow road (which alone leads to growth in Christ-like virtues)." It was averred this departure is "made manifest by frequent ebullitions of temper, love of money, and the appearance of hypocrisy," which prevented them from submitting "to such Leadership."

In anguish, Mrs. Eddy called a meeting of the Association and requested attendance by the eight students. They did not appear. She sent word, asking them to meet with her in private. They refused. After almost a month of fruitless effort to persuade the students to appear, the Association drafted and approved, among others, this resolution:

Resolved, that the charges made . . . in a letter, signed by J. C. Howard, M. R. Rice, D. B. Dawson, and five others, of hypocrisy, ebullitions of

temper and love of money, are utterly false, and
the cowardice of the signers in refusing to meet
her, and sustain or explain said charge, be treated
with the righteous indignation it justly deserves.
That while we deplore such wickedness and abuse
of her who has befriended them in their need and
when wrong, met them with honest, open rebuke,
we look with admiration and reverence upon her
Christ-like example of meekness and charity, and
will, in future, more faithfully follow and obey her
Divine instructions, knowing that in so doing we
offer the highest testimonial of our appreciation
of her Christian Leadership.

Already forces were at work seeking to destroy, and destroy utterly, what she was trying to build. Yet it was not
surprising that there should be deserters. All students, including Mrs. Eddy, were newcomers from established denominations. As such they were not accustomed to living in
a climate of self-discipline. Bereft of the trappings of ecclesiasticism, hers were teachings that demanded obedience not
to the edicts of church councils but to the law of God. What
Mrs. Eddy was trying to build needed strong and uncom-
promising leadership if it was to survive.

The defecting students confused firmness with temper,
although Mrs. Eddy was strict. She had to be. She knew if
what was promised by Christian Science was to be fulfilled
unswerving adherence to the teachings was imperative. In
Science and Health (p. 167) she wrote:

It is not wise to take a halting and half-way position or to expect to work equally with Spirit and
matter, Truth and error. There is but one way—
namely God and His idea—which leads to spiritual

being. The scientific government of the body must be obtained through the divine Mind. It is impossible to gain control over the body in any other way. On this fundamental point, timid conservatism is absolutely inadmissible. Only through radical reliance on Truth can scientific healing power be realized.

In *Rudimental Divine Science* (p. 17) she recalled her own experience:

> ... The Discoverer of this Science could tell you of timidity, of self-distrust, friendlessness, toil, agonies, and victories under which she needed miraculous vision to sustain her, when taking the first footsteps in this Science. The ways of Christianity have not changed.

Late in 1882 a man named Julius A. Dresser, who was a former patient of Phineas P. Quimby, was living in California when he heard of Mrs. Eddy's work in Boston. As quickly as he could Dresser went to Boston, where he attended Sunday services in Hawthorne Hall, saw with his own eyes an absence of vacant seats, obtained a copy of *Science and Health,* made inquiries about the sales of the book, checked on the activities at the Massachusetts Metaphysical College, and set about making his own plans to promote his own interests.

On February 8, 1883, he opened his attack by means of a letter which was published in the *Boston Post.* In this letter, which was signed "A.O.," Dresser accused Mrs. Eddy with stealing from Quimby the "healing through a mental method which [she] claims to have discovered." On February 19, 1883, the same newspaper published another letter.

This letter, initialed "E.G.," was a vigorous denial of the charge. It drew a reply. The reply, signed by Dresser, was published in the *Boston Post* on February 24, 1883, and stated in part:

"The undersigned is a quiet, humble citizen of Boston, who seeks no controversy with anybody. But when he knows positively that truth is being outraged and dragged in the dirt, he will step forward and uphold the truth and let error become, as it always does, its own destroyer. . . . I will call as a witness the same Mrs. Eddy whom 'E.G.' speaks of.

"This lady was a patient and a student of the late Dr. P. P. Quimby, of Portland, Me., in the winter of 1862 and '63. She was then known as Mrs. Patterson, wife of Dr. Patterson, dentist. The writer [Dresser introduced Mrs. Eddy to Quimby] of this communication was a patient and student of Dr. Quimby's at different times, from the year 1860 to 1865, including the period when Mrs. Patterson-Eddy was acting in the same capacity. . . . Mrs. Patterson-Eddy knows positively that the assertions of 'E.G.' in last Monday's Post are a tissue of falsehoods."

Mrs. Eddy replied at once:

> We had laid the foundation of mental healing before we ever saw Dr. Quimby; were a homeopathist without a diploma, owing to our aversion to the dissecting room. We made our first experiments in mental healing about 1853, when we were convinced that mind had a science which, if understood, would heal all diseases, we were then investigating that science, but never saw Dr. Quimby until 1862. . . .
>
> We never were a student of Dr. Quimby's, and Mr. Dresser knows that. Dr. Quimby never

had students to our knowledge. He was a humanitarian . . . He was somewhat of a remarkable healer, and at the time we knew him he was known as a mesmerist. We were one of his patients. He manipulated his patients, but possibly back of his practice he had a theory in advance of his method and, as we now understand it, and have since discovered, he mingled that theory with mesmerism.

We knew him about twenty years ago and aimed to help him. We saw he was looking in our direction and asked him to write his thoughts out. He did so, and then we would take that copy to correct, and, sometimes, so transform it that he would say it was our composition, which it virtually was, but we always gave him back the copy and, sometimes, wrote his name on the back of it. . . .

The exchange of letters between Dresser and Mrs. Eddy attracted more than a little attention in Boston. Appointing himself as their spokesman, Dresser gathered together various other mental healers, more than one hundred in all, and used his association with them to promote his claims for Quimby in every possible way. Joining in his attacks on Mrs. Eddy were a number of clergymen. Encouraged by Dresser, George A. Quimby began making claims for his father's papers which left a false impression that they were in his father's handwriting rather than in the handwriting of various copyists. Thereupon Mrs. Eddy offered to pay the costs of publication under certain conditions:

MR. GEORGE A. QUIMBY, son of the late Phineas P. Quimby,— over his own signature, and before a

witness,—stated, in 1883, that he had in his possession at that time *all* the manuscripts written by his
father. I hereby declare, to expose the falsehood
of parties publicly intimating that I have appro-
priated matter belonging to the aforesaid Quimby,
that I will pay the cost of printing and publishing
the first edition of those Manuscripts, with the author's name attached:

Provided,—that I am allowed first to examine
said Manuscripts, and that I find they were Mr.
P. P. Quimby's own compositions, and not mine,
that were left with him many years ago,—or that
they have not, since his death, in 1865, been stolen
from my published works; and also, that I am
given the right to bring out this one edition under
copyright of the owner of said Manuscripts, and
that all the money accruing from the sale of said
book shall be paid to said owner. Some of Mr.
Quimby's purported writings, quoted by J. A.
Dresser, were my own words, as nearly as I can
recollect them.

There is a great demand for my book, Science
and Health. Hence Mr. Dresser's excuse for the delay in publishing Quimby's Manuscripts—namely,
that this age is not sufficiently enlightened to be
benefited by them (?)—is lost; for if I have copied
from Quimby, and my book is accepted, this acceptance creates a demand for his writings.

MARY BAKER G. EDDY.[3]

The offer was not accepted, nor were the Quimby papers
published until 1921, some years after George A. Quimby's
death. Back in 1901, even while maintaining that Mrs.

---

[3] *The Christian Science Journal,* June, 1887.

Eddy's system of healing was an outgrowth of Quimby's, he had written: "The *religion* which she teaches certainly *is hers,* for which I cannot be too thankful; for I should be loath to go down to my grave feeling that my father was in any way connected with 'Christian Science.'" Having no substance, the Dresser-inspired charges quickly lost headway.

Historians have filled libraries with the deeds of warriors who left behind a dynasty, a legend, a sword—Mary Baker Eddy spoke of a man who left behind simple teachings. In all her writings she dwelt on these teachings, and in *Science and Health* (p. 131) she pointed out: "The central fact of the Bible is the superiority of spiritual over physical power." Likewise, it is the central fact of her own teachings.

In a house down the street and across from the Massachusetts Metaphysical College lived a little girl whose bright smile often cheered Mrs. Eddy. On one particular morning, Mrs. Eddy saw a doctor's carriage leaving the house. Waiting a moment, or two, Mrs. Eddy left her own home and, crossing the street, rang the bell of the house. A weeping woman answered. In answer to Mrs. Eddy's inquiry, the woman said the child was so sick that the doctor had said she could not get better. Mrs. Eddy asked to see the child. Going to the bedroom, she sat quietly in prayer. After a few minutes the little girl was restored, was out of bed, was romping around the house, and was smiling again.

Mrs. Eddy was called to treat a baby suffering from what appeared to its parents to be a serious malformation. Paying no attention to the deformity, Mrs. Eddy said to the mother, "You fell before this child was born." Shaking her head, the mother replied, "No, Mrs. Eddy, I never fell while I was carrying the child."

Declaring the truth, "There is no effect from prenatal shock or fear," Mrs. Eddy turned away from the baby, which was immediately healed. Not until then did the mother remember. "Yes, I do recall that two days before this child was born I fell down two steps, but I had forgotten about it."

The thirteen-year-old daughter of a Boston family had a growth on her neck which was so large that she could not turn her head without turning her entire body. Mrs. Eddy was asked to help. The growth disappeared, leaving no trace excepting for a scar where a doctor had lanced it previously.

CHAPTER SEVEN

"Teach All the Students You Can Get"

T HIS period, these years of the eighteen-eighties, was a period when what once seemed an impossible hope emerged from the obscurity of a few scattered communities in Massachusetts and New Hampshire—and with ever increasing assurance was moving into the highways of the world. It did not just happen.

In this period there was a great deal of confusion in the public mind regarding Christian Science. At different times following her Discovery in 1866, Mrs. Eddy referred to her teachings as Moral Science, Mental Science, Divine Science, Christian Healing, Mind Healing, and Metaphysics before using the words Christian Science. She was not alone in using the words. Breaking away, rebellious students continued to call themselves Christian Scientists, continued to call themselves Christian Science healers, and set up schools to teach others.

Nor was *The Christian Science Journal* the only publication so identified. There was the *International Magazine of Christian Science,* which was the successor to *Truth: Magazine of Christian Science,* of which there were three issues.

Nor was Mrs. Eddy's Christian Scientist Association the only such association. Former students formed what they called the International Christian Scientist Association.

In Vermont and Maine, New Hampshire, Massachusetts, Connecticut, and New York there were scores of persons soliciting public patronage and calling themselves mental healers or mental physicians. Beyond these, there were hypnotists, mesmerists, and spiritualists, all advertising themselves mental healers. So far as the public was concerned, it was disposed to make no distinction—and was beginning not to make one.

To set her teachings apart from all other teachings, Mrs. Eddy selected ten students, taught them, and graduated them from the Massachusetts Metaphysical College as teachers in August, 1884. It was the first Normal Class. In the next three years she taught other Normal Classes, graduated additional teachers, and instructed them: "Teach all the students you can get (ready and fit for being taught)."[1]

Returning to their homes after graduation, these teachers began moving out from their own communities. One such teacher went to Iowa, South Dakota, and Minnesota. In the records of her Association are these jottings, made by one of her students:

"As there was little demand for Christian Science work in Austin, the suburb of Chicago where she was living, she said she would go where people did want it ... she was called to ... Iowa; and within two weeks, in Dubuque, she had fifty patients ... in a short time, in Mount Vernon, she had one hundred patients ... in Olive, ... people came from all around for healing ... some days ... the rows of vehicles about the hotel were three or four deep ..."

In a dozen communities in the three states the story of the introduction of Christian Science was much the same:

[1] Judge Clifford P. Smith, *Historical Sketches.*

"Noticing many people calling on one of the guests at the hotel where she was stopping, the woman asked the clerk for the reason and he said a Christian Science healer was there and people were coming to be healed. Suffering from a claim of stomach trouble for years, she asked for treatment, and was healed."

The teachings spread very rapidly over midwestern states, but not without opposition, particularly from former students of Mrs. Eddy. One day the teacher who left Chicago to go to Iowa went to Cedar Rapids to find that in her absence a stranger had come into the town, was teaching what she said was the same thing as Christian Science, was practicing what she said was Christian Science healing, and was conducting what she said were Christian Science services. The pretender finally departed, but not until she had caused a good deal of strife.

Joining in the attacks on the teachings were voices from a hundred pulpits and the pens of scores of critics. In *Zion's Herald,* in December, 1884, the Reverend L. T. Townsend of Boston University addressed an open letter to Mrs. Eddy, saying in part:

"If you, or the president of your college, or your entire college of doctors will put into place a real case of hip or ankle dislocation without touching it, I will give you one thousand dollars. Or, if you, or your president, or your entire college, will give sight to one of the inmates of South Boston Asylum for the Blind, that sightless person having been born blind, I will give you two thousand dollars."

Another Boston clergyman, Reverend Stacy Fowler, wrote in the *Homiletic Review:*

"While 'healers' are multiplying it is evident that the science is waning. Mrs. Eddy . . . may teach the principles . . . in twelve lessons, but she cannot impart her power, her personalism, in twelve, nor in twelve hundred lessons. . . . The real *ictus* is her personalism. Her pupils are but feeble imitators of their teacher. Hence the spell is losing its charm. The movement is losing its momentum. In its present form it is an epidemic, and as an epidemic it will pass away. . . ."

Regularly, at meetings of the Boston clergy, she was the topic of discussion. At one meeting of the Boston Methodist Preachers group, one speaker referred to what he called the "Boston craze and Mrs. Eddy," saying:

"This woman claims to be the originator of a new system of philosophy and healing. Were there consistency enough in her teachings to constitute a philosophy it would be called a crude attempt to resuscitate the defunct idealism of the nihilistic type which appeared in the middle ages. Her views upon all metaphysical matters—we speak very mildly— are a self-contradicting hotchpotch."

Regularly, on Sundays, the clergy of Boston and the surrounding area assailed her as "a Jezebel teaching free love," "a daughter of Lucifer denying the efficacy of prayer," or "an irreverent publicist disclaiming God by denying a personal Christ, or Saviour."

Mrs. Eddy used the columns of *The Christian Science Journal* to restate her beliefs and the mails to invite hostile clergymen to attend classes at the Massachusetts Metaphysical College as her guests, to hear what was taught there, to ask questions and satisfy themselves as to the nature of the Christianity that was taught. As for the challenge to put in place a dislocation and restore sight to the blind, she reminded the clergyman that she had performed more difficult tasks fifteen years before. She then continued, "At present I am in another department of Christian work,—where 'there shall no sign be given them,' for they shall be instructed in the principle of Christian Science that furnishes its own proof." It was her way of saying to him that God, not Mary Baker Eddy, is the healer.

She could have suggested to the unbelieving that they could see for themselves by attending Christian Science Sunday services which were being held in Hawthorne Hall and where, coming in carriages, the crippled often left swinging crutches over their shoulders.

The attacks continued. The clergy said she was rewriting the Bible and supported the claim by saying *Science and Health* "is the Christian Science Bible." They must have known better, although the allegation still is heard. *Science and Health* is what Mrs. Eddy called it and designed it to be. It is a textbook. As such, it is read *with* the Bible for the purpose, as stated in the *Christian Science Quarterly,* of "corroborating and explaining the Bible texts in their spiritual import and application to all ages, past, present and future." Mrs. Eddy wrote *Science and Health* because she felt the great need for such a book.

Years before her own healing, Mary Baker Eddy was convinced that "the Scriptures have both a spiritual and literal meaning," [2] and closer study of the Bible confirmed this belief. In so believing, she was in full agreement with many distinguished Bible scholars. The day did not pass that she did not open the Scriptures for careful perusal. She sought understanding, and as with the prophet Samuel, she let no word heard in prayer fall to the ground.

Among the many attacks was one made in Tremont Temple, in Boston, on February 26, 1885. The Reverend Joseph Cook read a letter from the Reverend A. J. Gordon, a Boston clergyman, before a mass meeting of more than twenty-five hundred persons. The charges made were so intemperate that students pleaded with Mrs. Eddy to seek redress in the courts. Instead, she quieted them with words of brotherhood which she put on paper and published in

[2] *Science and Health,* p. 320.

the *Christian Science Journal* in May, 1885, under the title, "Love."

Mrs. Eddy did agree with her students when they expressed the wish that she would insist on being given an opportunity to appear before the Monday Morning Lectureship, as the Tremont Temple meetings were called, in reply to Reverend Gordon's attack. The Lectureship Committee refused, then reconsidered and extended an invitation in the theory, as stated in the March 19, 1885, issue of *The Congregationalist,* that "the best way of meeting the evil was to let it show itself."

On March 16, 1885, Mary Baker Eddy was presented to a hostile audience in Tremont Temple by the Reverend Joseph Cook. The introduction follows:

"It becomes my interesting duty to introduce to this audience, Mrs. Eddy."

Speaking without notes, Mrs. Eddy replied to the charges made against her by the Reverend A. J. Gordon. Taking up the charge that she did not believe in a personal God, she replied:

> I believe in God as the Supreme Being. I know not what the person of omnipotence and omnipresence is, or what the infinite includes; therefore, I worship that of which I can conceive, first, as a loving Father and Mother; then as thought ascends the scale of being to diviner consciousness, God becomes to me as to the Apostle who declared it—"God is Love"—divine Principle,—which I worship; and "after the manner of my fathers, so worship I God."

On the question as to whether she believed in the atonement of Christ, she declared:

I do; and this atonement becomes more to me since it includes man's redemption from sickness as well as from sin. I reverence and adore Christ as never before.

It brings to my sense, and to the sense of all who entertain this understanding of the Science of God, a *whole* salvation.[3]

Excepting for the applause of a few students who were given seats in the gallery of the Temple, a disapproving silence followed Mrs. Eddy as she stepped from the platform, walked down the aisle, and disappeared through a door that opened to the street.

In Chicago, the Right Reverend Samuel Fallows, a bishop of the Methodist Church, joined in the attack. Writing in *Mind in Nature* in the spring of 1885, the Bishop said: "The theory which is advanced by the one claiming to be the founder of the system is not worth the snap of a finger, and never cured a single case. . . .

"A theory that there is no personal God, no personal Devil, and no personal man, that matter is not real, that disease is only a belief of 'the mortal mind,' with all the rest of the peculiar notions grouped under 'Metaphysics,' has no more to do with the recovery of the sick than Tenderden Steeple with the formation of the Goodwin Sands. The one thing for which Mrs. Eddy deserves credit, is in hitting upon a novel plan to cause a *concentration* of one mind upon another for the well being of the body."

In the next issue of the magazine, Bishop Fallows continued his attack:

". . . I did not deny at all, as some seem to think, that cures were performed by persons going through the *modus operandi* of 'metaphysics.' But admitting that within a cer-

3 *Miscellaneous Writings*, p. 96.

tain limit, there have been bodily cures effected, it by no means follows that the notions of Mrs. Eddy on God, man, soul, 'mortal mind,' materia medica, science, 'metaphysics,' the Holy Scriptures, etc., etc., have the slightest connection with the recovery of the sick. Numbers of the 'metaphysicians' have looked into Mrs. Eddy's works and gone straightway into the healing business. They claim to have done as wonderful things as those who think they *understand* the system.

"I repeat with greater emphasis than before, that the *religious theory* which Mrs. Eddy places at the bottom of her system, a theory which I hold to be utterly *un*-Christian, never cured a case of sickness. It is simply the telepathic power of one mind over another, in harmony, of course, with the Divine law of restoration, which she and her followers are using."

In the June, 1885, issue of *Mind in Nature,* Mrs. Eddy replied:

> . . . As the founder, at this period, of Christian Science, I attest that he [Bishop Fallows] utterly fails to comprehend my statement of it. His explanation of one mind transferring its thoughts to another mind, thereby affecting the body, the human giving aid to the divine in its method of healing, is no more correct than to say a man assists the fall of an apple under the law of gravitation. It is virtually a denial of divine power to attribute all healing to mortals, implying it is done, either by mortal mind, or by a drug clad with more power than Deity. . . .
>
> To perceive the spiritual side and meaning of nature, one should understand *"metaphysics,"* as Paul expressed metaphysics—"absent from the

body and present with the Lord"—wherein we
learn the nothingness of matter, sensualism, sickness, sin and death, and the great somethingness
of Spirit, through the discipline, purification and
sanctification whereby the facts of Spirit are discerned, and the pure in heart see God. Propor-
tionately as the realities of Spirit appear, do the
so-called pleasures and pains of the body disappear;
to admit the unreality of matter tends to support
the great facts of Spirit, eternal Life, Truth and
Love. . . .[4]

Most, but not all, Boston pulpits were closed to her. In
the West Church, on Cambridge Street, the Reverend
Cyrus D. Bartol preached two sermons in her defense. He
came to see Mrs. Eddy, and left saying, "I have preached
the living God for forty years, but never felt His presence
and power as you do." Andrew Preston Peabody, professor
of Christian Morals at Harvard University, preached at a
number of Christian Science services at Hawthorne Hall.

With his wife, the Reverend Orrin P. Gifford, of the
Warren Avenue Baptist Church, accepted an invitation to
attend classes in the Massachusetts Metaphysical College
and, while not becoming a Christian Scientist, did gain
respect for the teachings and rebuked his fellow clergymen
for their attacks. Edward Everett Hale visited Mrs. Eddy
and wrote that she told him "more truth in twenty minutes
than I have heard in twenty years."

Away from Boston, as well as in Boston, there were many
rumors. In Boston Mrs. Eddy was reported as suffering from
pneumonia, or smallpox, or dropsy, or brain fever, or lum-
bago, or a combination of diseases and as being under the
care of medical doctors; in Missouri, a St. Louis newspaper

---

[4] For complete text, see Appendix III.

printed a dispatch from Boston saying, "Mrs. Eddy poisoned herself, leaving a will in which she bequeathed all her property to Susan B. Anthony, the suffragette." There were widely circulated stories that she had become a drug addict, and the rumors were so persistent that Mrs. Eddy used the columns of the *Journal* to say:

> To quench the growing flames of falsehood, once in about every seven years I have to repeat this,—that I use no drugs whatever, not even cofea (coffee), thea (tea), capsicum (red pepper); although every day, and especially at dinner, I indulge in homoeopathic doses of *natrium muriaticum* (common table salt). . . .

In Syracuse, New York, A. J. Swarts was getting a great deal of newspaper attention not so much because he said he was "a Christian Science practitioner long before Mrs. Eddy ever heard of it, and she borrowed from me"; as because he offered to "undertake to cure, in seven treatments, twelve invalids suffering from diseases medical doctors call incurable." He was arrested and charged with "practicing medicine without a license" but was released when he persuaded the court that his "system of cure did not come under any medical law of the State of New York." He left town after teaching a class and collecting what he could from each member. Up to that time Mrs. Eddy had never heard of him.

Mary H. Plunkett, a former student, was one of the organizers of the *International Magazine of Christian Science* and the National Association of Christian Scientists, both headquartered in New York City. In April, 1889, the publication carried a "Special Notice" which was signed by John J. T. Plunkett and Mary H. Plunkett, and which said "we . . . from the most profound conviction of duty, do jointly declare our marriage contract null and void."

In the May, June, and July issues of the publication, Mrs. Plunkett signed long articles on the subject of "Marriage and Divorce." Known in New York City as "the high priestess of Christian Science," Mrs. Plunkett's articles were regarded by New York newspapers as a defense, by a Christian Scientist, of "free love" and as showing a contemptuous disregard for the laws of the land. Also, there was another "Special Notice" signed by Mrs. Plunkett:

"Since our forms were made up, a matter of vital gravity to the Science has come before the public. It is too late for us to notice it this month, but the July number will contain a full account. Meanwhile let us be slow in judgment, remembering that all great discoveries and reforms were first, a private opinion; second, a little group of believers; third, a target for misrepresentation and abuse; and lastly a fact accomplished. Wait!"

In the July issue the "matter of vital gravity to the Science" was explained, but not briefly. Fourteen and one-half pages of the publication were needed. Using frequent quotations from *Science and Health,* but wrenching the quoted words from their original moorings, Mrs. Plunkett defended the "spiritual marriage," as she called it, of herself and A. Bentley Worthington, treasurer of the *International Magazine of Christian Science* and of the National School of Christian Science.[5]

Without exception, New York newspapers denounced the "wedding," the participants, and Christian Science. Adding to the untidy mess was the discovery by the press that Worthington was a several-times-married man, had not di-

[5] The school had classrooms in New York and Chicago. In these classrooms it was taught that "Christian Science is the science of spirit. The science of spirit is the essence of all religions and philosophies. Spirit is causation, hence back of all the arts and sciences there is Christian Science, the science of the sciences."

vorced his most recent wife, and, under another name, was wanted by the police on a twenty-five-year-old charge of embezzlement. Worthington disappeared before the police arrived at his honeymoon rendezvous. Before long, the publication was discontinued, the schools were closed, and Mrs. Plunkett disappeared from public view.

While reporters in New York were kept on the run by the rapidly changing affairs of Mary H. Plunkett, reporters for Boston newspapers were absorbed in a developing drama in a courtroom in Malden, Massachusetts. On trial, charged with manslaughter, was Mrs. Abby H. Corner, a Christian Scientist. She was accused of "causing the death of her daughter, Mrs. Lottie James, by neglecting to provide proper medical assistance at the time of her confinement."

The testimony did not support the charge. An autopsy disclosed that death would have been the outcome, the result of hemorrhages, had medical men been in attendance. Mrs. Corner was acquitted.

In Boston, membership in the Christian Scientist Association was almost evenly divided over a proposal to pay the legal costs incurred by Mrs. Corner in defending herself. The sum involved was two hundred dollars. Some members argued that payment was an obligation of the Association; others contended payment was an obligation of individual Christian Scientists. Mrs. Eddy was asked to make a decision. She favored individual subscriptions, saying she thought it unwise to establish a precedent such as would follow the use of Association funds. Her advice was heeded—for a time.

Although conscious of its existence, Mrs. Eddy was not fully aware of the nature of the rebellion that was beginning to take form with the membership of the Association.

In addition to giving prayer-filled hours to thoughts of disbanding the Association, of closing the Massachusetts Metaphysical College, and of the reorganizing of her

Church, Mrs. Eddy had placed herself under a heavy writing schedule in these harassing years.

In 1885, she published a treatise entitled *Historical Sketch of Metaphysical Healing;* in 1886 and 1887 she revised the pamphlet, calling it *Historical Sketch of Christian Science Mind Healing.* A wide distribution was made of each printing. In 1887, she published *Christian Science: No and Yes* and *Rudiments and Rules of Divine Science,* and, in the same year, a third book, *Unity of Good and Unreality of Evil,* was brought out.

Beyond these there was the textbook. Between 1883 and 1885 there were nine printings, making fifteen in all, of *Science and Health.* There was little resetting of type, and such changes as were made were for purposes of clarification rather than for additional text. Gross sales since 1875 approximated 14,500 copies. This total may seem small when compared with today's mass distribution in the manufacturing of books. Nonetheless, it was a total that today would be considered substantial considering the seriousness of the subject.

In 1885 there were signs that a new printing was needed. In September of that year Mrs. Eddy went to see John Wilson at the University Press to tell him of her wish to revise the textbook to include new material. In her mind was the thought of publishing *Science and Health* in one volume instead of two, as in the previous fifteen editions.

Also, she was in need of editorial help. In talking over these matters with Wilson she was told that what she was most in need of was a proofreader, rather than someone to act as a messenger, so to speak, between the printing establishment and herself. Mrs. Eddy was interested. Wilson suggested James Henry Wiggin, a retired Unitarian minister, who was one of the proofreaders at University Press.

Accepting the suggestion, Mrs. Eddy employed Wiggin

and put into writing, on several occasions, instructions covering his responsibilities. He was told, for instance, never to change her meaning in any way but just to bring it out. Also in the proofs he was to do no more than to make needed corrections in grammar. He was cautioned, too, to send all proofs to her, making no alterations whatever after she had sent the proofs to press.

Wiggin worked for Mrs. Eddy in his spare time, and it was not long before dissident students were circulating a story that "a man named James Henry Wiggin, a retired preacher who is a proofreader on the Boston Globe, and not Mary Baker Eddy, is the author of *Science and Health.*" In his volume, *Mary Baker Eddy and Her Books,* William D. Orcutt spoke of his surprise when first hearing the story and quoted from the "Random Recollections" of William B. Reid, head bookkeeper of University Press:

"When it was decided that it would be economy to have the copy prepared for the printer, thus saving charges for what would have been figured as 'alterations from copy,' if done after the type had been set up, Mr. Wiggin was detailed to do the work (punctuation, capitalization and general smoothing out as to construction of sentences) , and as he did this on his own time, the payment for these services were made by Mrs. Eddy, we having no interest in the matter.

"This was well-known to those in our office, as well as in our proofreading department, and caused many a smile among us when we read, from time to time, the repeated assertion that Mr. Wiggin had written the book, and it tickled him more than perhaps any one else to read that he was the *author* (instead of corrector). . . . I frequently dined with Mr. Wilson and Mr. Wiggin. . . . I can recall more than one occasion when the talk would turn on the topics of the day (Christian Science being then one of the leading subjects), the glee with which Mr. Wiggin would refer to the suspicion that he was the author (and it would be some 'glee,' as he had a laugh in keeping with his size), when he would say to Mr. Wilson, 'Wouldn't it have been fine if I had, and could give you all the printing?'

"I suppose that this claim is one of the lies that does not stay nailed, and for, perhaps, personal reasons is dragged into the light of day from time to time; but, nevertheless this *was* a lie!" [6]

The sixteenth edition of *Science and Health,* which was the first printing on which Wiggin worked, was published in 1886. It was a single volume containing two new chapters, as well as other new material. The new chapters were "The Apocalypse," and "Genesis."

The "a" in the wording "With a Key to the Scriptures," as used in the previous nine printings, was dropped. The title of the sixteenth edition was *Science and Health With Key to the Scriptures.* It became the permanent title.

Between 1886 and 1890 thirty-two editions were printed from the 1886 plates. In all, at the close of 1890, forty-eight editions of *Science and Health* were in print. The teachings of Mary Baker Eddy were taking hold.

[6] Strangely enough, it was a story that was believed by Wiggin's son, the late Albert W. Wiggin, Chairman of the Chase National Bank, New York, which became the Chase Manhattan Bank, one of the large financial institutions of the world.

Several years before his passing, I talked with Mr. Wiggin about his father's association with Mrs. Eddy and listened to the banker's insistence that his father wrote the textbook. I offered proof that contained his father's denial of the authorship, as well as photostats of Mrs. Eddy's instructions to him as proofreader. The son was not at all impressed. Only annoyed. N.B.

CHAPTER EIGHT

A Mission Only She Could Complete

L ACKING one, twenty-five years had passed since her own
healing. Mary Baker Eddy had come to know the price
of her discovery.

To be lied about was part of the price; vilification and
persecution were parts; envy, the most evil of evils, was
part; poverty was part; to be spat upon as she walked the
streets of Lynn was part—but, gaining strength with each
encounter, she weakened the attacks made upon her by her
conduct and became sure, as she had been sure since the
first taunt, that the moment of hatred's crowning triumph
would be the moment of its final collapse.

To Mary Baker Eddy truth had a deeper tone than falsehood. Testing values by higher standards, she found in the
disciplines of truth new strengths, new freedoms, and new
mastery over the materialism of a physical world. Rejecting
every counsel that tried to make a highway out of a detour,
she patiently sought the ways of the Creator.

She was not of those who look but do not see; who hear
but do not listen; who talk but do not do.

She accepted the words and works of the Nazarene as
God's great purpose unfolding. As she perceived, it was a
purpose that seemed to have become clouded; then, quite
early in the fourth century, it seemed to have been lost in
mankind's preoccupation with the material world about it.

Losing sight of God in the resultant confusion, mankind became persuaded into accepting illusions for substance, mysticism for worship, hope for understanding.

Although mankind still was fascinated by the very thing that obscured the eternal Design, Mrs. Eddy was not dismayed. Believing Christian Science was identical with what had disappeared more than one thousand five hundred years before, she set out to reinstate that which had been lost.

The real work was ahead. Behind was disappointment, but progress too.

It may be assumed that Mrs. Eddy was not greatly put out by the angry voices attacking her teachings. A wise woman, she realized that in singling her out for attack her enemies were helping to establish her in her rightful place as the Discoverer and Founder of Christian Science.

She knew she was offering a religion that promised much but demanded much. She knew growth would depend not upon numbers but upon the conduct of Christian Scientists—and that this conduct was of the greatest importance, for it is the sum of growth. She found comfort in what she stood for and encouragement in the desire of more people to stand with her. There would be disloyalty, and there would be persecution. These things she expected, and she spoke of them.

In an address (*Miscellany*, p. 151) to her church in Concord, New Hampshire, in 1889, she said: "Rest assured that the injustice done by press and pulpit to this denomination of Christians will cease, when it no longer blesses this denomination."

To the congregation of First Church of Christ, Scientist, in Atlanta, Georgia, she wrote (*Miscellany*, p. 191): "Be patient towards persecution. Injustice has not a tithe of the power of justice. Your enemies will advertise for you. Christian Science is spreading steadily throughout the world. Persecution is the weakness of tyrants engendered by their fear, and love will cast it out . . ."

In *Science and Health* (p. 29) she taught: "Christian experience . . . bids us work the more earnestly in times of persecution, because then our labor is more needed."

When in June, 1888, Mrs. Abby H. Corner, the Christian Scientist, was acquitted of manslaughter, a plot to remove Mrs. Eddy from her post of leadership in her own Church had reached ominous proportions. There were a number of events that may have encouraged the plotters into believing this was the time to strike.

In the May issue of the *Journal* Mrs. Eddy announced her intention of not attending the annual meeting of the National Christian Scientist Association in Chicago in mid-June, saying:

> . . . I shall not be present at the National Christian Scientist Association in Chicago, June 13; but my sympathies will go out largely to my students on that occasion, I even thank beforehand those who, with deathless love, are struggling Godward; and I warn those who are halting or getting blind, neither to stop and rest on my personality for all they achieve, nor to abuse it; but to remember always that Love fulfills God's law, and destroys sin as well as sickness, and that there is no other door by which to enter into Christian Science. . . .

In a meeting in Tremont Temple on the afternoon of June 6 her opponents displayed so much unexpected strength during a discussion of church matters that Mrs. Eddy felt impelled to invite a few students upon whose loyalty she was sure she could depend to attend another meeting, this one in her own home in the evening of the same day. Together they reviewed the situation and made plans to meet it by having William B. Johnson, secretary of the National Christian Scientist Association, acquaint certain western members [1] with the events of the afternoon in Tremont Temple, as well as in Boston.

Leaving for Chicago two nights later, Johnson took with him a letter:

Boston, June 8, 1888.

My dear Students.

Listen to this faithful student. Our vice-president in Boston is heading a new faction. Ask Mr. Johnson about it who bears this letter.

As ever your faithful Teacher,
M. B. G. Eddy.

Two or three days afterwards, with but a few knowing she was going, Mrs. Eddy, accompanied by Mrs. Laura E. Sargent, left Boston en route to Chicago. On the train Mrs. Eddy surely gave deep prayerful attention to the emerging disorderliness within her own community.

It was clear that disagreement over the use of Association funds for paying the costs of defending Mrs. Corner against the charge of manslaughter was no more than an excuse to obstruct. It was equally clear that the real motive for the disagreement was opposition to her intention to build a church edifice in Boston.

Word of Mrs. Eddy's arrival was carried in the Chicago newspapers along with the information that she would be on the platform of Central Music Hall, at State and Ran-

[1] Mrs. G. W. Adams, Mrs. J. H. Bell, Reverend George P. Day, Mrs. Hannah A. Laramie, Mr. and Mrs. John Linscott, Mrs. Caroline D. Noyes, Mr. and Mrs. Bradford Sherman, and Mrs. Elizabeth Webster.

dolph streets (present location of the Marshall Field Building) with one hundred of her students on the morning of June 14, when there would be a program of addresses by students on Christian Science.

On the designated morning the auditorium of Central Music Hall was filled with more than eight hundred members of the National Christian Scientist Association. Visitors crowded along the sides of the auditorium and sat in the balconies; among them were many who were sick or crippled. Seated on the platform were one hundred students, while below, immediately in front of the platform, was a filled press table.

With Mrs. Sargent, Mrs. Eddy was in the antechamber removing her wraps preparatory to taking her place on the platform when Reverend George P. Day, pastor of the Christian Science Church in Chicago and a member of the committee-in-waiting, came into the antechamber, saying:

"Now, Mrs. Eddy, the audience is assembled, the students are all assembled, and you are to speak first on the program."

Startled, Mrs. Eddy protested, explaining she was not prepared to speak because she was not supposed to speak.

"Yes, I know," returned Day, "but the plans were changed. It's just been announced to the audience that you will speak."

Realizing she was in the presence of disloyalty, Mrs. Eddy stood quietly for a moment, remote in prayer, then walked on the platform and took her place with her students. When she arose to speak, men and women in different parts of the hall began hurling questions at her, with the pastor [2] of her own church in Chicago being one of the most persistent questioners.

[2] Not long afterwards Day resigned his pastorate and withdrew from the Movement.

As one who was there wrote in her diary:

"Patiently, Mrs. Eddy bore this expression of malice until, suddenly, she faced her persecutors. Looking out and beyond their personalities, she opened her Bible at the Ninety-first Psalm, and began a marvelous exposition thereof, saying in substance and in part:

" '. . . Past, present, future, will show the word and might of Truth—healing the sick and reclaiming the sinner—so long as there remains a claim of error for Truth to deny or to destroy. Love's labors are not lost. The five personal senses, that grasp neither the meaning nor the magnitude of self-abnegation, may lose sight thereof; but Science voices unselfish love, unfolds infinite good, leads on irresistible forces, and will finally show the fruits of Love. Human reason is inaccurate; and the scope of the senses is inadequate to grasp the word of Truth, and teach the eternal. . . .' [3]

"While her voice rang out over the audience, her hearers were so transported by the vision of Truth opened up to them that even the stenographer forgot to take notes. At the conclusion of her address the audience sprang to its feet, several throwing away crutches, and men and women rushed to the platform . . . so great was the press that students hurried Mrs. Eddy from the platform lest she be swept off her feet."

In its account of the meeting, the Chicago *Times* spoke of the audience reaction: "The audience rose enmasse and made a rush for the platform. There were no steps provided for getting on the rostrum but that did not deter those who wanted to shake hands with the idolized expounder of their creed. They mounted the reporters' table and vaulted to the rostrum like acrobats."

The Chicago *Tribune* referred to the address as one that

[3] For full revised text, see *Miscellaneous Writings*, pp. 98–106.

"depended largely upon its logic for its force"; the Chicago *Inter-Ocean* said:

"Christian Scientists, as an organization, are of comparatively recent origin. . . . They stand for themselves, and are practical illustrations of the truths they teach. It must be admitted that the countenances of most of them showed evidence of high thinking, as if they attained to that condition wherein the spirit has obtained ascendancy over the body.

"The audience was composed of a goodly number of men and young women, but the women of middle age constituted the majority. Many of the latter were white-haired; their faces were cheerful and serene, and they looked very much as if they had come into possession of the most coveted secret of happiness, for which the sordid, selfish world without was struggling and contending in vain.

"The Rev. Mary B. G. Eddy stands at the head of the movement in Boston, where she has a strong and enthusiastic following. Her admirers, however, are not confined to the East, but are everywhere, and her presence in Chicago has very generally called them together. . . ."

Mrs. Eddy returned to Boston to learn that, in her absence, thirty-six students had withdrawn their support; in addition, they had gained possession of the records of the Christian Scientist Association and had given them to George J. Tufts, an attorney, for "safekeeping." Taking advantage of William B. Johnson's presence in Chicago, one of the deserting students had gone to the Johnson home, had told Mrs. Johnson that a special meeting of the Association had been called and there was need for the records. Unsuspecting, the secretary's wife produced them.

Planning to expel Mrs. Eddy from her own Association and from her own Church, the defecting students apparently believed that by having possession of the records they were making their position impregnable. Instead of giving ground, as they thought she would, Mrs. Eddy instructed Johnson to call a meeting of the Association, and to schedule it for June 27, "for the purpose [of giving] certain members opportunity to comply with the Constitution, Article 2, Section 1, and the By-Laws on Fellowship, Section 1." These two clauses read:

Article 2, Section 1, of the Constitution:

Members hereby pledge themselves to live peaceably with all men, so far as is consistent with justice, and truth, and do unto others as they would that others should do unto them. To remember the Ten Commandments, and never to interfere with the rights of Mind. It is expected that all members will express their views, by voting for or against any question. It shall be the privilege of all members to act independently, and exert an influence to restrain error and promote truth. Unwillingness to do this, will be considered as disqualifying them for Christian Science.

The By-law on Fellowship, Section 1:

It shall be the duty of Christian Scientists to befriend and help each other in times of need, and, so far as is consistent with justice and truth, to defend the reputation of members of this Association. If they have aught against other members, it shall be their duty to faithfully tell them of it, and so seek a reconciliation.

Speaking for Mrs. Eddy, Calvin A. Frye wrote to members of the Association on July 14, saying in part:
"I regret the necessity of informing you that the ring-

leaders of another faction are trying by falsehoods, and in-
sinuations, to mislead the members of the Christian Scientist Association. They insisted on an appropriation for Mrs.
Corner, but when the test came for individual subscription
for her, and $170.00 (we are told) was pledged, not one of
them contributed a cent.[4]

"Our President called a special meeting for a Christian
adjustment of this endeavor to break us up, and notices
were addressed to every member in the New England and
Middle States. . . . These notices were either intercepted in
the mail, or they who did receive them, say they did not, because they were afraid to meet what they had said, and stayed
away. . . ."

In a letter under date of August 22, 1888, William B.
Johnson wrote to all members of the Association and, in
this letter, quoted Mrs. Eddy as saying:

> I have no conception of what some members of
> the Association are hinting against me, and I will
> be present on the 27th inst. to hear what they have
> to say. Conscious of my own integrity in all things
> I call on members of this Association who have
> aught against me, to tell me of it, and even after
> they have broken this rule of the Church of Christ,
> and the commandments of God, and not "first hav-
> ing told their brother his fault," I will give them
> another opportunity to deal justly. This same in-
> justice to others has been bitterly complained of
> to me by the very members who are now dealing
> with me thus.
>
> I have earnestly counselled my students not to
> be guilty of this great wrong which has caused
> much discord. I have set them a different ex-

[4] The Association finally paid the bill.

ample, and told them first of their faults and avoided telling them to others. I will now give them one more opportunity to deal justly, and I will listen patiently and charitably to all they have to say against me, and in return I will ask only this: that those who have spoken of their great obligation to me will now be simply just to me. . . .

At the first special meeting called on behalf of Mrs. Corner, I was absent, not because I was unwilling to help her, but because she needed no help, and I knew it. I was not at the second special meeting because it was impossible for me to be and go to the meeting of the National Association at Chicago; also I wanted this conspiracy to come to the surface, it has. . . .

None of the rebellious students attended the meeting, thus leaving their teacher without an answer to her plea to "those who have spoken of their great obligation to me . . . be simply just to me."

In despair, because it left only a handful of loyal students in Boston, Mrs. Eddy gave serious consideration to locating in Chicago.

Through a night of prayer she came to see that the road she was on, however strewn with obstacles it appeared to be, would be the same road with no obstacle removed were she to go to Chicago or elsewhere. Leaving Boston, she would be starting again on a low level, because wherever she went there would go with her the realization that in leaving Boston she was admitting failure, not only for herself but, more importantly, for the cause she represented.

And, too, she came to see that inciting the rebellion was the same enemy whose swift arrival she learned about after her first spiritual healing. She had learned, too, in the years that followed, that she was never out of its sight. Nor would she ever be. She was a constant threat to its aspirations. The enemy was hatred.

Working in the universe of eternal law, she was thinking in its terms as she set about the task of safeguarding her teachings and her church, not only from doers of evil but also from the tamperers and from the faint of heart. Already she had protected the contents of the textbook, *Science and Health With Key to the Scriptures,* by copyright and by trademark which would identify her teachings.

Now she was setting out to examine more closely her church and its organizational structure. She had long held the conviction that upon her was laid a mission no one could complete but herself. On what she did in the gathering crisis depended her teachings and her church. These, her teachings and her church, would unfold in their great purpose and be builded in their great reality, or they would disappear.

In his book, *Twelve Years With Mary Baker Eddy,*[5] Irving C. Tomlinson recalled a conversation with Mrs. Eddy in which she told him of an experience when she was a patient under the care of Phineas P. Quimby, in Portland, Maine, in 1862:

" 'In the absence of Dr. Quimby ... a man was brought to the hotel where I was staying, who was in a pitiable condition. He had sometime previous met with an accident and he was well-nigh broken to pieces. His knees and ankles were out of place and he was suffering untold agonies. The proprietor of the hotel came to me and besought me to do something for the poor sufferer. At first I thought

[5] Copyright, 1945, The Christian Science Board of Directors; published by The Christian Science Publishing Society.

I could not. Then I said, "God can do it." I went to his bedside and lifted my thought silently to God. At the conclusion of my prayer I said, "Now you can arise and open the door for me." The man arose, and with the iron clamps he wore rattling as he walked, went and opened the door.' "

But before investigating Quimby's practices, she investigated homoeopathy, spiritualism, mesmerism, and hypnotism; and, as she testified before the Masters in 1907, "I found that human will was the cause of disease instead of its cure; . . . and that the Divine Mind was the Healer; then I found through the Scripture that . . . God did the healing." [6]

And long before that—in her own childhood, "she often listened with joy to these words, falling from the lips of her saintly mother, 'God is able to raise you up from sickness' "; [7] and, as a child, she had proof of the words. They were words and proof that left an indelible impression on her mind.

These and other experiences were behind her conviction, as she wrote in Science and Health (p. 107), that "God had been graciously preparing me during many years for the reception of this final revelation of the absolute divine Principle of scientific mental healing." Now, in 1888, in spite of constant attack from without and rebellion within, the movement had gained in strength and in numbers. On hand was an accumulation of activities that had no place in the structure that was forming in her mind.

Being first in her prayers, her church was first in her thought. In her thought a church is "God's gift, foundation and superstructure [to which] no one could hold a wholly

[6] Mrs. Eddy, and the Late Suit in Equity. Copyright, 1908, by Michael Meehan.
[7] Science and Health, p. 359.

material title." [8] Having protected her teachings by copyright that identified and protected them, she was determined to protect her church in perpetuity.

It was a desire long in her mind. She took the first step toward bringing it to fruition in 1867, when she impressed upon her first student, Hiram S. Crafts, the need, if he was to heal, to rid his prayers of all human personality and to depend completely upon God. As she did with Crafts, so was she setting out to do in her church and in the organizational structure of which her church would be the "foundation and superstructure."

In the intervening years she had permitted the admission of practices that, to her, were of a nature similar to those which caused Jesus to say "suffer it to be so now." It was not a sudden decision. All who called themselves Christian Scientists, including herself, were from other denominations. Some had been attracted to her teachings because, in them, they found healing; others had come because they observed the healings; others because they found comfort in her words; attracted by curiosity, others came to see, but came back to listen; others because, in her teachings, they perceived a religion which, by bringing healing for the ills that beset mankind, was eternal—not new and not old.

In setting out to remove all sense of human personality —including her own!—from the church and from the organic structure surrounding the church, she first had to prepare **her** students for the appearance of a new form of church government. Continually she impressed upon her followers the inaccuracy of thinking that she, as a person, was the government of her church; rather, she sought to demonstrate that she only served as an instrument in the living temple of spiritual law, which the government of God is.

[8] *The Christian Science Journal*, July, 1892.

To the task she brought a mind already disciplined.

In 1888, the Christian Science movement was made up of a number of organizations, all small, all poor, and all vigorous. There were a few churches similar to the one in Boston, all of which held services in rented halls. There was one church edifice. It was located in Oconto, Wisconsin. Built in 1886 at a cost of one thousand dollars, it seated a hundred persons.

There were several Associations, and their number was increasing. First among them was the Christian Scientist Association, which was formed by Mrs. Eddy, and six students on July 4, 1876. Not then but later the Association became a formal body holding regular meetings and operating under bylaws, rules, and a constitution, all of which were approved by Mrs. Eddy and submitted to the membership for approval.

In the Constitution, Mrs. Eddy included a carefully worded account of her discovery, saying:

> ... a Divine principle and given rule applicable to every condition of man, and constituting the Divine plan of his salvation from sin, sickness and death exist in the order of Eternal life, Truth and Love, and that Jesus demonstrated for man's example and his redemption, this holy principle of Divine Science, healing the sick, casting out devils, error, and raising the dead; clearly showing by this Divine understanding and proof, the indivisibility of Science and Christianity.[9]

[9] Commenting on this paragraph, Clifford P. Smith said in his book, *Historical Sketches,* "The foregoing quotation is from the constitution as first printed, in which the capitalization and punctuation may have been furnished by the printer."

On April 12, 1879, the Association met and, as Mrs. Eddy wrote in *Retrospection and Introspection* (p. 44), "voted to organize a church to commemorate the words and works of our Master, a Mind-healing church, without a creed, to be called the Church of Christ, Scientist, the first such church ever organized."

Although not all the members of the Association did become members of the church, the Association did keep a watchful eye on the affairs of the church, supported it financially, directed its progress, and opened the way for related activities. Through it Mrs. Eddy promoted *The Christian Science Journal,* which led to The Christian Science Publishing Society, the Committee on Publication, the Reading Rooms, and, indirectly, a number of other activities.

Directly, the Association was responsible for the forming, by Mrs. Eddy, in 1886, of the National Christian Scientist Association, which, as Mrs. Eddy wrote in *Retrospection and Introspection* (p. 52), was organized "to meet the broader wants of humanity, and provide folds for the sheep that were without shepherds." In organizing, the members voted: "The purpose and object of this National Association is to give students' students an equal footing with others in Christian Science and to promote unity and brotherly love. Charters will be granted by this National Association to the minor Associations."

The National Association had its first meeting in New York City on February 11, 1886; its second annual meeting was held in Boston; its third was in Chicago. At its fourth annual meeting, in Cleveland, it received a letter from Mrs. Eddy in which she turned over to it for use as its official organ *The Christian Science Journal,* including all funds belonging to the publication. Ownership of the magazine remained with Mrs. Eddy, along with management editing.

The "minor Associations" were made up of teachers and their students, Mrs. Eddy having given such permission to those among her own students whom she deemed qualified to form such Associations.

In Boston, in 1887, acting independently, several church members banded together to open a "Free Dispensary of Christian Science Healing" at 3 Boylston Street. Using rented rooms as a headquarters, the students fanned out through the poorer sections of the city, calling on the sick and discouraged, treating them, giving them hope, and inviting them to visit the Dispensary. Almost always their words brought disbelieving laughter—yet there were times when disbelieving laughter was suddenly stilled. Before long the Dispensary became known as a place of healing.

On Easter Sunday, April 21, 1889, Mrs. Eddy announced that a Christian Science Dispensary would be operated under the auspices of the Church of Christ, Scientist, and the individual efforts of church members were discontinued as having served their purpose. In June, 1889, the National Christian Scientist Association adopted a resolution stating: ". . . In all places where Churches of Christ (Scientist) or Christian Scientist Associations exist, all dispensary work should be conducted under the auspices of such church or association, and that its conduct in such cases independently of such organizations, be discountenanced."

The Dispensary in Boston was located at 7 Temple Street, several rooms being needed. On Sunday afternoon there were Bible classes for "instruction in the spiritual sense of the Scriptures"; Sunday and Wednesday evenings were given over to "addresses, conversation and inquiry about Christian Science healing"; "the Dispensary was open daily from 9 a. m. to 9 p. m. for the reception and treatment of patients in Christian Science"; in separate rooms there were "conversations on Christian Science every evening from 7:30 to 9:30."

Christian Science literature was offered for sale, and individual church members used the Dispensary as a starting point in their house-to-house coverage of different parts of the city "for the purpose of talking Christian Science to the inmates and inviting them to come to the Bible class and other meetings" as well as for "physical healing." If they could afford to do so, applicants were expected to pay something for the literature or for the healings. If they were not able to pay, there was no charge.

After a few weeks Christian Scientists were requested to stay away from the Sunday and Wednesday evening services. The full facilities of the Dispensary were needed for the newly interested.

The Dispensary, the Associations, the Massachusetts Metaphysical College, *The Christian Science Journal,* the Church—these were among the activities Mrs. Eddy was examining closely.

CHAPTER NINE

Marking Out Guidelines

O F immediate concern to Mrs. Eddy was a situation involving a strip of land on which she hoped to build the edifice which would serve as The Mother Church for Christian Scientists the world over.

The strip of land was at Caledonia and Falmouth Streets in Boston and in the precise language of the Registry of Deeds was described thus:

"Beginning at the junction of Falmouth Street and a forty-foot street now called Caledonia street; thence running Southwest on said Falmouth street one hundred and sixteen and eighty-eight hundredths feet; thence Northwest at a right angle to a point where a line drawn at right angles to said forty-foot street at a point thereon one hundred and sixteen and fifty-five hundredths feet Northwest from the point of beginning meets the said boundary at right angles to Falmouth street, sixty-six and seventy-eight hundredths feet; thence at an obtuse angle on said line at right angles to said forty-foot street sixty-seven and thirty-five hundredths feet to said forty-foot street; thence Southeasterly on said forty-foot street one hundred and sixteen and fifty-five hundredths feet to the point of beginning; containing seven thousand, eight hundred and twenty-eight square feet more or less, and subject to the agreements and restrictions mentioned in a deed recorded in Suffolk Registry of Deeds Lib.

1719, Fol. 83 so far as the same are now legally operative."

It was new land that only recently had been strewn with boulders and grass and patches of sand that belonged to its former occupants, the marshes and tidewaters of the Back Bay district. Reclaimed land, although likely enough Mrs. Eddy did not inquire into these particulars. Her concern was of more recent origin.

In 1885 members of the Christian Science Association began making contributions toward a church edifice. In another year two thousand dollars had been raised by subscriptions, and a majority of the members of the Association were to use the sum as down payment on the property at Falmouth and Caledonia Streets. The property was valued at sixty-eight hundred dollars, and the owners were willing to accept a three-year mortgage, payable July 1, 1889, for the balance of forty-eight hundred dollars. Over Mrs. Eddy's strong objections the Association approved the terms.

Basing her objections on her firm belief that "God's gift, foundation and superstructure" was something to which "no one could hold a wholly material title," it was unsuitable that she would advise a transaction that included a mortgage. She offered to buy the property, thus relieving the Association of any responsibility. The offer was refused. The wish was to raise the money by holding a fair, and the fair was held in Horticultural Hall on December 19–21, 1886.

More than five thousand dollars represented the profit, but before the money could be used to pay off the mortgage, the treasurer of the building fund disappeared, and the money disappeared with him. When Mrs. Eddy was told, she asked that no effort be made to apprehend the man. She told the committee she was sure the missing treasurer was an honest man, and, being sure of that, she was of the opinion that his inability to escape from his own conscience was sufficient punishment.

Her wishes were followed, and she closed the incident by urging her students to accept her counsel that if it was right that the Church of Christ, Scientist should rest on a spiritual foundation, a way would be found to meet the mortgage.

Already and with no one knowing her purpose, she had employed a lawyer to search the laws of Massachusetts in an effort to find a statute which would provide a way for her to establish her church as "God's gift, foundation and superstructure to which no one could hold a wholly material title."

When employed, the attorney was less than optimistic and sought to dissuade her, saying he knew of no statute that would meet her requirements. She insisted. After a long search the lawyer found a little-known provision in Chapter 39 of the Public Statutes of Massachusetts which stated:

"The deacons, church wardens, or other similar officers of churches or other religious societies, and the trustees of the Methodist Episcopal churches appointed according to the discipline and usages thereof, shall, if citizens of this commonwealth, be deemed bodies corporate for the purpose of taking and holding in succession all the grants and donations, whether of real or personal estate, made either to them and their successors, or to their respective churches, or to the poor of the churches."

With sanction of the Commonwealth of Massachusetts in hand to build a church edifice and make of it a "holy gift," she waited for her students to redeem their pledge. Months passed, and months became years, until it was December, 1888. On the fourth day of that month, acting under Mrs. Eddy's instructions, Baxter E. Perry, a Boston attorney, quietly purchased the mortgage, using money that, just as quietly, Mrs. Eddy had given him.

The day the mortgage was due—July 1, 1889—came and went. Nothing was done. August came. Still no word from the church members. Mrs. Eddy told Perry to notify Alfred Lang, now treasurer of the church building fund, that the lot would be offered for sale at a public auction on August 3. There was no acknowledgment by Lang, nor did he or any other church member appear at the auction. On August 3, the sole bidder was George Perry, son of the attorney. His bid was approximately five thousand dollars. Title to the lot was turned over to him on August 6, 1889. For a while, the matter rested.

The time had come, Mrs. Eddy was sure, to begin the task of accustoming her followers for the years when she would not be present in person to direct the affairs of the Christian Science movement. More and more she was marking out guidelines for them to follow; more and more she was delegating authority.

On March 5, 1889, in a "leave-taking" report to sixty-five primary class students of the Massachusetts Metaphysical College, she disclosed her hope for a "church universal" in her time:

> I want to say, too, to my students everywhere, whether they have attended my classes or have received instruction through reading my books, that they can become members of the "mother church" here in Boston, and be received into its communion by writing without their personal presence.

To a student who inquired about the union of Christian Science churches with other Christian churches she said:

... I want to promote the union of the church. ... The Christian church is sacred to me; just as the Jew held all that had the name of God written on it, so all that calls itself by the name of Christ, I love, and hold sacred.

How shall we best promote union with Christ, and draw all the churches that are called by that holy Name nearer to him?

I look to Christ for guidance. Jesus did not carry his church—the Jewish—with him. He could not build his on their foundation; neither can we. They are founded on personal sense and credal doctrines about God. How can we proceed on our way without the life of Christianity, the recognition of God, Good, as all? ... We cannot afford to remain in the fetters of a personal sense of God. Then we plant ourselves on matter rather than Spirit, ... and must say as Martin Luther said, "Here I stand, I cannot do otherwise, so help me God, Amen."

Another member of the class inquired about the duties of pastors in Christian Science churches, a rule having been adopted on February 17, 1889, stipulating "all students of Christian Science must drop the title of Reverend and Doctor, except those who have received these titles under the *laws* of the *state*." In reply to a question, Mrs. Eddy said:

The ordination of the pastor is not an essential to the reception of members from other churches, or of new members. The old membership ceases when the new begins. The pastor is not the church; it is the church that they come into, and that does not depend on the pastor. You are delegated by the church to perform this duty, and your action has as much validity as the action of a chairman or moderator of any meeting, who is appointed *pro tem.* The person, any person, so delegated can receive new members just as effectively as an ordained pastor.

There were some grumblings. Mrs. Eddy advised the dissatisfied: "My beloved brethren will some time learn the wisdom of this By-law." Seeking freedom from the demands upon her, she left Boston a few days later and went to Barre, Vermont. Here she remained for a month, waiting and listening. Returning to Boston, she first gave consideration to taking up residence in Roslindale, a suburb, but finding no suitable location, moved to Concord, New Hampshire, renting a house at 62 North State Street.

It was good to be back in the surroundings of her birth. There was peace here. Not far from here her mother's soft voice had sung her to sleep; not far from here, with her brother Albert, she had watched the seasons come to the Merrimack Valley—the perfume of summer flowers, the colored banners of autumn, the doors of winter creaking open to spring. Laughing waters rushing down the creek that crossed a meadow. Here, seventy miles from Boston, with no automobiles and almost no telephones, she could ponder the decisions only she could make, uninterrupted by the uninvited.

From Concord, she used the July, 1889, issue of the *Journal* to say:

> Inquiries are coming in from the "four quarters"—For what purpose has Mrs. Eddy relinquished certain lines of labor in the field of Christian Science and called others to the work? Is she writing her history? or completing her works on the Scriptures? She is doing neither, but is taking

a vacation, her first in twenty-five years. She is taking no direction of her own or others, but her desire is that God may permit her to continue to live apart from the world, free from the toil and turmoil in which her days have been passed for more than a quarter century.

And in the August issue of the *Journal* notified the field:

Take Notice: No correspondence relating to any matter of organization, or aught connected with Church, Christian Scientist Associations, or matters relative to individuals,—in fine, no question relating to our cause except those involving the real essence or animus of Christian Science, will be considered by Mrs. Eddy, Dr. Foster-Eddy, or Mr. Frye.[1]

At the same time she wrote to Julia Bartlett on the same subject:

Now I repeat that whatever questions in any of the C. S. organizations come up—no reference be made to me, for I hereby state that I *will not* entertain the question nor consider it, and why?

Because under the counteracting mental influences, if I do this, my counsel is liable to be either carried out too late, or misunderstood, or carried out only in part, and because of all these things the wisdom and necessity of it is not seen nor the good it might do accomplished and many will say she is a "hard master." I have borne this many

---

[1] Attracted by the spiritual healing of a friend in 1887, Ebenezer J. Foster, a graduate of Hahnemann Medical College, Philadelphia, Pa., enrolled in the Massachusetts Metaphysical College. Winning his teacher's confidence, he became Mrs. Eddy's adopted son on November 5, 1888, and changed his name to Foster-Eddy.

years and think at this period of my retirement
it should be seen that this is why I left the field.
Again my students must learn sooner or later to
guard themselves, to *watch* and not be misled.

Prior to leaving Boston, she resigned as Pastor of the
church in Boston, saying to the members:

Beloved Brethren:—For good and sufficient reasons I again send you my resignation, which must
be final of the Pastorate of the Church of Christ,
Scientist, Boston, and recommend that you secure
a Pastor to enter upon this labor in early Autumn.
One who will take full charge of this dear Church,
look after its interests, receive and attend to applications for membership, hold regular communion service, and in all respects discharge the duties
of a Pastor. Also I beg that you will give such an
one a sufficient salary to enable him to give his
whole time to the duties which belong to this
responsible office.

On November 23, 1889, she led the members of her
church to a second step.

This morning has finished my halting between
two opinions. This Mother Church must disorganize and now is the time to do it and form no new
organization but the spiritual one. Follow Christ
Jesus' example and not that of his disciples. Theirs
has come to naught in science, ours should establish Science but not material organizations. . . .

The next day, William B. Johnson notified the church
members:

The annual meeting of the Church of Christ (Scientist), Boston, will be held in the Christian Science Reading Room, No. 210 Hotel Boylston, 24 Boylston Street, Monday, Dec. 2, 1889, at 7:30 P.M.

At this meeting the question will be laid before the Church:—to consider the advisability, and take action thereon, of dissolving the organization of the Church on the basis of material and human law, and of remaining together henceforth on a plane of spiritual law in accordance with the higher teachings we are constantly receiving.

Per order of Business Committee,

Wm. B. Johnson, Clerk

On December 2, 1889, the Church Board met and adopted these five resolutions:

(1) That the time has come when this Church should free itself from the thraldom of man-made laws, and rise into spiritual latitudes where the law of love is the only bond of union.

(2) That the Regulations and By-Laws of this Church be and are hereby declared to be, in all their articles and clauses except that part of Article 1 which fixes its name, null and void.

(3) That the Corporation be and is declared dissolved and that the present Clerk of the Church be hereby requested to take the steps necessary to give legal effect to this resolution.

(4) The members of this Church hereby declare that this action is taken in order to realize more perfectly the purposes of its institution as an organization viz. growth in spiritual life and the spread of the "glad tiding"—and that they will

continue as a Voluntary Association of Christians knowing no law but the law of Love, and no Master but Christ in the exercise of all the ministrations and activities heretofore performed by them as a Church of Christ (Scientist).

(5) That the members of this church hereby make loving recognition of the services and guidance of the founder and late pastor of the church, and also the expression of their grateful thanks to those who in the capacities of assistant pastor or otherwise have fostered its growth.

More than two months previously, on September 23, 1889, not long after she had recommended the setting "aside of all that is ceremonial even in appearance in our church," she had acted to dissolve the Christian Scientist Association of the Massachusetts Metaphysical College.

Beloved Students:—

I have faithfully sought the direction of Divine wisdom in my advice herein given, namely, that you vote TODAY to dissolve this organization.

1st. Because the teacher who organized this first Christian Science Association has retired from her place in the College, and no longer prepares the students for entering this Association.[2]

[2] In the nine years of its existence (1881–1889 inclusive) the College had one teacher and three assistant teachers. The one teacher was Mary Baker Eddy. The assistant teachers were Asa Gilbert Eddy, Ebenezer J. Foster Eddy, and General Erastus N. Bates.* Asa Gilbert Eddy taught two terms; Ebenezer J. Foster-Eddy taught Primary, Normal, and Obstetrics classes, one term; General Bates taught one class.

* When discharged from the Army at the close of the War Between the States, Bates was told by the medical doctors that he faced invalidism for his remaining years. Healed in Christian Science, he became a student of Mrs. Eddy and devoted his life to the Cause.

2nd. Because new students whom others have taught may not receive the reception that her students have received from this associated body. They may not consider them students of the same grade, and this may incite improper feeling between my students and the students of other teachers. I regret to say that there has been much discord in the past, between students connected with this Christian Science Association, and it would seem more natural for them to harmonize than different grades of students; hence the precedent does not favor the hope for future harmony.

3rd. Because it is more in accord with Christian Science for you to unite on the basis of Love and meet together in bonds of affection, from unselfish motives and the purpose to benefit each other, and honor the cause. Therefore I strongly recommend this method alone, of continuing without organization, the meeting together of the students of the Massachusetts Metaphysical College.

I most earnestly desire that the present reputation of my College shall be sustained, and go into history honoring God and whomsoever He hath anointed with peace on earth and love for the whole human family.

Affectionately your Teacher,

Mary B. G. Eddy

On October 29, 1889, Mrs. Eddy called a special meeting of the Massachusetts Metaphysical College Corporation at which time "it was unanimously voted: That as all debts of the Corporation have been paid, it is deemed best to dissolve this Corporation, and the same is hereby dissolved." Copies of the resolution, accompanied by a note from Mrs. Eddy, were mailed to her students:

> Beloved Student: You are again called to accept, without a present understanding, a marked providence of God. Our Master said: "What I do thou knowest not now, but thou shalt know hereafter."
> Trust Him in this unlooked-for event, and He will sooner or later show you the wisdom thereof. I have acted with deliberation. For the past two years this change has seemed to me the imperative demand of Christian Science in consonance with the example of our Master. Trusting that you also will discern the wisdom of this advanced step and coincide with this act of the Corporation.
>
> I am affectionately yours,
>
> Mary B. G. Eddy

There were many among her critics who received the news of the closing of the Massachusetts Metaphysical College as a sure sign of the approaching collapse of the Christian Science movement. What they did not know, and probably would not have believed had they been told, was that Mrs. Eddy had closed her college at the peak of its popularity and its prosperity. There were more than three hundred applications on hand, and each day's mail added to the total. There were applications that came from all over the United States, from Canada, and from Europe.

In 1889 Mrs. Eddy disengaged herself from five organizational responsibilities. She resigned the presidency of the two Christian Scientist Associations, resigned the editorship of *The Christian Science Journal,* the pastorate of her church in Boston, and her position as teacher in the Massachusetts Metaphysical College.

In the midst of disorganization (although none but she saw it) the permanent form of the government of The Mother Church was beginning to appear. Behind was whatever was provisional or impermanent. In its stead was coming a form of church government unique in the world. Spiritual in its conception and impersonal in its administration, it would be a government of Rules and Bylaws that, as Mrs. Eddy wrote, "were impelled by a power not one's own, were written at different dates, and as the occasion required." [3]

It would be a church whose teachings she knew would not at first please mankind but would please God. They were teachings that would give mankind increasing understanding of its Creator. In so teaching she was not unlike Paul, who said to the Galatians:

"For do I now persuade men or God? or do I seek to please men? for if I yet pleased men, I should not be the servant of Christ."

"The servant of Christ"—so, too, did Mary Baker Eddy look upon herself. She saw in every healing the presence of God, the liberation of mankind from the tyranny of its belief in matter, and the affirmation that spiritual consciousness, not breath and not a heartbeat, is the eternal element.

By disengaging herself from organizational responsibilities, Mrs. Eddy was freeing her time and her thought, that she might give full attention to her most important work, her textbook—*Science and Health With Key to the Scriptures.* It was a textbook that would provide the inmost nature of the church she was bringing into existence. It would be a church that would not be governed by human opinions

---

[3] *Manual of The Mother Church.*

but a church that, in perpetuity, would be governed by the precepts of God.

From its faint beginnings in 1872 when her outline was rejected by a Boston publisher, her book, a disappointment in its first and second printings, had gone into forty-eight printings, all but six of which were in the previous six years. In Europe, in Canada, and in the United States the verdict was the same. No longer was it necessary for so many to lean on her convictions to support their own. It was not acceptance contrived by propaganda. All the propaganda had been against her teachings. It was an acceptance produced by study of the book itself.

The manufacturing order for the fiftieth edition of *Science and Health* was entered into the records of the University Press on July 2, 1890. But before July 2, 1890, Mrs Eddy had been in touch with John Wilson, head of the printing establishment, advising him of her forthcoming manuscript, and with the Reverend James Henry Wiggin, advising him of her wish that he continue in her employ as a proofreader. She notified Wiggin on June 14, 1890, "I shall request Mr. Wilson to send the proofs to you and then you to me and I to him."

William G. Nixon, who had come from Pierre, South Dakota, to be publisher of *The Christian Science Journal,* was asked by Mrs. Eddy, in 1890, to serve as publisher of *Science and Health,* as well as of her other books. Nixon was her first publisher. His name appears on the title page of the fifty-first edition of the textbook, the fiftieth edition having been published under her supervision. The appointment relieved her of a great deal of time-consuming detail.

Prior to the coming of Nixon, it was the practice of the University Press (as William Dana Orcutt recalled in his volume *Mary Baker Eddy and Her Books*) to send shipments directly to Mrs. Eddy for wrapping and mailing.

These shipments were in addition to those from the bindery to other addresses but all required her personal attention. Taking into account the immediate success of the revised edition, the burden would have been extraordinarily heavy because within the year, *Science and Health* was in its fifty-second edition.

The fiftieth edition was the first to carry marginal headings; replacing the use of poetry or verse at the head of each chapter, as in previous editions, were Biblical quotations; five chapters appearing in previous editions were dropped; [4] seven new chapters were introduced; [5] chapters were rearranged.

The chapter headings and their arrangement in the fiftieth edition follow:

"Science, Theology, Medicine"; "Physiology"; "Footsteps of Truth"; "Creation"; "Science of Being"; "Christian Science and Spiritualism"; "Marriage"; "Animal Magnetism"; "Some Objections Answered"; "Prayer"; "Atonement and Eucharist"; "Christian Science Practice"; "Teaching Christian Science"; "Recapitulation."

Key to the Scriptures: Genesis, Apocalypse; Glossary and Index.

With the exception of two, these chapter headings remain unchanged ("Christian Science and Spiritualism" now has this heading: "Christian Science versus Spiritualism"; "Animal Magnetism" now has this title: "Animal Magnetism Unmasked"). However, in later editions, Mrs. Eddy rearranged the chapters into their present sequence:

[4] "Wayside Hints"; "Imposition and Demonstration"; "Healing and Teaching"; "Platform of Christian Scientists"; "Reply to a Critic."
[5] "Science, Theology, Medicine"; "Christian Science and Spiritualism"; "Some Objections Answered"; "Prayer"; "Atonement and Eucharist"; "Christian Science Practice"; "Teaching Christian Science."

"Prayer"; "Atonement and Eucharist"; "Marriage"; "Christian Science versus Spiritualism"; "Animal Magnetism Unmasked"; "Science, Theology, Medicine"; "Physiology"; "Footsteps of Truth"; "Creation"; "Science of Being"; "Some Objections Answered"; "Christian Science Practice"; "Teaching Christian Science"; "Recapitulation." Key to the Scriptures: Genesis; The Apocalypse; Glossary; Fruitage, which contains about one hundred pages of Christian Science healings; and an Index.

As she recalled in the Preface to the fiftieth edition, Mrs. Eddy "closed her college, October 29, 1889, . . . with a deeply-lying conviction that the next two years of her life should be given to the preparation of this edition of her work on *Science and Health.*"

In the two years she made many changes in successive editions although most of the changes were in the fiftieth and fifty-first editions.

It was in those years that Orcutt began his publishing career under John Wilson, at the University Press. So it was natural that the day came when Wilson sent him to Concord "to discuss with Mrs. Eddy personally a matter she had previously taken up with him.

"I was shown into the study, and after a brief wait a slight, unassuming woman entered the room, giving me a smiling welcome which placed me completely at my ease.

". . . 'So you are the young man who has been helping my friend John Wilson during his son's absence,' she said. 'He has told me a great deal about you. Please sit down. I am glad to know you.'

". . . Her interest in me at the beginning was due to her belief that I was an essential piece to be fitted into her friend's design for living, to repair a break that had occurred. If she, as John Wilson's friend, could help him to accomplish this, she intended to do so. That was her idea of what friendship meant.

"After a few moments of general conversation we turned to the proof sheets I had brought with me, and the questions Mr. Wilson had wished settled were answered with promptness and directness. At first, one might have been deceived by her quiet manner into thinking that she was easily influenced. There was no suggestion to which she did not hold herself open. If she approved, she accepted it promptly; if it did not appeal, she dismissed it with a graciousness that left no mark—but it was settled once and for all. There was no wavering and no uncertainty." [6]

For William Dana Orcutt it was the beginning of a memorable friendship.

[6] *Mary Baker Eddy and Her Books,* by William Dana Orcutt. Copyright, 1950, The Christian Science Publishing Society.

CHAPTER TEN

Every Hill Ascended

THESE were years when there were many troublemakers. There was Mrs. Josephine C. Woodbury; there was Joshua F. Bailey; there was Mrs. Augusta E. Stetson; there was William G. Nixon. There were others, quite a few of them.

After giving birth to a son, Mrs. Woodbury announced that this was the result of an "immaculate conception" and called her offspring the Prince of Peace. Although this was obviously ridiculous, the lunacy of the woman was used by Mrs. Eddy's enemies in an effort to deface her teachings.

As Editor of *The Christian Science Journal* for a period of six months, Joshua F. Bailey advised his readers to (1) use the Rotherman Version of the New Testament in preference to Mrs. Eddy's choice of the King James Version; (2) refrain from reading the Bible "for three months or more [after entering Christian Science]. Don't open it even, nor think of it. But dig day and night at *Science and Health"*; and (3) "burn every scrap of 'Christian Science literature,' so-called, except *Science and Health,* and the publications bearing the imprint of the Christian Science Publishing Society in Boston."

Letters streamed into the office of the Publication Committee of the National Christian Scientist Association, all in vigorous protest to the Editor's inept statements. Bailey resigned but after resigning persuaded the Publication Committee to form a "General Association for Dispensing Christian Science Literature," whereupon Bailey used the *Journal* to call upon all Christian Scientists to join with him in the distribution of selected reading material. At the same time, and in the same request, he gave the impression that failure to buy a copy of the new edition of *Science and Health* would be regarded as an act of disloyalty to Mrs. Eddy.

In accord with her wish to be undisturbed during the period of revising her textbook, Mrs. Eddy was not immediately told of Bailey's obtuseness. When told, she acted promptly. In the July issue of the *Journal* appeared this card:

> Since my attention has been called to the article in the May *Journal,* I think it would have been wiser not to have organized the General Association for Dispensing Christian Science Literature.
>
> 1. Because I disbelieve in the utility of so widespread an organization. It tends to promote monopolies, class legislation and unchristian motives for Christian work.
>
> 2. I consider my students as capable, individually, of selecting their own reading matter and circulating it, as a committee would be which is chosen for this purpose.
>
> I shall have nothing further to say on this subject, but hope my students' conclusion will be wisely drawn, and tend to promote the welfare of those outside, as well as inside this organization.
>
> Mary B. G. Eddy

In the same issue of the *Journal* was a "Notice" of the dissolution of the General Association for Dispensing Christian Science Literature. Bailey was without a vehicle for further improvisations.

Nevertheless, some of Bailey's words have remained in the vocabularies of critics of Christian Science. Years have elapsed, but critics still argue that by advising newcomers to Christian Science not to read their Bibles "for three months, or more," Bailey was subordinating the Scriptures —and, in his capacity as Editor, he was speaking with authority as well as with the consent of Mrs. Eddy, else his statement could not have appeared in *The Christian Science Journal.*

Neither argument is based on fact. Bailey could not speak with authority on Christian Science because he had no such authority. Nor was Mrs. Eddy's consent needed before an article could be published in the *Journal.* In June, 1889, she had turned over such responsibilities to the National Christian Scientist Association.

Having lost access to the columns of the *Journal,* Bailey began scheming with Mrs. Augusta E. Stetson, a student who later was to cause a great deal of anguish to Mrs. Eddy. Their hope was to get possession of the publication. The opportunity—or what they thought was the opportunity— came in November, 1892.

On the first day of November, 1892, William G. Nixon resigned as Manager and Publisher of the *Journal.* In his letter of resignation he said: ". . . On assuming my duties as publisher, there was not a dollar in the treasury . . . today there is cash in the treasury to the amount of over six thousand dollars ($6,000), with all our bills paid to date. . . ."

Nixon's resignation came as a surprise, but more surprising was the glowing report of the *Journal's* financial condition, and most surprising was the attack on Mrs.

Eddy. This attack disclosed itself in the statement "not a dollar in the treasury," which continued: ". . . unpaid printing and paper bills . . . not to mention a contingent liability of many more hundreds represented by unearned *Journal* and *Series* ¹ subscriptions paid by subscribers in advance, which sum of money had been disbursed in the course of business prior to my coming."

Joseph Armstrong, who succeeded Nixon, turned over the financial records of the publication to a firm of auditors. In their report the auditors showed assets amounting to $9,953.67, of which $8,032.92 was in cash, and liabilities of $7,591.43, leaving a balance of $2,362.24 against which were some bills which had not been presented. Also, despite Nixon's assurance that "all bills (are) paid to date," the audit disclosed "bills not paid" amounting to $2,253.01. These were not the only aberrations in Nixon's statement.

In the resignation of Nixon, Joshua Bailey and Mrs. Stetson thought they saw the moment of opportunity to take control of the *Journal;* nor were they at all discouraged by the findings of the auditors, which were published in March, 1893. They continued their clandestine efforts among the members of the National Christian Scientist Association until September 20, 1893.

On this day the Association, holding its first meeting in three years, received a letter from Mrs. Eddy:

> My dear Students:—I have a unique request to lay before the National Christian Scientist Association. It is this: Will you decide by vote, whether or not I already am the owner of the *Christian*

---

¹ This was a twelve-page publication issued twice monthly from May 1, 1889 until May 1, 1891. Called the *Christian Science Series,* it contained articles and poems.

Science Journal, which seems to have fallen into my hands by reason of your prior vote to disorganize this Association? But however this may be, I see the wisdom of again owning this Christian Science waif. Therefore I respectfully suggest to this honorable body the importance of voting on this question.

Affectionately yours,

Mary B. G. Eddy

On the same day the following motion was made, seconded, and passed unanimously:

"That it be declared by this Association of Christian Scientists to be its understanding that the *Christian Science Journal* is now owned by Rev. Mary Baker G. Eddy, its donor and original proprietor. . . ."

In the November, 1893, issue of the *Journal* it was explained that Mrs. Eddy took this unusual way "to make doubly sure that (the *Journal*) belonged to her, and that no person had, or could have, any legal claim on the *Journal*. . . ." In the same issue Mrs. Eddy published this statement:

My Beloved Christian Scientists:—Please send in your contributions as usual to our *Journal.* All is well at headquarters and when the mist shall melt away you will see clearly the glory of the heaven of love within your own hearts. Let this sign of peace and harmony be supreme and forever yours. . . .

With confirmation of Mrs. Eddy's ownership, Bailey and Mrs. Stetson abandoned their efforts to get control of the *Journal.*

These, also, were the years when she placed her teachings, and her church, beyond the reach of troublemakers.

In these years Mary Baker Eddy was doing precisely what she had been doing for a long time. She was looking into the future, when she would not be present in person to protect her teachings and her church.

From childhood she had known that every hill ascended brings into view a loftier one; and, always between, there is a valley to be crossed. This was the history of Christianity. Through its first three centuries, and for twenty-five added years, Christianity consisted of teachings which few believed although the sick were healed, the leper was cleansed, and the dead were raised.

A missionary named Paul had carried the teaching of the One who was crucified across a pagan world while ascending the hills of Syria and Celicia and Galatia, of Macedonia, until he was in Rome itself. For more than two hundred and fifty years after Paul, there followed a host of bishops scattered along the Mediterranean, each interpreting the Scriptures to fit his own prejudices until, in 325, at the Council of Nicaea, the bishops met, and agreed, not unanimously, but by majority vote, on what all should say in the name of Christianity.

No longer were the sick healed, the leper cleansed, and the dead raised. Instead, came pageantry, ritual, robes of authority, and fear. Afterwards came the Dark Ages, the Inquisition and the Reformation, all contributing to the hills and valleys that make up the history of Christianity.

More than fifteen hundred years after the Council of Nicaea, and eighteen hundred years after Paul's execution in pagan Rome, Mary Baker Eddy discovered what she deeply believed was the lost element of Christianity —healing—and began her long struggle against the now entrenched forces of ecclesiasticism, scholasticism, and materialism. After twenty-six years of evangelical work, the great hour for the reorganization of her church was near. The year itself was 1892.

In 1889, in addition to moving from Boston to Concord that she might be undisturbed in expanding and clarifying *Science and Health,* Mrs. Eddy sought solitude that she might be ready for the duty that bound her.

In August, 1889, in *The Christian Science Journal,* she had addressed a letter to the Boston congregation suggesting to it a new use for *Science and Health.* The letter read:

ORDER OF CHURCH SERVICE

TO THE CHURCH OF CHRIST (SCIENTIST), BOSTON.

Beloved Brethren:—I recommend that you lay aside all that is ceremonial even in appearance in our Church and adopt this simple service.

Before the sermon read one hymn, sing once. Read selection from a chapter in the Bible, and, if agreeable to pastor and Church, a corresponding paragraph from *Science and Health.* Repeat alternately the Lord's Prayer, the pastor repeating the first sentence and the audience the following one. Unite in silent prayer for all who are present. Close with reading hymn, singing, silent prayer, and the benediction.

Yours lovingly in Christ,

Mary B. G. Eddy.

The permanent form of church services was beginning to appear. It was the result of patient work.

In February, 1890, in the *Journal* was this statement:

The dissolution of the visible organization of
the Church is the sequence and complement of that
of the College Corporation and Association. The
College disappeared, "that the spirit of Christ
might have freer course among its students and all
who come into the understanding of Divine Science"; the bonds of organization of the Church
were thrown away, so that its members might
assemble themselves together and "provoke one
another to good works" in the bond only of Love.

Although seeking "no new organization but the spiritual
one" Mrs. Eddy was completely aware that if the church
she envisioned was to endure throughout her absence, in
person, in all the years of the future, it would have to be
established on a proper legal foundation. There need be
no conflict. Nor, as she disclosed the way, should there be.

The church Mary Baker Eddy was envisioning was not
one in which human voices would be heard uttering human
opinions from a pulpit, but one in which the Bible and the
Christian Science textbook, with its interpretive spiritual
passages, would be the only preachers.

She knew that, if undiluted, her teachings would be out
of reach of the conniving Herods, whenever and wherever
they might be. She knew that the church, the textbook, and
the *Church Manual* would stand together or fall together.

They would stand together or fall together because, with
the Bible and the textbook as the only preachers, they would
form the shield that would safeguard the teachings, just as
the *Manual* would be the shield that would protect the
church and the textbook.

Ten months after Mrs. Eddy had recommended to the
members of The Mother Church that they "lay aside all that
is ceremonial even in appearance in our church . . . Before

the sermon ... read selections from a chapter in the Bible, and if agreeable to pastor and Church, a corresponding paragraph from *Science and Health* ..." Mrs. Eddy received a letter from Caroline D. Noyes, a member of the Chicago church, saying, in part:

"Recognizing that *Science and Health* is both our Teacher and Healer, we resolved to take it into our pulpit and make it our Preacher also, by reading selections from it, together with appropriate passages from the Scriptures in place of a sermon. ... In two months both church and Sunday school have doubled in number."

Continuing, the Chicago student wrote: "It is apparent ... that the numerous group of Scientists who are waiting ... for a pastor or speaker to establish services, can proceed at once with possibly greater advantage to themselves than could be realized with a speaker. They are certain to gain strength through reliance on their own efforts, and from participation in the worship."

At the time there were about twenty Christian Science churches and sixty Christian Science societies with a total attendance of but a few thousand. It was a group that, in its entirety, was made up of men and women who had come into Christian Science from other denominations. What Mrs. Noyes did not realize was that Mrs. Eddy was working toward the same end of having the Bible and *Science and Health* as the only preachers in her church and had been for some time, but Mrs. Eddy also knew her followers were not ready to accept such a drastic change in church services.

In the August, 1891, issue of *The Christian Science Journal,* she gave the first public intimation of her desire to remove all human opinions from the teachings of her church. Following the use of the textbook in association with the Scriptures in Sunday services in the Chicago church, Mrs.

Eddy watched closely to see that thought was not confused and confidence unsettled among all who listened.

Knowing that only a small minority of her followers was qualified to select the proper citations from the two books, and believing it her duty to prevent the mutilation of both books—the Bible and *Science and Health*—Mrs. Eddy reminded all churches and all societies that her writings were protected by laws of copyright, hence "it is not right to copy my book and read it publicly *without my consent.*"

In the same communication she offered "as a gift to my noble students,—working faithfully for Christ's cause on earth,—the privilege of copying and reading my works for Sunday service, provided, they each, and all destroy these copies at once, after said service. Also, that when I shall so elect, and give suitable notice, they desist from further copying my writings, as aforesaid"; and gave her reason for the instruction: "This injunction . . . is intended to forestall the possible evil of putting the divine teachings contained in *Science and Health* into human hands, to subvert or to liquidate." [2]

In October, 1891, in the *Journal,* Mrs. Eddy published this "Notice":

> Question: "Shall we continue to read in the pulpit, on Sunday, extracts from *Science and Health?*"
>
> "If you comply with my terms relative to these Sunday services, published in the August issue of this year's *Journal,* you should. I have consented to this as above, and see no other causes than those designated in August *Journal* for changing the form you had already adopted for your Sunday sermons. I gave no permission for you to use my

---

[2] Full text, *The Christian Science Journal IX* (August, 1891), p. 182.

writings as aforesaid, except it be in place of a sermon delivered in your established pulpits."

Her words were closely read in the widening circle of churches. In churches, such as the one in Chicago, pastors were free to use the Bible and the textbook instead of a sermon, if they so wished. However, this privilege was confined solely to pastors of "established pulpits."

Waiting another two months, but continuing to be careful not to lead too fast, Mrs. Eddy announced another change in the "Order of Church Services" for *all* Christian Science churches:

> That there be uniformity among Christian Scientists in their Church services, I submit the following Order of Exercise:
>
> Anthem.
>
> Pastor announces that he will read from the Bible, and from *Science and Health*.
>
> Reading.
>
> Lord's Prayer and Spiritual Version repeated alternately.
>
> Pastor commences the first line of the Prayer, and repeats it with the Church; then he responds to it with the version. Next, the Church repeats the second line of the Prayer and Pastor responds, and so on to the end.
>
> Pastor reads Hymn.
>
> Singing.
>
> Sermon.
>
> Collection.
>
> Pastor reads Hymn.
>
> Singing.
>
> Benediction.
>
> Mary B. G. Eddy

There were a number of changes in the new order of services. Two books, the Bible and *Science and Health,* were in authoritative positions; The "Lord's Prayer and Spiritual Version"[3] appeared for the first time in church services; these being the most important changes.

The Lord's Prayer with its spiritual interpretation, as first used in church services, follows:

Our Father, which art in Heaven,
Our eternal supreme Being, all-harmonious.
Hallowed be Thy name.
Forever glorious.
Thy Kingdom come!
Ever-present and omnipotent!
Thy will be done in earth, as it is in Heaven.
Thy supremacy appears as matter disappears.
Give us this day our daily bread;
Give us each day the living bread;
And forgive us our debts, as we forgive our debtors.
And Truth will destroy the claims of error.
And lead us not into temptation, but deliver us from evil;
Led by Spirit, mortals are freed from sickness, sin and death.
For Thine is the Kingdom and the power and the glory forever. Amen.
For Thou art all Substance, Life, Truth, and Love forever. So be it.

[3] As used for the first time in church services, the Prayer with its spiritual interpretation was as published in the 1891 edition of *Science and Health.* The Prayer with its spiritual interpretation first appeared in the first edition of *Science and Health.*

Mary Baker Eddy's spiritual interpretation of the Lord's Prayer was not a single act; nor was her Order of Church Services a single act, nor the writing of *Science and Health,* nor the development of the *Church Manual,* nor the conception of her church. In their final form, all were the work of years as, dwelling in the chapel of prayer, Mrs. Eddy discovered more and more about the eternal structure in which only permanent values are found.

Perceiving that the strength of her church was not in numbers but in teachings, not in cathedrals nor edifices many but in one church which would be called *The Mother Church,* Mary Baker Eddy knew that internal antagonisms were insidiously at work.

That was not a new experience. Principle is always under attack in this world.

To Mrs. Eddy, the important thing was not what was being attempted but its effect on her followers. Some would act in confusion, which would suit the purposes of the conspirators; some would act in faith, believing that in her teachings was truth.

In 1889, after recovering the land on Falmouth Street on which to build the edifice of The Mother Church, Mrs. Eddy had instructed Ira O. Knapp to transfer title to the property to three trustees under terms of a deed of trust which Concord lawyers had drawn up at her request. The trustees were Alfred Lang, Marcellus Munroe, and William G. Nixon.

In the *Journal* (January, 1890) it was announced that a church edifice would be built on the lot, and that work would be started when subscriptions reached the sum of twenty thousand dollars. Following this announcement, the Christian Scientist Association of the Massachusetts Metaphysical College voted unanimously to make the edifice "strictly a Memorial Church . . . in the heart of the very city where the Founder and Teacher of this Science has had the hardest battles to wage against error; where at its early inception she stood alone, sole advocate and defender of the Cause. . . ."

Mrs. Eddy put a stop to the proposal by writing in the November, 1890, issue of the *Journal:*

> I object to such a departure from the Principle of Christian Science, as it would be, to be memorialized in a manner which should cause personal motives for building the First Church of Christ (Scientist) in Boston.
>
> Contributions to this Boston Building Fund should be made on a higher plane of thought.
>
> The lot of land that I gave this church, was, for the purpose of building thereon a house for the worship of God, and a home for Christian Scientists.
>
> The true followers, who worship "in Spirit and in Truth," will contribute to this Building Fund from a similar motive, and thus abide by the Principle of Christian Science which we acknowledge.
>
> Mary B. G. Eddy

The proposal to build a Memorial Church was abandoned; another idea took its place. This was an idea which proposed a structure that would be a combined church edifice and publishing building. The idea found strong support among the trustees and little support among the directors. Of the trustees, Lang and Nixon were as one.

Persuading Munroe to join with them, Lang and Nixon also persuaded the Directors to agree to the building of a combined church and office building, the plans for which were published in the March, 1892, issue of the *Journal.* Responding, Mrs. Eddy wrote the Directors:

> All that I have counseled has worked well for Church and Cause. Your only danger now lies in the past being repeated. . . .
>
> I wrote to you, Miss Bartlett, and others not to organize a church! Then it was reported that I gave the order to organize, but I did not.
>
> Now your salvation as a people whose God is the Lord lies in being wise as a serpent. Again I repeat do not . . . change your present materially disorganized—but spiritually organized— Church, nor its *present form* of church *government.* . . .
>
> The lot I paid for, the taxes on it, the expense of Lawyer, etc., are all straight, *legally* and forever settled. No man can make it otherwise any more than evil can destroy Good.
>
> Affectionately,
>
> M. B. G. Eddy

Standing firm, the Directors resisted the efforts of the trustees to disregard Mrs. Eddy's counsel against reorganizing the church that they might erect a combined edifice and office building, whereupon the trustees appealed to the membership of the church.

The trustees told the membership they had visited a lawyer to make inquiries as to the legality of Knapp's title to the property and had been told that "no individual, or body, has a title to the property." On the lawyer's advice they sought permission from the directors for the lawyer to examine the church records that necessary steps might be taken to legalize the title. They met with refusal. They made a second request and met with a second refusal. After much questioning and long listening, a majority of the members voted with the trustees and against the directors.

When told of the action Mrs. Eddy advised the members that, by reorganizing, they were inviting the loss of their form of church government and title to the lot. She sobered them further by adding: "Let the church reorganize . . . let her pass on to her experience, and the sooner the better. When we will not learn in any other way, this is God's order of teaching us, His *rod alone* will do it."

CHAPTER ELEVEN

A Great Purpose Unfolding

B ELATEDLY realizing that Mrs. Eddy was willing to let them blunder if she could effect their good, the church members met again on June 1, 1892, reversed themselves, and voted acceptance of the deed of trust; and, with thirty thousand dollars already contributed, they adopted resolutions calling upon the trustees to begin building operations at once.

The trustees objected, protesting that the title to the land on which the church was to be built was "imperfect" and saying that "had they had free access to Mrs. Eddy during the past three months," the imperfections in the title "would have been in a way to cure, and the Church edifice would ere this have been begun. . . ."

In reply, the directors informed all who had made contributions: "If the Deed was not strictly sound and Mr. Nixon knew it as he said he did from the first he had no right to get your money for building on land to which he had not a clear title." They continued: "When Mrs. Eddy was led to fear there were flaws in the Deed she begged the Trustees to put your money in the building and then have the title made sound. For if the Deed is broken before this is done the Trustees can claim the money which they have deposited in their own names and nobody but themselves can take it out of the banks. This is why she urged them to

go to building or else stop calling for building funds, until
they had a clear title.

"Mr. Knapp is ready to give a sound title to the land on
the terms of his Deed and as Mrs. Eddy wished to give it; but
they will either have it on their own terms or as they say no
title at all, and yet continue to receive your money."

Planning among themselves to buy another plot of land
on which would be built a church that would be free from
the restrictions of the Deed of Trust, the trustees circulated
a letter soliciting support for their position and, in so doing, called attention to findings of the Massachusetts Title
Insurance Company, of Boston. Having examined the Deed
of Trust, the title company expressed the opinion that the
Trust, as set up by Mrs. Eddy, was "a public charity"; being
so, the land on which the church was to be built was under
the control of the Supreme Court of Massachusetts because
there was no formal church organization qualified to hold
property.

Despite dissenting legal opinions, Mary Baker Eddy was
secure in her heart that the Deed of Trust she signed was
in accordance with the statutes of the Commonwealth of
Massachusetts. With the appearance of opposition, she employed a firm of lawyers to search the laws of Massachusetts
for the purpose of confirming her conviction there was legal
permission that would permit her church to own property
and still free it from corporate limitations.

The lawyers found the little-known law which provided
the protection Mrs. Eddy was sure existed. Even while the
lawyers were searching, Mrs. Eddy was calling upon the
trustees: "Delay not to build our Church in Boston; or else,
return every dollar that you ... have had no legal authority
for obtaining—to the several contributors, and let them, not
you, say what shall be done with their money."

The demand was made in an article in the *Journal* in

July, 1892. The article, revised by Mrs. Eddy in its permanent form, appears in *Miscellaneous Writings*, pp. 139–142. In it, Mrs. Eddy explained:

As with all former efforts in the interest of Christian Science, I took care that the provisions for the land and building were such as error could not control. I knew that to God's gift, foundation and superstructure, no one could hold a wholly material title. The land, and the church standing on it, must be conveyed through a type representing the true nature of the gift; a type morally and spiritually inalienable, but materially questionable—even after the manner that all spiritual good comes to Christian Scientists, to the end of taxing their faith in God, and their adherence to the superiority of the claims of Spirit over matter or merely legal titles.

No one could buy, sell, or mortgage my gift as I had it conveyed. Thus the case rested, and I supposed the trustee-deed was legal; but this was God's business, not mine. Our church was prospered by the right hand of His righteousness, and contributions to the Building Fund generously poured into the treasury. Unity prevailed—till mortal man sought to know who owned God's temple, and adopted and urged only the material side of this question.

The lot of land which I donated I redeemed from under mortgage. The foundation on which our church was to be built had to be rescued from the grasp of legal power, and now it must be put back into the arms of Love, if we would not be found fighting against God.

The diviner claim and means for upbuilding the Church of Christ were prospered. Our title to God's acres will be safe and sound—when we can "read our title clear" to heavenly mansions. Built on the rock, our church will stand the storms of ages; though the material superstructure should crumble into dust, the fittest would survive,—the spiritual idea would live, a perpetual type of the divine Principle it reflects. . . .

On August 19, 1892, Ira O. Knapp and Flavia Stickney Knapp, his wife, gave a quit claim deed to the lot at Falmouth and Caledonia streets. For the first time since its purchase in 1886, the lot was in Mrs. Eddy's name. Already Lang, Nixon, and Munroe had learned that the Deed of Trust was legal and that their idea of soliciting funds for building a combination church and office building was a violation, had agreed to return all contributions to the donors, and had resigned as trustees.

In 1878, when Mary Baker Eddy revised *Science and Health,* there were those who insisted the textbook "should not be made public, but," as she wrote in *No and Yes* (p. 3), "I obeyed a diviner rule."

She saw, as she had seen from the beginning, that possession of her discovery could not be embraced in selfish protection but was a gift that had to be shared, if it was not to be lost again. And as with *Science and Health,* so with The Mother Church, it, too, was a gift to be shared with all who were eligible.

With title to the lot on which her church was to be built now in her name, Mrs. Eddy wasted no time effecting her plans. On August 22, 1892, she wrote letters to twelve students, asking them to meet in the home of Julia Bartlett on

August 29, at twelve noon, for the purpose of organizing The Mother Church, The First Church of Christ, Scientist, in Boston, Massachusetts.

Including the four Directors (Ira O. Knapp, William B. Johnson, Joseph S. Eastaman, and Stephen A. Chase), the twelve whose privilege it was to establish The Mother Church were: Julia Bartlett, Ellen L. Clarke, Janet T. Colman, Mary F. Eastaman, Ebenezer J. Foster-Eddy, Eldora O. Gragg, Flavia S. Knapp, and Mary W. Munroe. Each of the twelve was chosen by Mrs. Eddy.

In a new Deed of Trust, which was read to the assembled twelve in Julia Bartlett's home on August 29 and which was executed by Mrs. Eddy two days later, on September 1, 1892, were included these two paragraphs:

This deed of conveyance is made upon the following express trusts and conditions which the said grantees by accepting this deed agree and covenant for themselves and their successors in office to fully perform and fulfil.

1. Said grantees shall be known as the "Christian Science Board of Directors," and shall constitute a perpetual body or corporation under and in accordance with section one, Chapter 39 of the Public Statutes of Massachusetts. Whenever a vacancy occurs in said Board the remaining members shall within thirty days fill the same by election; but no one shall be eligible to that office who is not in the opinion of the remaining members of the Board a firm and consistent believer in the doctrines of Christian Science as taught in a book entitled *"Science and Health,"* by Mary Baker G. Eddy beginning with the seventy-first edition thereof.

And, too, this paragraph:

4. Said Board of Directors shall not suffer or allow any building to be erected upon said lot except a church building or edifice, nor shall they allow said church building or any part thereof to be used for any other purpose than for the ordinary and usual uses of a church.[1]

In transferring title to the land on which The Mother Church was to be built to The Christian Science Board of Directors, in establishing the Board as "a perpetual body or corporation," and in bestowing upon its members responsibility to fill whatever vacancies occurred within their midst, Mary Baker Eddy broke with traditional forms of church government—and, stipulating that no structure should "be erected upon said lot except a church building, or edifice," she had the lot at Falmouth and Caledonia streets sealed off, making it the continuing location of The Mother Church.

In making The Christian Science Board of Directors a self-perpetuating body, Mrs. Eddy placed its members beyond the range of voices of intrigue within or without the Movement. Designing her Church for its great purpose, she was basing it firmly, building it strongly, and modeling it on a master plan in which her teachings would be clearly outlined through all the future.

Having conferred most unusual powers upon the Directors, Mrs. Eddy then called upon them to meet with the eight others she had chosen to organize The Mother Church. As a body of twelve, these students were instructed

[1] For full copy see *Church Manual*, pp. 128–135, and *The Cross and the Crown*, copyright 1952, by Norman Beasley. Published by Duell, Sloan and Pearce.

to agree upon twenty other students who, after she had given her approval, would be invited into church member-ship and who, along with the twelve, would be known as First Members.

In so instructing the twelve, Mrs. Eddy told them not to "name anyone bearing a tablet." Since 1888, when thirty-six students took advantage of her absence in Chicago to resign as members of the Christian Scientist Association of the Massachusetts Metaphysical College, to gain possession of the Association records by trick, and to drop their church memberships, she was watchful over the efforts of some of these same students to regain the position of influence they once had.

Most, if not all, had returned as regular attendants at church services, had sided with Lang, Nixon, and Munroe in the efforts of the former trustees to violate the conditions of the Deed of Trust, and, in various ways, such as by offer-ing contributions to the Building Fund, had sought to shorten the probationary period which they had to com-plete before being eligible for church membership. By cautioning against naming "anyone bearing a tablet," she was referring specifically to these thirty-four students. Her words were heeded. None was named a First Member.

On September 23, 1892, the twelve students [2] Mrs. Eddy had chosen to establish The Mother Church met quietly in Boston and elected as First Members twenty other students. All were approved by Mrs. Eddy. They were:

Calvin A. Frye, Edward P. Bates, Eugene H. Greene, David Anthony, Hanover P. Smith,[3] Mrs. Josephine Curtis Otterson, Mrs. Grace A. Greene, Mrs. Caroline S. Bates,

[2] One of the chosen twelve, Mrs. Ellen L. Clarke, was absent unavoidably but had approved the full list of twenty.

[3] Smith, a deaf-mute since birth, was healed by Mrs. Eddy while she was living in Boston. Later he became a Christian Science lecturer.

Mrs. Emilie B. Hulin, Mrs. Caroline W. Frame, Mrs. Elizabeth P. Skinner, Mrs. Augusta E. Stetson, Mrs. Henrietta E. Chanfrau, Mrs. Emily M. Meader, Mrs. Berenice H. Goodall, Mrs. Annie V. C. Leavitt, Mrs. Laura E. Sargent, Mrs. Ann M. Otis, Mrs. Mary F. Berry, Miss Martha E. S. Morgan.

In addition to the foregoing names, the minutes of this historic meeting contain the Tenets of the Church:

> Tenets to be subscribed to by those uniting with "The First Church of Christ, Scientist" in Boston, were read by the President [Ebenezer J. Foster-Eddy]. The Tenets were adopted, and ordered to be written in the book containing the records of this Church.

Tenets
OF
The First Church of Christ, Scientist,
BY
Rev. Mary Baker G. Eddy.

To be signed by those uniting with "First Church of Christ, Scientist."

1. As adherents of Truth, we take the Scriptures for our guide to eternal Life.

2. We acknowledge and adore one Supreme God.

We acknowledge His Son, the Holy Ghost, and man in His image and likeness. We acknowledge God's forgiveness of sin, in the destruction of sin, and His present and future punishment of "whatsoever worketh abomination or maketh a lie." And the atonement of Christ, as the efficacy of Truth and Love. And the way of Salvation as demonstrated by Jesus casting out evils, healing the sick, and raising the dead—resurrecting a dead faith to seize the great possibilities and living energies of the Divine Life.

3. We solemnly promise to strive, watch, and pray for that Mind to be in us which was also in Christ Jesus. To love the brethren, and, up to our highest capacity to be meek, merciful, and just, and live peaceably with all men.

When living in Lynn in 1879 Mrs. Eddy obtained a charter for her first church. She wrote twenty rules of membership. In 1892, when she organized her new church, The Mother Church, she wrote six rules of membership. There would be more, but they were yet to come. Now, although discerning the readiness of her students for definite direction, she was leading a step at a time, each step leading to the next, and each leading forward. "First the blade, then the ear, after that the full corn in the ear."

The six rules adopted at the September 23, 1892, meeting were:

1. The annual meeting of THE FIRST CHURCH OF CHRIST, SCIENTIST, IN BOSTON, shall be held on the first Tuesday evening in October in each year for the choice of officers for the ensuing year; listening to the reports of the Treasurer, Secretary, and Committees, and for the transaction of any church business that may properly come before the meeting.

2. Quarterly meetings of this church shall be held on the Saturday evening next preceding the Communion Sunday in each quarter, beginning

with the Saturday next preceding the first Sunday in January, 1893.

3. Applications for membership, coming from the students' students, must include the names and recommendations of their teachers. All applications for membership must be addressed to the pastor or the clerk of the church. If to the pastor, he shall hand the letters to the clerk, who shall read them at the quarterly church meeting, and the First members shall vote on admitting these candidates. Candidates for membership with this church shall be elected by a majority vote.

4. The names of the members elected at a quarterly meeting of this church shall on the following Sunday be read from the pulpit and the Communion service be held.

5. The Communion shall be observed by this Church on the first Sunday in October, January, April and July—by special exhortation, Hymns, Singing, and silent prayer.

6. Members of this church cannot be members of other churches except they are of the same denomination as this church.

Most important of the six rules was Rule 3 with its stipulation that "applications for membership, coming from the students' students, must include the names and recommendations of their teachers . . . and the First members shall vote on admitting these candidates."

By so ruling, Mrs. Eddy gave to the First Members, all chosen by herself, the function of screening all applicants for membership. Before many months, 349 applicants were awaiting membership; in little more than a year, there were 1,502.

In organizing her Church, Mary Baker Eddy sought only those ways that, to her, were based on Spiritual law. In Spiritual law she saw the true way—the way of the great Teacher, the only way in which her Church would prosper. In these teachings was found the Science of the higher Force that destroys evil, substitutes continuing right for whatever is wrong, and prophesies the future.

But work remained that only she could do—a post had to be held that only she could guard. Nothing could release her from a jot of her responsibility nor lift one ounce of her burden from her shoulders.

Although she had written in the *Journal* (March, 1892), "if our Church is organized, it is to meet the demand, 'suffer it to be so now,' " she *knew* in September of the same year that a permanent organization would be needed.

This she disclosed following publication of the *Church Manual* in 1895, when she wrote:

> Heaps upon heaps of praise confront me, and for what? That which I said in my heart would never be needed,—namely, laws of limitation for a Christian Scientist. Thy ways are not as ours. Thou knowest best what we need most,—hence my disappointed hope and grateful joy.... Of this I am sure, that each Rule and By-law in this Manual will increase the spirituality of him who obeys it, invigorate his capacity to heal the sick, to comfort such as mourn, and to awaken the sinner.[4]

By so writing, she again evidenced her readiness to accept the guidance of prayer over *"that which I said in my heart would never be needed,—namely, laws of limitation for a Christian Scientist."* Nor did she exclude herself from

4 *Miscellany,* pp. 229–30.

the Rules and By-laws of the *Church Manual*. In April, 1922, in the *Journal*, Adam H. Dickey, who served as her secretary in 1908, recalled knowing "no one who ever expressed such a high regard for the Manual . . . nor do we know anyone who has obeyed it more willingly or more implicitly than did Mrs. Eddy. She has been known to correct some simple thing she herself was doing on finding that it was not in accord with the Manual of The Mother Church."

As devotion to God was the essential part of her character, so was part of that devotion expressed in a determination to protect the teachings. The more she listened in prayer, the more she realized her own "present feeble sense of Christian Science"; [5] and as she said in *Retrospection and Introspection* (p. 84), "Centuries will intervene before the statement of the inexhaustible topics of *Science and Health* is sufficiently understood to be fully demonstrated."

Yet she knew there would be a few who would think of themselves as being beyond the need of the discipline that is inherent in organization. Since the first years of her teaching she had encountered such disputants. They caused her anguish but did not cause her to deviate from her course. To her, as Judge Clifford P. Smith recalled after talking with her in 1909, "organization is necessary for a religion or church which intends to attain much size."

As Judge Smith also wrote, "She said she had always, from the time of the first organization of the Christian Scientist Association, felt this to be true. She said she now saw that it was essential, and without it the Christian Science movement would be left unprotected.

"She continued by saying that the organization should fit the occasion; that is, the Christian Science movement needed an organization corresponding to its character and

[5] *Science and Health,* p. 577.

purpose. She spoke of the Christian Scientists who go about saying we need no organization as 'not knowing what they are talking about.' She also said, in substance, 'Organization is a simple matter, for all of its importance. It is simply a matter of doing things by working together.'

"In closing, she spoke of its being desirable that I be well informed on this subject, and to use what she had given me in writing. In later years, when the entire organization of The Mother Church was threatened, I appreciated the value of what Mrs. Eddy had said to me and . . . had advised me to be well informed on the subject." [6]

In 1919, the trustees of The Christian Science Publishing Society disputed the authority of The Christian Science Board of Directors (as contained in the *Church Manual*), took their case to the Supreme Judicial Court of Massachusetts, and lost.

Organization was a subject often in Mrs. Eddy's thought; in her writings there is much instruction. All were published prior to the day of Judge Smith's interview in 1909. She knew that spiritual gifts are not subject to organization but human dispositions are. Unhappily, despite Mrs. Eddy's wishes, there still remain a few who consider themselves so advanced in Christian Science as to have no need for its protective discipline.

The building of the edifice at Falmouth and Caledonia streets was, as Joseph Armstrong [7] wrote in his small book, *The Mother Church,* "so great a demonstration of Christianity and Christian Science as to leave on the world's thought an indelible mark, which must be given a place in history."

[6] *Permanency of The Mother Church and Its Manual.* Revised Edition. Copyright, 1954, The Christian Science Publishing Society.
[7] In 1893, Armstrong became a member of The Christian Science Board of Directors. He succeeded Joseph S. Eastaman.

In September, 1893, the situation was as follows:

The building plans the Directors had accepted called for an expenditure of about $200,000. On hand was about $40,000. Contributions had almost ceased. Under the terms of the deed, there could be no borrowing nor could any promise of payment be made beyond the funds in hand.

Having chosen plans that called for the use of New Hampshire stone in the edifice, the Directors turned their attention to building costs and learned that under a new code costs had gone up nearly one-third in Boston. Not only that, but under the new code, plans for all new buildings had to be approved by the city engineers; also, no building permit could be issued until the builder had accepted drawings for a completed structure.

In this dilemma, the Directors went to Concord to see Mrs. Eddy. Instead of being discouraged by the information, she urged them to move ahead and quickly, assuring them that when money was needed it would be forthcoming.

Returning to Boston, the Directors learned that the architect was dissatisfied and wanted a substantial down payment instead of a fee, with one half payable when construction contracts were signed and the balance when the edifice was completed. After some discussion, the Directors bought the plans and retained the architect as a consultant.

The building code required full specifications of construction. The Directors could not supply them. After examining partially completed architectural drawings and listening to the explanation of the Directors, the City Engineer waived the requirement and issued the building permit.

In October the Directors let contracts for excavation, pile driving, and stone foundations. The work was completed and paid for before the coming of heavy winter weather. The excavation was boarded over pending the resumption of work in the spring. Meanwhile, the Directors were in receipt of a letter from Mrs. Eddy in which she suggested that the church be completed before the end of 1894 instead of by September 1, 1897, as permitted by the terms of the deed of trust.

Calling in the builders, the Directors asked for estimates on the cost of walls, including brick and stone exteriors. Although all bills had been paid and subscriptions were coming in, the estimate of fifty-seven thousand dollars was beyond their means. Bank deposits amounted to much less.

While still puzzling over how to build the walls and stay within the terms of the deed, the Directors received another letter from Mrs. Eddy. In this communication she suggested the inclusion in the contract of a provision permitting them to stop work at any level above the Auditorium floor. The proposal was made, accepted by the builders, and the contract for the erection of the walls was signed on December 6, 1893.

Almost at the same time she suggested the foregoing step to the Directors, Mrs. Eddy wrote to a selected number of her students:

                    Pleasant View, Concord, N. H.

My beloved Student:

I have prepared a subscription list for building the Mother Church. The names to be placed thereon I have *carefully selected*. All who sign it agree to pay $1000. It is dated December 25, 1893, for my Christmas gift. It reads the same as the slip enclosed. I give this opportunity to as many as I can readily reach of my faithful students to sign, that I may put their names which are attached to the sums severally paid, with my name, and "Science and Health," and my card of thanks, into a box placed in the Corner Stone of our Church. I shall name this donation as an extra bequest to the Church Building Fund, presented to me for this object, in demonstration of their love for their Teacher, and their devotion to our cause —by my fellow laborers in Christian Science. This box with its sacred contents and associations is to be placed as above named in our monumental Church.

When I receive your name on the slip enclosed I shall send it to the Treasurer, Mr. S. A. Chase, who will paste it on the subscription list. Please send in time, for your name and the amount you give, to be memorized as specified. The Treasurer will receipt to you for $1,000.

Also for important reasons keep this transaction a sound secret till the time comes for its denouement, the laying of the Corner Stone. Please sign your name twice,—one signature is to be pasted on to my subscription list, the other remains on the enclosed slip.

With great love,

Mary Baker Eddy

Please reply at once.

This was not a call for alms. Far from it. It was a call for self-examination. With the exception of only a very few, not many students were able, financially, to do more than sign pledges for future fulfillment. Most students were of limited means; a majority were women. Nevertheless, they could have had no glowing sense of self-approval in returning their signed pledges.

They surely sensed or knew that to complete the building of The Mother Church not only was for the good of all Christian Scientists but also for their own good as individuals. Before the spring of 1894 was much more than half over nearly all the pledges had been redeemed, adding forty-four thousand dollars to the Building Fund and permitting work to proceed following a delay caused by a dispute between the builders and suppliers over the amount of iron needed.

On May 21, 1894, the day selected by Mrs. Eddy, and following a simple ceremony also requested by her, the Corner Stone was set in place. It was a ceremony that consisted of silent prayer followed by the audible rendition of The Lord's Prayer. Sealed within the Stone was a copper box containing these articles, each wrapped in oiled silk: The King James Version of the Bible in the finest morocco binding; in similar binding, a copy of the eighty-fourth edition of *Science and Health With Key to the Scriptures* by Mary Baker G. Eddy; other writings by Mrs. Eddy—*Retrospection and Introspection, Unity of Good, No and Yes, Rudimental Divine Science, People's Idea of God, Christian Healing, Historical Sketch of Christian Science Mind Healing, Defense of Christian Science,* Christian Science Series (five numbers), in manuscript form, and an address written by Mrs. Eddy for the occasion; the June, 1894, issue of *The Christian Science Journal;* Christian Science Quarterly Lessons (April, May, June, 1894) ; three cards containing names of students who contributed a thousand dollars each to the Church Building Fund; a grateful acknowledgment by Mrs. Eddy; and the names of the Board of Directors written by hand by Mrs. Eddy.

In the manuscript sealed within the Corner Stone, and written by her for the occasion, Mary Baker Eddy disclosed a great Purpose unfolding:

> ... without pomp or pride, laid away as a sacred secret in the heart of a rock, there to typify the prophecy, "And a man shall be as an hiding place from the wind, and a covert from the tempest; ... as the shadow of a great rock in a weary land:" henceforth to whisper our Master's promise, "Upon this rock I will build my church; and the gates of hell shall not prevail against it.". . .[8]

The remaining days of May, the summer months, the months of autumn, and the weeks of December were not uneventful.

Iron floor beams were delivered late, and when delivered, were found to be too long. The stone in the walls was chipped away to make them fit. Iron columns for the walls were defective; a month was lost before a supplier could be found whose product was approved by the City Engineer. Not being paid on time by the builder, masons threatened to strike. The strike was averted by passing the hat among Christian Scientists on the premises and advancing the money, but a railroad strike stopped shipments of iron for the roof.

In October the building operations were so far behind schedule that the contractors were saying the church would not be ready for occupancy before May, 1895. At Mrs. Eddy's request, Director Joseph Armstrong began giving full time to the work. On November 1, there was no roof on the building, no windows, no doors; five days later there was a heavy snowfall, followed by very cold weather. Di-

[8] *Miscellaneous Writings,* p. 144.

rectors and church members kept the floors clean by constantly sweeping them and shoveling the snow through the empty window frames, thus permitting the men to continue working, but not for long. Within a day or two, only a couple of men showed up, the foreman reporting that the rest of the men "are not willing to work in this kind of weather." A full crew was found so that by the last week in November the work had progressed to a point that permitted the plasterers to begin.

The plasterers were agreeable, but the contractor said that the structure had to be "clear of all other work for at least six weeks." The contractor and plasterers were persuaded to work with the other trades and were paid extra wages to work Saturday afternoons and Saturday evenings until midnight.

Scarcely was that matter settled when the city closed Caledonia Street to vehicular traffic that it might begin installing sewers. With only Falmouth Street available for unloading, workmen protested the crowded conditions and threatened to quit. After much persuasion they withdrew their threat. In October a contract was signed for the delivery of pews. December came and the order remained unfilled.

The Directors sent a representative to Michigan where the manufacturer's plant was located. The representative was told that, in sending in his order, the salesman had noted the pews would not be needed "before the spring of 1895."

Acknowledging the salesman's miscalculation, the manufacturer put his entire force to work on the order. On December 21 the pews were in Boston. These were but *some* of the obstacles that were overcome.

Just before midnight on Saturday, December 29, everything was in place. The church was ready for services on the following day.[9] There was more than enough money in the bank to pay all bills.

From Concord, on December 19, Mrs. Eddy again wrote the Directors:

> My beloved Students, The day is well nigh won. You will soon rest on your arms. Thank God you have been valiant soldiers—loyal to the heart's core. "Who is so great a God as our God?"
>
> Present no contribution box on Dedication day. When you know the amount requisite and have received it for finishing the church building—close all contributions and give public notice thereof.
>
> Hold your services in the Mother Church Dec. 30, 1894, and dedicate this church Jan. 6th. The Bible and *Science and Health With Key to the Scriptures* shall henceforth be the Pastor of the Mother Church. This will tend to spiritualize thought. Personal preaching has more or less human views grafted into it. Whereas the pure Word contains only the living, health-giving Truth.
>
> With love, mother,
>
> Mary Baker Eddy

A few days later, Mrs. Eddy again wrote the Directors, giving a new order of Sunday services:

> 1. A Hymn.
> 2. Silent prayer, followed by the audible repetition of the Lord's Prayer, and its spiritual in-

[9] On December 18, 1894, Mrs. Eddy requested the holding of "the first services in God's temple, December 30, 1894"—and they were held. The first services were communion services presided over by Septimus J. Hanna who, on this same day, resigned as pastor and began his first term as First Reader of The Mother Church.

terpretation given on page 322 of *Science and Health, With Key to the Scriptures.*

3. Hymn.

4. The announcement by one of the Readers of the Bible Lesson for the day, the subject, golden text, and footsteps thereof; the reading responsively of the lesson text, followed by the reading of the expository notes by the readers, who shall be a man and a woman, one reading the Bible references, and the other the quotations from *Science and Health, With Key to the Scriptures;* this reading to be done alternately.

5. The collection and an anthem, or solo.

6. A Hymn.

7. The benediction.

From the above it will be seen that the quotations from the Bible and textbook are not to be written, but read directly from the books.

This change in the services has reference only to the Mother Church, and is not to be adopted by branch churches until further notice.

The day of dedication was mild, and snow was falling as the first of five services [10] began at nine o'clock on the morning of January 6, 1895. At four-thirty o'clock in the afternoon the final service was ended. An estimated five thousand persons were in attendance at the five services. The church seated a few more than nine hundred persons at each service. Of the estimated five thousand in attendance, about three thousand were from places other than Boston.

[10] For full account of services see pp. 591–610, *The Cross and The Crown.* Published 1952, Duell, Sloan and Pearce, New York.

CHAPTER TWELVE

The Shield That Protects
Her Teachings

FROM the moment of her realization that if she was to be heard she would have to have a church of her own, it was Mary Baker Eddy's hope that the teachings themselves would preclude the need for rules and bylaws of church government. Reluctantly, she came to see that this hope called for a spiritual quality that was beyond the reach of mortals.

In 1879, when she formed her church, Mrs. Eddy wrote out the rules of membership and continued to write them, by hand, until in the early summer of 1895 it became clear that this method was no longer practicable. There were Christian Science churches, several hundred of them, in the Middle West, the West, the South, the East, New England, in Canada, and in Europe.

In 1895, Mrs. Eddy published the first edition of the small book without which there could be no Christian Science churches and no Christian Science movement. The small book is called the *Church Manual of The First Church of Christ, Scientist, in Boston, Mass.* In its first edition it contained thirty-eight pages; in its permanent form, it contains eighty-one pages of By-laws with an Appendix of thirty additional pages.

Years of prayer went into the writing of these Rules and

By-Laws. Beginning with handwritten directions, they took the form of a printed four-page folder in 1892 and became a *Church Manual* in 1895. Final changes were made by Mrs. Eddy in 1908.

Thus what once were a few rules written on a sheet of paper and seen only by a few persons became the shield for a Movement that proclaims how much alive faith is that a woman's understanding of God should become the marching song of multitudes.

When the problem of writing the *Church Manual* presented itself, Mrs. Eddy did what she always did when faced by a decision affecting her teachings. Deep-rooted in the eternal verities, she sought the sanctuary of prayer—and listened. The great witnesses in the Kingdom of Spirit have always done that, have always listened.

In the Book of Joshua (1–7) is instruction: "Only be thou strong and very courageous (30–21) that thou mayest observe to do according to all the law, which Moses my servant commanded thee: turn not from it to the right hand or to the left, that thou mayest prosper whithersoever thou goest."

In the Book of Isaiah (30–21) again is instruction: "And thine ears shall hear a word behind thee, saying, This is the way, walk ye in it, when ye turn to the right hand, and when ye turn to the left."

And as it was with the *Church Manual,* so was it with *Science and Health.* Each book discloses the spiritual distance this woman traveled in these years of grace. The unfoldment of each book was the same—in the beginning, a few sheets of paper on which were written her thoughts and, finally, the printed word in its incommutable form.

Sixteen years separated the first and permanent editions of the *Church Manual;* thirty-five years separated the first and permanent editions of *Science and Health.* Each book has its purpose. One is the textbook; one is the shield. In serving the Cause of Christian Science they are inseparable.

In the evolution of the *Church Manual,* as in the evolution of *Science and Health,* the changes made were not changes in the basic teachings. Rather, they were paragraphs of clarification with, as Mrs. Eddy said, "detail so requisite to demonstrate genuine Christian Science, and which will do for the race what absolute doctrines destined for future generations might not accomplish." Hence, all the changes were important.

The first edition of the *Church Manual* contains both Church Rules and By-laws. There are nine Rules and fourteen By-laws. In its permanent form, the *Manual* contains only By-laws, of which there are thirty-five.

In the back of the first edition, as in the permanent *Church Manual,* is printed a copy of the Deed of Trust [1] by which Mrs. Eddy conveyed the land for the edifice of The Mother Church to The Christian Science Board of Directors. Also, there are other paragraphs, written by Mrs. Eddy, which are not contained in the permanent book.

Within these paragraphs is a By-law of instruction to the Directors, First Members, the Finance Committee of the Church, and the Treasurer, covering the making of an annual report of "the amount of Church Funds on hand, the amount of its indebtedness, and of its expenditures for the last year."

Between brown, hard covers, the 1895 *Church Manual* was a book seven and one-half inches long by five inches wide. It contained thirty-eight pages, was copyrighted by The Christian Science Board of Directors.

In the first edition, and in several editions thereafter, responsibility for the government of The Mother Church was divided between The Christian Science Board of Di-

[1] For the full text of the Deed of Trust see the *Church Manual.*

rectors and the First Members,[2] with the latter being the principal governing body.

The Directors were: Ira O. Knapp, Joseph Armstrong, Stephen A. Chase, and William B. Johnson. All were First Members, so as Directors and as First Members they participated in all decisions affecting the government of The Mother Church. All decisions were subject to Mrs. Eddy's approval.

Some Rules and By-laws needed only a few words of change, but these were very vital words. For instance, in Article II, Section 1, of the By-laws of the 1895 *Church Manual,* Mrs. Eddy wrote:

> I, Mary Baker Eddy, ordain the *Bible,* and *Science and Health With Key to the Scriptures,* Pastor over the Mother Church,—The First Church of Christ, Scientist, in Boston, Mass.,—so long as the Church is satisfied with this Pastor.

The permanent By-law reads:

Article XIV

THE CHRISTIAN SCIENCE PASTOR

Ordination. SECTION 1. I, Mary Baker Eddy, ordain the BIBLE, and SCIENCE AND HEALTH WITH KEY TO THE SCRIPTURES, Pastor over The Mother Church,—The First Church of Christ, Scientist, in Boston, Mass.,—and they will continue to preach for this Church and the world.

---

[2] In 1901, at Mrs. Eddy's request, the First Members adopted this By-law: "The business of The Mother Church hitherto transacted by the First Members shall be done by its Christian Science Board of Directors." From 1903 until 1908 the First Members were called Executive Members. As such, they had no church function except to serve as Readers or as President. In 1908 the title of First Member was abolished.

Unmentioned in the first edition, the *Church Manual* itself receives specific attention in the permanent edition. The closing By-law (Article XXXV) states:

> For The Mother Church Only. Section 1. The Church Manual of The First Church of Christ, Scientist, in Boston, Mass., written by Mary Baker Eddy and copyrighted, is adapted to The Mother Church only. It stands alone, uniquely adapted to form the budding thought and hedge it about with divine Love. This Manual shall not be revised without the written consent of its author.
>
> Seventy-third Edition the Authority. Sect. 2. The Board of Directors, the Committee on Bible Lessons, and the Board of Trustees shall each keep a copy of the Seventy-third Edition and of subsequent editions of the Church Manual; and if a discrepancy appears in any revised edition, these editions shall be cited as authority.
>
> Amendment of By-Laws. Sect. 3. No new Tenet or By-Law shall be adopted, nor any Tenet or By-Law amended or annulled, without the written consent of Mary Baker Eddy, the author of our textbook, *Science and Health*.[3]

There were many who doubted when the first *Manual* was issued, and who continued to doubt, that it was possible to write a permanent set of rules that would serve the church through all history. On February 27, 1903, Mrs. Eddy took note of the uncertainty and wrote to The Christian Science Board of Directors:

[3] Published in 1908.

Beloved Students: I am not a lawyer, and do not sufficiently comprehend the legal trend of the copy you enclosed to me to suggest any changes therein. Upon one point however I feel competent to advise namely: Never abandon the By-laws nor the denominational government of the Mother Church. If I am not personally with you, the Word of God, and my instructions in the By-laws have led you hitherto and will remain to guide you safely on, and the teachings of St. Paul are as useful to-day as when they were first written.

The present and future prosperity of the cause of Christian Science is largely due to the By-laws and government of "The First Church of Christ, Scientist" in Boston. None but myself can know, as I know, the importance of the combined sentiment of this Church remaining steadfast in supporting its present By-laws. Each of these many By-laws has met and mastered, or forestalled some contingency, some imminent peril, and will continue to do so. Its By-laws have preserved the sweet unity of this large church, that has perhaps the most members and combined influence of any other church in our country. Many times a single By-law has cost me long nights of prayer and struggle, but it has won the victory over some sin and saved the walls of Zion from being torn down by disloyal students. We have proven that "in unity there is strength."

With love as ever
Mary Baker G. Eddy

N.B. I request that you put this letter upon our Church records M. B. E.

When she made the final changes in the *Church Manual,* Mary Baker Eddy gave her followers a form of government that is unique in church history. She accepted what came to her in prayer as divine instruction and never doubted that when put to the test the *Manual* would "be acknowledged as law by law," as she said to Clara Shannon, a member of her household. Yet, in her household, there were those who were troubled, and the thing which troubled the most concerned the Church when Mrs. Eddy was no longer present in person to watch over it.

One day at Chestnut Hill, William R. Rathvon, who afterwards became a member of The Christian Science Board of Directors, brought up the subject while talking with Henry M. Baker, who was Mrs. Eddy's cousin and who also was a lawyer of note in New Hampshire. "General Baker," inquired Rathvon, "for some time I have been quite concerned about how certain parts of our *Manual* would function if Mrs. Eddy could not supply her assent or signature as it requires. I thought best to ask you as a lawyer and one in whom Mrs. Eddy has every confidence.

" '... You need not be at all uneasy,' were his reassuring words. 'It is a matter of common law in a case of this kind, where it is physically impossible to carry out specified conditions by the one named, that the next in authority assume that jurisdiction. And in this case the next in authority is the Board of Directors of The Mother Church. Any competent court in the land will uphold the *Manual* just as Mrs. Eddy intends it to function whether her signature is forthcoming, or not.' " [4]

Judge Septimus J. Hanna and Archibald McLellan, who had joined Rathvon in questioning the lawyer, were persuaded; and so was Rathvon. But there remained uncer-

---

[4] *Permanency of The Mother Church and Its Manual.* The Christian Science Publishing Society. Copyright 1954.

tainty. In the *Manual* (Article XXV, Section 1) is this
By-law:

> The Board of Trustees, constituted by a Deed
> of Trust given by Rev. Mary Baker Eddy, the Pas-
> tor Emeritus of this Church, on January twenty-
> fifth, 1898, shall hold and manage the property
> therein conveyed, and conduct the business of
> "The Christian Science Publishing Society" on
> a strictly Christian basis, for the promotion of the
> interests of Christian Science.

It began to be argued that under this By-law the Board
of Trustees had final authority, in Mrs. Eddy's absence,
over all publishing activities. After a number of years of
uncertainty the Board of Trustees brought suit, claiming
that The Christian Science Board of Directors did not have
authority in all matters affecting The Mother Church.

On November 23, 1921, The Massachusetts Supreme
Judicial Court dismissed the suit, saying:

"The last several editions issued during the life of Mrs.
Eddy contained provision that 'This Manual shall not be
revised without the written consent of its author.' Since
the Church Manual on its face purports to be the work
of Mrs. Eddy as author . . . it is apparent that there can
now, since the decease of Mrs. Eddy, be no change in the
provisions of the Church Manual in accordance with its
terms."

Article VIII, Sect. 28, of the Church By-laws reads:

> NUMBERING THE PEOPLE: Christian Sci-
> entists shall not report for publication the number
> of the members of The Mother Church, nor that of
> the branch churches. According to the Scripture

they shall turn away from personality and numbering the people.[5]

Mrs. Eddy agreed with the Unitarian Emerson who said,
"Whenever the appeal is made—no matter how indirectly
—to numbers proclamation is then and there made that religion is not. He that finds God a sweet enveloping thought
. . . never counts his company."

Mary Baker Eddy never counted her company. She knew
that whatever the religion, when its membership is publicly
proclaimed, it is a faith that has substituted human preoccupation with the authority of numbers for reliance on
the authority of God. As such, it has its parallel with Jesus'
parable of the prodigal son, on whom Mrs. Eddy wrote,
"Like him, we would find our Father's house again—the
perfect and eternal Principle of man." [6]

While Mrs. Eddy still was here in person others were
fretting over the absence of legal phraseology in the *Manual*, seeming to fear that this lack weakened the position
of the Church in the event of litigation. They seemed not
to understand that writing the *Church Manual* was not an
assignment for a lawyer, no matter how skillful. It was an
assignment only Mary Baker Eddy could undertake and
complete. Not the Mrs. Eddy the public saw on her daily
carriage rides but the Mary Baker Eddy who could be
found only in her writings.

It was only this Mary Baker Eddy who could devise By-
laws to meet the requirements of the Church that was
envisioned.

[5] Among the several admonitions in the Bible against numbering the
people is this instruction in Chapter One of the Book of Numbers: "For
the Lord had spoken unto Moses, saying, only thou shalt not number the
tribe of Levi, neither take the sum of them among the children of Israel
. . . and the Levites shall keep charge of the tabernacle of testimony."

[6] *Miscellaneous Writings*, p. 369.

One illustration of the acceptance by Christian Scientists of Mrs. Eddy's statement: "Those who look for me in person, or elsewhere than in my writings, lose me instead of find me" (*Miscellany*, p. 120), is the attitude of The Christian Science Board of Directors toward Article 1, Sect. 5, of the *Church Manual*. It reads:

> The Christian Science Board of Directors shall consist of five members. They shall fill a vacancy occurring on that Board after the candidate is approved by the Pastor Emeritus. A majority vote or the request of Mrs. Eddy shall dismiss a member. Members shall neither report the discussions of this Board, nor those with Mrs. Eddy.

As Christian Scientists, the members of this Board can have only one understanding of that instruction. Involved is a sense of obedience. It is a sense that is spiritual. As such, it is inviolable. The Christian Science Board of Directors are Mary Baker Eddy's representatives, in perpetuity.

As the shield that protects the writings of Mary Baker Eddy from the hands of the revisionists, the *Church Manual* also protects the *foundational trusts* of the Christian Science Movement. On November 14, 1904, Mrs. Eddy wrote to the superintendent and teachers of The Mother Church Sunday School, saying, in part: "It is a joy to know that they who are faithful over foundational trusts, such as the Christian education of the dear children, will reap the reward of rightness, rise in the scale of being, and realize at last their Master's promise, 'And they shall be all taught of God.' " [7]

The *foundational trusts*, so to speak, that carry on the

[7] *Miscellany*, p. 230.

mission of the Founder of Christian Science are seven; and the seven may be identified thus:

1. The Mother Church, with its Christian Science Board of Directors. (They represent the Cause, and the government of The Mother Church as prescribed in the *Church Manual*.)
2. The branch churches. (They represent the preaching ministry of the Movement.)
3. The Christian Science Publishing Society. (This is the publishing and distribution aspect of the Movement.)
4. The Christian Science Board of Education and the teachers. (They represent the teaching and instructive aspects of the Movement.)
5. The Christian Science practitioners. (This is the healing aspect of the Movement.)
6. The Christian Science Board of Lectureship. (This is the missionary aspect of the Movement.)
7. The Committee on Publication. (This is the corrective and protective aspect of the Movement.)

Article I, Section 6, of the *Church Manual* reads: "The business of The Mother Church shall be transacted by its Christian Science Board of Directors." Inasmuch as the interests of The Mother Church are world-wide, the Directors have many things to do. They meet three times a week, usually from 9:30 to 12:30 A.M., and reconvene for two hours in the afternoon. Always there are special or urgent items on the agenda of each day, at times as many as twenty or thirty.

It is necessary for the Directors to keep in close touch with the executive and administrative heads of the many activities and departments of the church. Requiring constant attention are questions from more than thirty-five hundred churches, societies, and college organizations, problems that arise in the work of thousands of practitioners, as well as the problems of unnumbered thousands of church workers and laymen.

There is the responsibility for watching over the different publications to make sure they are properly edited, the responsibility for the maintenance of church property, as well as the responsibility for the supervision of all other activities.

Each week, the Trustees of The Christian Science Publishing Society meet with the Directors; also, there are weekly meetings with the Editors of *The Christian Science Monitor,* the *Journal,* the *Sentinel,* and the *Herald.* There are specified times when the affairs of The Christian Science Benevolent Associations are before the Board; times when the Finance Committee of The Mother Church, the Manager of the Committees on Publication, the business manager of The Christian Science Publishing Society, the Board of Lectureship, the Treasurer of The Mother Church, the Clerk of The Mother Church, as well as others who are engaged in the affairs of the church, meet separately with the Board.

There are periodical meetings of the Trustees under the Will, also meetings with the Trustees who come under Clause VI of the Will of Mary Baker Eddy. In addition, there are visits with members of The Mother Church who come to Boston from the far places of the earth; there is the always waiting correspondence.

In the years of her ministry, Mary Baker Eddy wrote almost all her letters by hand. How many in the aggregate no one really knows. More than fourteen thousand are in the Archives of The Mother Church, and they are being added to constantly.

No communication or letter written by Mrs. Eddy that has come into the possession of the Board has ever been destroyed. All are carefully bound, indexed, and kept in a secure place that they may be preserved and be readily available for incumbent Directors, and their successors in office, when faced by any problem touching or affecting the Cause.

Each Board meeting is opened by silent prayer followed by the audible rendition of the Daily Prayer, which is the daily duty of all members of The Mother Church: " 'Thy kingdom come'; let the reign of divine Truth, Life, and Love be established in me, and rule out of me all sin; and may Thy Word enrich the affections of all mankind, and govern them!"

One of the distressing duties of the Directors is the task of disciplining a member of The Mother Church. Mrs. Eddy found it no less distressing. While realizing "A slight divergence is fatal in Science," [8] she chose to reason with an offender, but when reason and patience failed she did not hesitate to act. The Directors do likewise.

While she was here in person, Mrs. Eddy placed upon the Directors full responsibility for the maintenance and continuance of her teachings in all their purity. Again she notified her followers on October 12, 1909:

> My province as a Leader—as the Discoverer and Founder of Christian Science—is not to interfere in cases of discipline, and I hereby publicly declare that I am not personally involved in the affairs of the church in any other way than through my written and published rules, all of which can be read by the individual who desires to inform himself of the facts.[9]

[8] *Rudimental Divine Science,* p. 17.
[9] *Miscellany,* p. 359.

As meaningful life with God is the destination in Christian Science, so, in physical science, "the supreme task of the physicist," as Albert Einstein once said, "is to arrive at those universal elementary laws from which the cosmos can be built up by pure deduction."

To emphasize the need for always making sure of arriving at the right destination in physical research, Charles Francis Kettering, when director of General Motors Research Laboratories, often used this illustration:

"Two men boarded an early evening train in Detroit. The destination of one man was Boston, the destination of the other man was New York. They had dinner together and spent the evening together talking in the club car. At eleven o'clock each went to his own coach, in separate parts of the train.

"The following morning one man was in Boston. The other man was in New York because, before boarding the train, each man had examined his railroad ticket. During the night, the train arrived in Albany where the coaches containing Boston passengers were disconnected from the New York coaches, shunted off the main track, and attached to a train leaving for Boston—all because a piece of steel, very thin at its thinnest point, was placed between the wheels of the Boston coaches and the rails."

So it is in Christian Science—"a slight divergence," as Mrs. Eddy said, "is fatal." Looking upon and speaking of her teachings as "divinely authorized," believing that the law of God is changeless and that it cannot be subtracted from nor be added to, she placed upon The Christian Science Board of Directors the entire responsibility of protecting her teachings from deviators, from tamperers, and from misinterpretation.

Were they to fail in that duty the Church of Christ,

Scientist, as Mary Baker Eddy established it, would no longer exist. This she knew.

That is why she accepted the post of Pastor Emeritus (in perpetuity) of The Mother Church, The First Church of Christ, Scientist, in Boston, Massachusetts. This is why she made The Christian Science Board of Directors accountable (also in perpetuity) to the Creator, as found in her writings. That was why she placed the teachings and the law of her church, as contained in the *Church Manual,* beyond the reach of personal interpretation.

Mary Baker Eddy knew there always are those (and always will be, so long as the world exists) who lie in wait seeking the opportunity to corrupt the careless and confuse the thoughtful. This she had no intention of permitting to happen.

To prevent it, she wrote the *Church Manual* and, in it, placed great responsibility upon the Directors, charged them with strict adherence to her teachings, but counseled firmness and patience—both!—in dealing with malcontents, even as she was strict, was firm, and was patient.

There was One who, when speaking of the wise man who built his house upon a rock, said "and the rains descended, and the floods came, and the wind blew, and beat upon that house; and it fell not; for it was founded upon a rock." In saying these things was not Jesus speaking of truth as the rock that gives footing in the swirling tide that is materialism?

Recognizing the origin of evil, Mary Baker Eddy saw that evil could gain a footing only in surroundings that were materialistic and could survive only in a world of materialism. Years before the words "atom" and "atomic force" became ordinary words in everyday conversation she was using them and pointing out that the powers of God are found only in the spiritual universe—and not in a force that drives missiles that take men into space or, rising from beneath the sea, search out cities and civilizations for destruction.

Blessed with an inner ear that caught the moral tone of the universe, she knew that disorderliness in the world is in exact proportion with the prevalence of materialistic beliefs, and she perceived that destructive ideas that are loosed in one part of the world lie in wait for all parts of the world.

In *Science and Health* (p. 28) Mrs. Eddy wrote: "If the Master had not taken a student and taught the unseen verities of God, he would not have been crucified. . . . Neither the origin, the character, nor the work of Jesus was generally understood. Not a single component part of his nature did the material world measure aright." Could not the same thing be said of her?

Of course Mrs. Eddy was not put to death, but she was denounced with a savagery seldom encountered. Surely, had she been content to keep her discovery to herself or to confine it to supper-table conversation in boardinghouses where she lived in Lynn, she would not have been spat upon in the streets nor been the center of venomous attacks from pulpit and press.

Believing that to do the work of God on earth is man's noblest privilege, she accepted her discovery as His work and looked upon it as her duty to share, to protect, and to treasure. It was because she believed so deeply in the teachings in *Science and Health* that she took such great pains to place these teachings beyond the hands of the revisionists. The many revisions in the teachings of the Master justified her concern over the preservation of her own. The inevitable result was loss in spiritual meaning.

In *Science and Health* (p. 139) , Mrs. Eddy wrote:

"The decisions by vote of Church Councils as to what should and should not be considered Holy Writ; the manifest mistakes in the ancient versions; the thirty thousand different readings in the Old Testament, and the three hundred thousand in the New,—these facts show how a mortal and material sense stole into the divine record, with its own hue darkening to some extent the inspired pages."

In 1903, she counseled the General Association of Teachers: "Adhere to the teachings of the Bible, Science and Health, and our Manual, and you will obey the law and gospel." [10] She asked no more of her followers than she required of herself.

Perceiving man as something higher than the dust, Mrs. Eddy's most cherished hope was to free the hearts and minds of men from the captivity of matter. She identified materialism as the source of evil and saw that only in materialistic surroundings could men be imprisoned in the chains of a sensualistic theory of life. Offering no compromise with matter and making no genuflections to custom, she stood her ground in proclaiming the Source from which flows the intelligence that steadily beats back the frontiers of evil.

She was familiar with the reply to the rich man who asked: "Good Master, what shall I do that I may inherit eternal life?" and Jesus replied: "Why callest thou me good? there is none good but one, that is God."

In Mrs. Eddy's teachings that which is good is of God, therefore is eternal; and that which is evil is material, therefore is temporal. Depicting as it does the qualities of Spirit, good is the value by which all else is tested. Good

[10] *Miscellany,* pp. 251–52.

is never lost, never vanquished; and, rising above the moment of seeming defeat, it becomes a stronger good—even as Jesus demonstrated in his three days of glorious achievement in the sepulchre.

These were teachings she was protecting in a *Church Manual* the coming of which the world could not avoid and the significance of which the world could not ignore. In placing upon The Christian Science Board of Directors sole responsibility in perpetuity for the preservation of her teachings and the management of her church, Mrs. Eddy informed the world that the new religion that had its present beginnings in 1866, which she named Christian Science, would be available, unchanged, so long as a copy of the *Bible* and a copy of *Science and Health* remain in the world.

Of the many wise decisions this inspired woman made, this was one of the wisest. It made certain that the element of healing which was an integral part of the teachings of Jesus would not be lost again. Deep within her were two assurances. One was the assurance that Christian Science was in complete harmony with the Christianity Jesus taught; the other was the assurance that the time would come when all Christians would find acceptable the instruction Jesus gave to the woman of Samaria at the well of Jacob: "But the hour cometh, and now is, when the true worshippers shall worship the Father in spirit and in truth: for the Father seeketh such to worship him. God is a Spirit: and they that worship him must worship him in spirit and in truth."

The time will come, she was sure, when, in his search for God, man will turn his eyes away from pageantry and ritual, will shut his ears to the voices of dogma, and begin to find within himself the Truth that awaits him.

At that time he will return to the simple teachings, knowing that a fisherman's boat is a sufficient pulpit and a hillside a sufficient altar "when two or three are gathered together in my name." He will know the way into the vast resources of Spirit is always open; know that advancement into the spiritual is the only true progress; know that in understanding of the spiritual is found the mastery of the physical.

At that time instead of many Christian denominations there will be but one.

CHAPTER THIRTEEN

Indifference to Earthly Claims

I N establishing a new order of services, Mary Baker Eddy
was introducing an inclusive ideal that would immunize
her church from personal opinions that seek to accomplish
what can only be achieved by spiritual perception.

Two readers reading Lesson-Sermons consisting solely
of Bible references and explanatory quotations from *Science and Health with Key to the Scriptures,* silent prayer,
the audible repetition by the congregation of the Lord's
Prayer and its spiritual interpretation as given in the Christian Science textbook, a solo, a benediction—this was the
service she designed to be the light by which all might see.

Twenty-seven in all, including Thanksgiving Day services, the Lesson-Sermons did not come to full flower all at
once. Seeking to "cover the essentials of Christianity," Mrs.
Eddy chose the subjects, used them (in their present Order) in her class teachings, and learned, as Bible Lesson
Committees of The Mother Church have since learned, that
she was able to treat each subject "an indefinite number of
times and each time [have practically] a new sermon." In
preparing her Lesson-Sermons her thoughts never moved
away from the words of Paul to his church in Galatia:

Do I seek to please men? for if I yet pleased men,
I should not be the servant of Christ. But I certify

you, brethren, that the gospel which was preached of me is not after man. For I neither received it of man, neither was I taught it, but by the revelation of Jesus Christ.

Reflecting Mrs. Eddy's instructions, a member of the Committee spoke of this same objectivity in the preparation of the Lesson-Sermons: "Christian Science sermons seek not to please men: for a preacher who seeks to please men is not the servant of Christ. The gospel preached from our pulpits is not after man, neither was it taught of man, but by the revelation of Jesus Christ." [1]

It was Mrs. Eddy's conviction, as the Committee member wrote: "There is no more effective way of teaching the Word than by means of these sermons. They bring in review the spiritual import of Scripture in its entirety. Its content from Genesis to Revelation, is expounded ... No attentive, sincere student, or earnest listener, whether Scientist or non-Scientist, can hear or read the alternate passages from the Bible and 'Science and Health with Key to the Scriptures,' without seeing the unity of the two."

However much the world may disagree, few persons have so influenced its thought since medieval times as Mary Baker Eddy.

Once denouncing her teachings, the Christian clergy is now accepting them in steadily increasing measure. The medical profession, which once uniformly ridiculed her healings, is more and more recognizing the soundness of their spiritual basis; no longer are legislatures openly hostile to her words—and the public practice of Christian Science is now legal in all fifty states of our Union and in many of the other free nations; in the armed forces, Christian Sci-

[1] *The Christian Science Sentinel*, March 20, 1902. Copyright by The Christian Science Publishing Society, Boston, Massachusetts.

ence chaplains serve side by side with those of other denominations; in actual circulation in more than one hundred nations are copies of *The Christian Science Monitor.*

Although her teachings still are not fairly dealt with, the time will come when they will be better understood, both within and without the Movement. Unfairness will disappear. Of ruling importance in bringing about this acceptance of her teachings was Mrs. Eddy's decision to do away with all personal preaching in her church. The decision was not quickly made.

Early, even while she was her church's only preacher and crowds were overflowing halls where she spoke, Mrs. Eddy was searching for words not her own. As in preaching, so was it in healing, as John C. Lathrop remembered her counsel:

> Now measure yourself and your growth by your works, not by your words. All I have ever accomplished has been done by getting Mary out of the way, and letting God be reflected. When I would reach this tone, the sick would be healed without a word.[2]

Seeking to do away with personal opinions in Christian Science services, Mrs. Eddy, in August, 1891, suggested the inclusion of Bible passages with their spiritual interpretation as written in *Science and Health* in Sunday services in her church in Boston. These readings were to precede the regular sermon. Before long she began to receive requests from churches in other communities that they be permitted to follow Boston's lead; and some went farther, their pastors requesting permission to use *Science and Health* as the source of Sunday sermons.

[2] *We Knew Mary Baker Eddy.* Copyright, 1943, The Christian Science Publishing Society.

In granting the privilege, Mrs. Eddy made one condition. Because the contents of the textbook were copyrighted, students were required to submit copies of all such sermons. Errors she patiently corrected. Instead of growing less frequent, the errors began to multiply until the contents of proposed sermons had little resemblance to what was written in *Science and Health*. Mrs. Eddy promptly withdrew the privilege.

There were many reasons for her action. All her reasons were compelling. One was paramount.

As she wrote in *Science and Health* (p. 342), "If Christianity is not scientific, and Science is not of God, then there is no invariable law, and truth becomes an accident"; and on page 207 of the textbook she cautioned, "Error of statement leads to error in action."

Having found—often after weeks or months and, in some instances, after years of prayer—the precise words that conveyed the spiritual meaning of passages from the Bible, she perceived in the careless paraphrasing by students the destruction of her teachings and, again, the loss of healing from Christianity.

Withdrawing from all work, she devoted herself to prayer. As a result, the Bible and *Science and Health with Key to the Scriptures* became the only preachers in The Mother Church and in all its branches. The Lesson-Sermons replaced personal preaching.

Certain it is that, having perceived the need for having "the Bible and the Christian Science textbook as our only preachers,"[3] Mrs. Eddy prayerfully studied the manner in which the Lesson-Sermons were to be presented—their purpose, their construction, and their spirit.

By so doing, she was opening the Scriptures and her understanding of them in their spiritual meaning, as inter-

3 *Christian Science Quarterly.*

preted in her textbook. The placing of them before Christian Scientist and non-Christian Scientist alike was not a single step but one of a series. First were her own "feeble attempts to state the Principle and practice of Christian healing." [4] As her understanding grew, there came with it the first edition of *Science and Health.* It was one product; but it also was a step.

In teaching in her home and in the Massachusetts Metaphysical College, she was opening the Scriptures to those who sought instruction even though after receiving they departed, each to his own notion.

Mrs. Eddy's was an advance along a line of steppingstones, each leading to the next, each with its problems— but each being a steady climb toward the Light, so that, in 1893, she was able to rebuke an impatient student: "You don't know, my dear, what patience is. I prayed for years for the revelation of a pastor for our Christian Science Church, one not influenced by the wiles of the devil." In the Bible and in her textbook she found this pastor.[5]

In their own study of the manner in which the Lesson-Sermons are to be presented, the members of the Bible Lesson Committee must keep these teachings before them:

> The Christian Science ground is that salvation that includes good health as well as good morals; that there must be a saving from sickness as well as sin; that there must be a redemption from all disease and discord, not through the portals of the grave, but through the 'triumphal arch of immortality.' (*Science and Health*)—that is, through Life.

[4] *Science and Health,* Preface p. ix.
[5] In 1895, the Bible and *Science and Health With Key to the Scriptures* became the only preacher in *all* Christian Science Churches.

Any sermons that fail thus to teach fall short of the sermonizing taught and practised by Jesus. On this ground, Christian Scientists sincerely invite comparison of their sermons and the results thereof with those of other systems. The Truth contained in the Christian Science sermons, *fully assimilated,* will destroy alike sin, sickness, and death.

These sermons further illustrate that the Christian Science text-book is truly textual. It is not a book which can be read as a story-book or continuous tale. Each paragraph, often each sentence, is a study in itself, for it states an infinite truth, an eternal fact, that has in it the very essence of Life.

With God being the introductory subject in her class teachings, it was natural that God would be first among the subjects of the Lesson-Sermons. Since the introduction of the Scriptures and the textbook as the only preachers in all Christian Science services, God has been the subject of scores of Lesson-Sermons, just as have been the twenty-six other subjects. There has been no duplication.

This does not mean that specific passages have not been repeated. They have been—but always in new surroundings and in a new light.

Not entirely, but largely, the character of each Lesson-Sermon is determined by the immediate purpose. If that purpose is "to show the true thought of God as revealed in the Scriptures," appropriate Scriptural passages, with explanatory citations from the textbook, are selected. There are so many passages from both books that, in combination, their arrangement is almost limitless.

If the purpose is "to show how the Heavenly Father is to be understood," or to show what is meant by "Principle," or "Soul," or "Love," or "Truth," or "Life," or any other synonym of God, the Scriptural passages and textbook explanations are joined.

Each sermon "has its parts or sections," and, as a member of the Bible Lesson Committee wrote: "Each of these parts deals with some one special phase of the subject under consideration, and each part helps to make the whole understood. . . ."

To illustrate how the Scriptures and the textbook fit together, the member of the Bible Lesson Committee explained, "in the sermon on . . . God as Love, the Bible text affirms that God is Love . . . a statement which *Science and Health* unfolds. In the sermon on Soul, one of the Psalms is quoted as saying, 'Bless the Lord, O my soul.' The correlative passages from our text-book uses the word Soul in two meanings: first, it is applied to Deity; next, where it refers to the Spiritual sense; . . . the Bible text may be figurative or symbolic, which the parallel passages . . . will make plain . . .

"Study reveals progress in each lesson; there is introduction, body, and conclusion. The first section may affirm the scientific fact regarding the subject, and the following sections in an orderly way explain this fact . . . It is seen, also, that each lesson denies the error and affirms the truth regarding the subject. The false teaching is suggested and the true teaching plainly set forth which destroys the false.

"Through the entire sermon there is the single theme or subject, even as in a grand anthem there is one theme which each note, chord, and harmony unfolds, develops, and strengthens. So each verse and sentence of our sermon echoes and re-echoes the divine Truth which, when heard, gives melody and harmony, and brings the eager listener into tune with the infinite Principle of all harmony.

"While it is not to be understood that the Golden Text and Responsive Reading [6] form a part of the sermon ... they do fulfil their mission. The Golden Text may be said to contain the fundamental thought with which the sermon deals. It is a general statement of Truth which the sermon elaborates. The responsive reading, while entirely separate from the sermon, deals with the same subject. While no part of the temple (sermon), it may be called the stairway which leads to the temple, warning the worshiper that he is drawing nigh unto the holy place."

The Lesson-Sermons, the titles placed upon them by Mrs. Eddy, and the order of their giving (with the exception of Thanksgiving Day services), follow:

God; Sacrament; Life; Truth; Love; Spirit; Soul; Mind; Christ Jesus; Man; Substance; Matter; Reality; Unreality; Are Sin, Disease, and Death Real?; Doctrine of Atonement; Probation After Death; Everlasting Punishment; Adam and Fallen Man; Mortals and Immortals; Soul and Body; Ancient and Modern Necromancy, *alias* Mesmerism and Hypnotism, Denounced [7]; God the Only Cause and Creator; God the Preserver of Man; Is the Universe, Including Man, Evolved by Atomic Force?; Christian Science; Lesson for Thanksgiving Day.

Accompanying her desire to remove all human opinions from her teachings, Mary Baker Eddy could have had but a single prayer in her heart in divining the subjects of the sermons to be preached in her church. That desire was that

[6] In all cases the Golden Text and Responsive Reading are quotations from the Bible.

[7] On November 27, 1910, Mrs. Eddy added the word "Denounced" to this Lesson-Sermon.

all who listened might grow to better understand God. As in His kingdom is found no plague of sin, or sickness, or death, so in her teachings.

In calling her teachings a Science, she raised the level of inquiry from one of speculation to one of certainty—for by discovering what she believed to be the rule of healing she opened the way to the understanding of that Truth which none has yet seen, but which each knows is the only possible answer. As the work of God's kingdom is inexhaustible, so are the means to do it. What else is this work but a Science?

The trip from her home in Concord had taken several hours so that evening was gathering when Mrs. Eddy, with two companions, arrived in Boston and went directly from the railroad station to The Mother Church. The day was April 1; the year was 1895.

Seeing her church for the first time, as she entered the door leading to the center aisle she paused and, by pausing, disclosed the true tranquillity that reveals itself in deep meditation. Then, moving away from her two companions and walking down the aisle, she sank to her knees in prayer on the first step leading to the platform.

Slowly rising to her feet, she walked up the steps and across the platform to the First Reader's desk where, softly in a humbly reverent voice, yet in tones plainly audible to the two women watching from the rear of the auditorium, she spoke the full words of the Ninety-first Psalm: "He that dwelleth in the secret place of the most High shall abide under the shadow of the Almighty. I will say of the Lord, He is my refuge and my fortress: my God, in him will I trust . . . ."

As she completed the sixteenth and final verse of the

Psalm, she moved behind the desk of the Second Reader; again her voice was heard, this time repeating the two verses of the Welsh hymn:

> Guide me, O Thou great Jehovah,
> Pilgrim through this barren land:
> I am Thine, and Thou art mighty,
> Hold me with Thy powerful hand.
> Bread of heaven! Bread of heaven!
> Feed me now and evermore.
>
> Open is the crystal fountain,
> Whence the healing waters flow;
> And the fiery cloudy pillar
> Leads me all my journey through.
> Strong Deliverer! Strong Deliverer!
> Still Thou art my strength and shield.

Concluding, this white-haired woman who passed with indifference all earthly claims to power and prestige returned to where her companions were waiting. She spent the night in Mother's Room in the church tower and, with her companions, left early the following morning. Only a few knew she had been in Boston and had spent the night in her church. There were two other visits.

The second visit was at the Sunday morning services on May 26. The services had begun and the congregation was singing when Mrs. Eddy entered the edifice. In the July issue of the *Journal* was this account:

"Her presence was unknown [to most] until her appearance in the aisle of the auditorium on her way to the pulpit. The services had proceeded as usual until they were more than half concluded when she stepped upon the platform. After listening to the organ and a solo . . . she stepped to the desk and without text or note addressed the congregation for upwards of twenty minutes. Her glowing words of kindly greeting, love, admonition, and warning were intently and eagerly listened to by all ... At the close of the benediction the audience were requested to remain seated until Mrs. Eddy passed out, as it would have been impracticable to have personally met all the large audience."

In part, she said:

... More love is the great need of mankind. A pure affection, concentric, forgetting self, forgiving wrongs and forestalling them, should swell the lyre of human love. . . .

Examine yourselves, and see what, and how much, sin claims of you; and how much of this claim you admit as valid, or comply with. The knowledge of evil that brings on repentance is the most hopeful stage of mortal mentality. Even a mild mistake must be seen as a mistake, in order to be corrected; how much more, then, should one's sins be seen and repented of, before they can be reduced to their native nothingness! . . .

Beloved brethren, Christ, Truth, saith unto you, "Be not afraid!"—fear not sin, lest thereby it master you; but only *fear to sin*. Watch and pray for self-knowledge; since then, and thus, cometh repentance,—and your superiority to a delusion is won.

Repentance is better than sacrifice. The costly balm of Araby, poured on our Master's feet, had not the value of a single *tear*. . . .[8]

[8] *Miscellaneous Writings.* Published by the Trustees under the Will of Mary Baker G. Eddy.

On January 5, 1896 Mrs. Eddy again visited her church; as before, few knew she would be present. It was Communion Sunday; again she talked without notes.

Also, as on the other Sunday, she left immediately after the closing of the service.

Many letters followed requesting there be more appearances in the pulpit of her church. In the February, 1896, issue of the *Journal* she instructed not only the members of The Mother Church but all her followers:

> The hour has struck for Christian Scientists to do their own work, to appreciate the signs of the times, to demonstrate self knowledge and self government, and to demonstrate as this period demands over all sin, disease, and death. . . .

The January 5, 1896, appearance was her last appearance in her church.

For a little more than two years after the introduction of the Bible and *Science and Health* as "the only preachers" in The Mother Church, Mrs. Eddy watched carefully and read carefully all letters and comments from the field relating to this momentous step. Then, in April, 1897, she wrote to all Christian Science churches (there were about three hundred) "respectfully requesting" them "to have the First Reader read the following, at the opening of the Bible Lesson on Sunday:"

> The Bible, and the Christian Science text-book, are our only preachers. We shall now read scriptural texts, and their correlative passages from our text-book,—these comprise our sermon.

> The canonical writings, together with the word
> of our text-book corroborating and explaining the
> Bible texts in their denominational, spiritual im-
> port and application to all ages, past, present, and
> future, constitute a sermon undivorced from truth,
> uncontaminated or fettered by human hypotheses,
> and *authorized* by Christ. . . .[9]

Also, in a little more than two years, interest in the
teachings had so increased that, on December 10, 1897,
Mrs. Eddy announced that all churches wishing to hold "a
second service on Sunday" could do so "but the *same* Sunday Lesson must be read, at both services, until April 1898."
The stipulation "until 1898" probably was for the purpose
of establishing in the minds of her followers that whatever
the chosen time or times and wherever the church, the
service or services on any particular Sunday would be
the same. And having established the rule, she never
changed it.

The year of 1898 did not pass without the making of
one more lasting change in the presentation of the Lesson-
Sermons. Up to this year, the First Reader read the Scriptural selections and the Second Reader read the correlative
passages from the textbook. In its December issue, the
Journal published a notice informing all churches that
henceforth the Second Reader would read from the Bible
and the First should read from *Science and Health.*

From 1866 on the years had all been eventful: the years
of 1897 and 1898 were among the most eventful. Anticipat-
ing a routine conference on the progress of her printing
schedule at University Press, William Dana Orcutt went to

[9] The present "Explanatory Note," also written by Mrs. Eddy, which is
contained in the *Christian Science Quarterly* is somewhat different, but not
different in meaning.

Concord in 1897 in response to a word from Joseph Armstrong, a member of the Board of Directors, telling of Mrs. Eddy's desire to see him "as soon as it was convenient."

They had completed their discussion covering the details involved in the publishing of her books, and, knowing of the demands upon her time, Orcutt was preparing to leave when Mrs. Eddy indicated a package lying on a table. At her suggestion he opened the package, and heard her say: "I have a new manuscript for you. These are writings of mine that have appeared during the past years which I consider essential to preparing Christian Scientists for the full understanding of Science and Health. There is nothing to discuss about style, as I want the new book to match Science and Health in every way, but I do urge you to put it through the press as rapidly as possible because I am asking my students to cease teaching Christian Science until after the volume has appeared." [10]

Realizing the importance Mrs. Eddy placed upon the new book, Orcutt, once he was back in his office, went over the manuscript with great care before turning it over to the compositors; and with, as he wrote, the "realization of how much this extraordinary woman had accomplished— even beyond what I had witnessed with such accumulating admiration and amazement."

Having told Orcutt of her intention to notify her students "to cease teaching Christian Science until after the" appearance of *Miscellaneous Writings*, Mrs. Eddy published the following three paragraphs in the March, 1897, issue of *The Journal*:

The Christian Scientists in the United States and Canada are hereby enjoined not to teach a

---

[10] *Mary Baker Eddy and Her Books*, William Dana Orcutt. Copyright 1950, by The Christian Science Publishing Society.

student Christian Science for one year, commencing on March 14, 1897.

'Miscellaneous Writings' is calculated to prepare the minds of all true thinkers to understand the Christian Science Text-book more correctly than a student can.

The Bible, Science and Health with Key to the Scriptures, and my other published works, are the only proper instructors for this hour. . . .

A year later, in March, 1898, she rescinded the order, using the *Journal* for this "Notice":

I hereby notify the field that on March 1st the year expires in which Christian Scientists were requested to abstain from teaching. To-day my message to you is that loyal students from the Massachusetts Metaphysical College who have proven themselves good and useful teachers may instruct two classes of not over thirty (30) students during this ensuing year. May our God that is Love teach us this year, and every year how to serve Him. May the dear, faithful laborers who are not required to teach this year "wait patiently on the Lord, and He will renew their strength" for that which is to come.

A month previously (February, 1898) Mrs. Eddy had used the *Journal* for another important announcement. It was an announcement that was in the form of a new Church By-law; and it said:

This Church shall establish a "Board of Lectureship." This Board shall consist of not less than three members. The candidates for membership shall be subject to the approval of Rev. Mary Baker Eddy. The members of this Board shall be elected annually by the Christian Science Board of Directors.

When the need is apparent, the Christian Science Board of Directors of the Mother Church may call on any member of this Board of Lectureship to lecture at such places and at such times as the Cause of Christian Science demands. Also the branch Churches of Christ, Scientist, through their clerks, may apply to any member of this Lectureship, for aid and it shall be granted them.

The lecturers' traveling expenses, and the cost of hall shall be paid by the church that employs them, unless the receipts from the lecture are sufficiently remunerative. The lecture-fee shall be left to the discretion of the lecturer.

The present candidates for the "Board of Lectureship," are as follows: Mr. Edward A. Kimball, C.S.B., Rev. George Tomkins, D.D., C.S., Rev. William P. McKenzie, C.S., Rev. Irving C. Tomlinson, C.S., Mr. Carol Norton, C.S.[11]

Before there was a Board of Lectureship, there was a Board of Missionaries, and before there was a Board of Missionaries,[12] the first lecturer and the first missionary was Mrs. Eddy herself. It was not a rewarding task in the sense that people crowded to hear her. More often than

11 Lecturers now travel the civilized world in meeting the invitations of branch churches and societies.
12 In 1895 a Board of Missionaries was formally established by The Mother Church "to supply sections that have no healers or teachers in Christian Science."

not, she was reviled or ridiculed or spat upon. Secure in the realization that the Light toward which she was moving had its source elsewhere than in herself, she did not even pause.

In 1866, not long after her own healing, as she recalled in *Retrospection and Introspection* (p. 40), she was invited to speak before the Lyceum Club in Westerly, Rhode Island, where a demonstration of her new-found Science of healing "so stirred the doctors and clergy that they had my notices for a second lecture pulled down, and refused me a hearing in their halls and churches."

When establishing the Board of Lectureship, Mrs. Eddy stipulated to the Directors and to the lecturers themselves that she was not to be consulted on what aspects of Christian Science were to be discussed, but she did make it clear she would keep in close touch with their work and would encourage them or admonish them as the need became apparent.

In addition, she admonished them at the start that they were not to quarrel with any religion but to "be charitable to all men . . . and to cement the bonds of Christian brotherhood, whose every link leads upward in the chain of being . . ."

CHAPTER FOURTEEN

"The Bright Smile of Welcome"

ONLY a God-inspired individual could have accomplished what was accomplished by Mary Baker Eddy in these years. Although in her seventies and eighties, years were never in her thought; never out of her thought was the task before her. It was a task that was not to be done for her own self, nor for God, but for all people, wherever they might be.

As she wrote in *Science and Health* (p. 494):

> Is it not a species of infidelity to believe that so great a work as the Messiah's was done for himself or for God, who needed no help from Jesus' example to preserve the eternal harmony? But mortals did need this help, and Jesus pointed the way for them. . . .

Nearly nineteen centuries later, she was pointing in the same direction.

These were some of her accomplishments in these years; although not necessarily the exact order of their appearance:

(1) Outlined the terms of, and signed, a Deed of Trust through which she created The Christian Science Board of

Directors; (2) organized The Mother Church, The First Church of Christ, Scientist, in Boston, Massachusetts; (3) built the original edifice of The Mother Church; (4) upon invitation was represented in the World's Parliament of Religions at the World's Fair, in Chicago, in 1893.

In time, not many years had passed since clergymen had contemptuously referred to her as the "prayerless Mrs. Eddy" because of her introduction of silent prayer into her church services. Now, many among those who were listening to Charles Carroll Bonney, President of the Parliament, extending a welcome to Christian Scientists had adopted silent prayer into their own church services.

In recognizing Mrs. Eddy's teaching that "God will heal the sick through man, whenever man is governed by God," [1] Dr. Bonney was saying:

"No more striking manifestation of the interposition of divine Providence in human affairs has come in recent years, than that shown in the raising up of the body of people known as Christian Scientists, who are called to declare the real harmony between religion and Science, and to restore the waning faith of many in the verities of the sacred Scriptures." [2]

In reply, Judge Septimus J. Hanna, who represented Mrs. Eddy, read selected paragraphs from her writings.[3]

The following day the Chicago *Tribune* stated: "The crowd in the Hall of Columbus yesterday morning was greater than at any time since the Parliament first opened. It was apparent the announcement that the cause of Christian Science would be presented attracted them."

(5) Wrote and published the *Church Manual;* (6) es-

[1] *Science and Health,* p. 495.
[2] *Miscellaneous Writings,* p. 312.
[3] Full text, Appendix II.

tablished The Christian Science Publishing Society; (7) assembled and published *Miscellaneous Writings;* (8) established the Bible and *Science and Health* as the only preachers in all Christian Science churches; (9) established the Christian Science Board of Lectureship; (10) established the Christian Science Board of Education; (11) established the Christian Science Quarterly; (12) established the Christian Science Committee on Publication; (13) established the *Christian Science Sentinel.*

In a letter to William P. McKenzie, trustee of the Publishing Society, dated August 20, 1898, Mrs. Eddy wrote: "The dignity of our cause and the good of [our] students demand of us to publish a weekly newspaper." On September 1, the first issue of *The Christian Science Weekly* was in the hands of subscribers.

On January 26, 1899, following receipt of a letter by Judge Septimus J. Hanna, editor, the publication appeared as *The Christian Science Sentinel.* In her letter to Judge Hanna, which was dated January 19, 1889, Mrs. Eddy said:

> Sentinel is the proper title for our Weekly... Also let me prophesy "Sentinel" and the motto with it describes the future of this newspaper. It will take that place and must *fill it* when numerous periodicals of our denomination are extant.

The motto Mrs. Eddy suggested was first heard upon the Mount of Olives when, after Peter and James, John and Andrew had inquired of the Master: "Tell us, when shall these things be? and what shall be the sign when all these things shall be fulfilled?" And Jesus answered them, saying: "What I say unto you I say unto all, Watch."

The words "what I say unto you I say unto all, WATCH," are the motto of the *Sentinel.*

(14) Made final revisions in *Science and Health*. They were extensive, resulting in a textbook of approximately seven hundred pages. Mrs. Eddy always sought clarity; thus more than half the pages in the previous edition contained deletions or rearranged sentences or expanded paragraphs—but never was there a change in thought. Chapters were shifted into permanent sequence; side headings were changed; lines were numbered; replacing the Index was a new chapter entitled "Fruitage," the material for this chapter having been selected by Edward A. Kimball and Rev. William P. McKenzie from a large number of testimonies made available to them by Mrs. Eddy.

Mrs. Eddy referred to the revisions in *Science and Health* (p. 361), saying:

> I have revised *Science and Health* only to give a clearer and fuller expression of its original meaning. Spiritual ideas unfold as we advance. A human perception of divine Science, however limited, must be correct in order to be Science and subject to demonstration. A germ of infinite Truth, though least in the kingdom of heaven, is the higher hope on earth, but it will be rejected and reviled until God prepares the soil for the seed. That which when sown bears immortal fruit, enriches mankind only when it is understood,—hence the many readings given the Scriptures, and the requisite revisions of *Science and Health with Key to the Scriptures.*

The new manuscript was its own evidence of long and prayerful concentration.

The printers printed *Science and Health* on paper that previously was used only for Bibles and prayer books. Permission to use this paper was obtained after years of persuasion by Mrs. Eddy to the effect that inasmuch as the two books were inseparable in Christian Science teachings, not only was it appropriate that the paper be the same but with increased sales for *Science and Health* there would be corresponding increased sales for the Bible.

Impressed by the argument, the Oxford University Press in England, sole distributor of Oxford India paper, finally consented but not before learning for themselves how much the expanding interest in Christian Science was stimulating sales of the Bible.

(15) Giving no hint of her purpose, Mrs. Eddy dispatched telegrams to approximately seventy students on November 15, 1898, promising "a great blessing" if they would be present in Christian Science Hall in Concord at four o'clock in the afternoon of the following Sunday. The telegrams went to individuals living in places as far from Concord as Kansas City, Missouri (about one thousand five hundred miles) ; and all but three or four were present when Edward A. Kimball read Mrs. Eddy's address of welcome:

> Beloved Christian Scientists:—Your prompt presence in Concord at my unexplained call witnesses your fidelity to Christian Science and your spiritual unity with your Leader. I have awaited your arrival before informing you of my purpose in sending for you, in order to avoid the stir that might be occasioned among those who wish to share this opportunity, and to whom I would gladly give it at this time if a larger class were advantageous to the students.
>
> You have been invited hither to receive from me

one or more lessons on Christian Science, prior to
conferring on any or all of you who are ready for it,
the degree of C.S.D., of the Massachusetts Metaphysical College. This opportunity is designed to
impart a fresh impulse to our spiritual attain-
ments, the great need of which I daily discern. I
have awaited the right hour, and to be called of
God to contribute my part towards this result.

The "secret place," whereof David sang, is unquestionably man's spiritual state in God's own
image and likeness, even the inner sanctuary of
divine Science, in which mortals do not enter without a struggle or sharp experience, and in which
they put off the human for the divine. Knowing
this, our Master said: "Many are called, but few
are chosen." In the highest sense of a disciple,
all loyal students of my books are indeed my students, and your wise, faithful teachers have come
so to regard them.

What I have to say may not require more than
one lesson. This, however, must depend on results.
But the lessons will certainly not exceed three in
number. No charge will be made for my services.[4]

Using the Decalogue and the Sermon on the Mount as
her subject, but drawing upon the whole Bible to point
up her words, Mrs. Eddy conducted two classes, one on
Sunday and one on the following day. In attendance were
sixty-seven students, almost evenly divided between men
and women.

Following custom, no notes were taken of her words and
no stenographic record was made. However there are many
written recollections of students who were among the in-

[4] *Miscellany*, pp. 243–44.

vited, and there was general agreement among them as to what she said. Recalling the two classes, George Wendell Adams wrote: "She dwelt at length on the point that there could be but one full and complete reflection of one God, and that this must be the basis of all scientific deduction. She indicated that only as her students grasped this fundamental fact that one God could have but one reflection did they have the right basic sense of Christian Science, and there was no other starting point."

During her first class, Mrs. Eddy emphasized the supreme importance of humility in whatever the work of her listeners and in whatever the work of *all* Christian Scientists. She recalled occasions in the first years after her discovery when the sick were healed before she was able to respond in person to the summons. Unable to persuade the benefactors that, despite her absence in person, the healings were the result of her prayers, she became so disturbed that on one occasion she prayed that the sick person who was calling "must not get well until I get there!"

The patient was sick when she arrived and no better when she left. Returning to her home she prostrated her thought in prayer, seeking forgiveness for her moment of human self-glorification. Having straightened out her own thinking regarding *her* relationship to the Eternal Father, the patient quickly responded to her ministrations.

There was a world-renowned physicist who would have understood Mrs. Eddy's emphasis on the supreme importance of humility. One evening, a few years before his passing, Albert Einstein was a guest at a small dinner party. Seated beside him was the wife of a friend, and the two were in earnest conversation when the woman inquired, "Dr. Einstein, if you could possess only one quality, what would it be?"

Without hesitation, Einstein replied, "Humility."

As Mrs. Eddy completed her second day of instruction (the opening class was of two hours' duration, the second lasted four hours) the more than three score students gathered about her insisting she accept payment in money for their greatly increased understanding. She refused, saying, "I do not want this class to be an affair of money at all."

(16) Wishing to make the contents of *Science and Health* more quickly available and thus more useful to its readers, Mrs. Eddy outlined her wishes for a concordance to Albert F. Conant, having chosen him for the difficult assignment. It was an admirable choice. As soon as the revised edition of the textbook was in plated form and ready for the presses, thereby "freezing" the lines as numbered, Conant began preparing his manuscript for the printer.

Having prepared his copy on cards, he met with Mrs. Eddy and with William Dana Orcutt (previously Mrs. Eddy had approved his method of references and subreferences) for a discussion on type faces. It was Mrs. Eddy's wish that they use type faces and sizes which would indicate at a glance where each word belonged. The University Press did not have certain bold-face types selected by Mrs. Eddy so the typesetting was done by Riverside Press, in Cambridge, Massachusetts, but under Orcutt's supervision. The concordance was printed by University Press.

In the Preface to the first concordance Mrs. Eddy wrote:

> For many years there have been calls for a more complete index to *"Science and Health with Key To The Scriptures,"* and although the index prepared by the late Rev. J. H. Wiggin about the year 1885 was quite large, neither it nor subsequent indices fully met the requirements of the students of our textbook. It finally became apparent that the only satisfactory way to meet this need was to

prepare a complete Concordance, which should include all prominent words and phrases which the student may desire to find. . . .

Mary Baker Eddy.

Pleasant View, Concord, N. H., May 15, 1903.

(17) Within a few years after its completion the edifice of The Mother Church was too small to serve all who sought to attend Christian Science services. Branch churches were formed in various suburbs of Boston—in Cambridge, Roxbury, Chelsea, and in other communities—and morning and evening services were held on Sunday in The Mother Church. There remained insufficient accommodations, so that in her annual Message to The Mother Church, delivered on June 15, 1902, after pointing out, "here allow me to interpolate some matters of business that ordinarily find no place in my Message," Mrs. Eddy said:

> It is a privilege to acquaint communicants with the financial transactions of this church, so far as I know them, and especially before making another united effort to purchase more land and enlarge our church edifice so as to seat the large number who annually favor us with their presence on Communion Sunday. . . .[5]

Communion services were attended by such numbers of people on June 15, 1902, that they were held in the Mechanics Building.

In response to Mrs. Eddy's suggestion "to purchase more land and enlarge our church edifice," Edward A. Kimball proposed the building of an auditorium to seat four or five

[5] Copyright, 1902, by Mary Baker G. Eddy. Copyright renewed 1930. Published by the Trustees Under the Will of Mary Baker G. Eddy.

thousand persons and, in effect, added: "Acting in behalf of ourselves and the Christian Scientists of the world, we agree to contribute any portion of two million dollars that may be necessary for this purpose."

The motion was seconded by Judge William G. Ewing and was approved without a dissent. In the church treasury was this sum: $33,756.29.

On June 9, 1906, there was an announcement in the *Sentinel*, signed by Stephen A. Chase, Treasurer, which read:

"The contributors to the building fund for the Extension of The Mother Church, The First Church of Christ, Scientist, in Boston, Mass., are hereby notified that sufficient funds have been received for the completion of the church building, and the friends are requested to send no more money to this fund. . . ."

On June 10, 1906, which was Communion Sunday, the extension was dedicated. The cost was approximately two million dollars.

On June 11, 1906, among the newspapers throughout Europe, Canada, and the United States that printed dispatches regarding the dedication of the extension was the *Boston Herald*:

"Five thousand people kneeling in silent communion; a stillness profound; and then, rising in unison from the vast congregation, the words of the Lord's Prayer! Such was the closing incident of the dedicatory services of the extension of The Mother Church, The First Church of Christ, Scientist, at the corner of Falmouth and Norway streets, yesterday morning. And such was the scene repeated six times during the day.

"It was a sight which no one who saw it will ever be able to forget. Many more gorgeous church pageantries have been seen in this country and in an older civilization; there have been church ceremonies that appealed more to the eye, but the impressiveness of this lay in its very simplicity; its grandeur sprang from the complete unanimity of thought and of purpose. There was something emanating from the thousands who worshipped under the dome of the great edifice whose formal opening they had gathered to observe, that appealed to and fired the imagination. A comparatively new religion launching upon a new era, assuming an altogether different status before the world! . . ."

Mrs. Eddy was not in attendance at the services.[6] Under date of April 8, 1906, she had dispatched this letter:

Will one and all my dear correspondents accept this, my answer to their fervid question: Owing to the time consumed in travel, *et cetera,* I cannot be present *in propria persona* at our annual communion and the dedication in June next of The Mother Church of Christ, Scientist. But I shall be with my blessed church "in spirit and in truth."

I have faith in the givers and in the builders of this church edifice,—admiration for and faith in the grandeur and sublimity of this superb superstructure, wherein all vanity of victory disappears and the glory of divinity appears in all its promise.

Mary Baker Eddy

Pleasant View, Concord, N.H. April 8, 1906

(18) While a visitor in Dresden in 1886, Mrs. Mary Beecher Longyear of Marquette, Michigan, introduced Christian Science to that part of Germany by bringing healing to a number of sick people and by addressing

[6] Mrs. Eddy never visited the extension but did drive by it in her carriage.

several gatherings. In late December, 1904, or in early January, 1905, when Mrs. Longyear called on Mrs. Eddy they discussed the possibility of setting up an institution where the sick might receive Christian Science treatment.

When living in Lynn, Mrs. Eddy shared her home with the poor, giving over five of the seven rooms in the frame building to them, saying, "Now you have a home offered you and no rent to pay for it So do not be cast down I thank God more for this than anything that I have a shelter if it is humble to go to in an hour of want and to welcome those who need a little time to meet the hour." [7] In Boston, on Easter Sunday, 1887, she announced the founding of a Christian Science Dispensary, at 7 Temple Street. It was the first of about thirty such places of healing in other cities.

Although the Dispensaries were closed in 1894, Mrs. Eddy encouraged Mrs. Longyear by suggesting that the institution be called a Sanatorium and that in addition to caring for the sick arrangements be made to train nurses to make sure that all treatment would be in accordance with Christian Science teachings.

Under date of January 15, 1905, Mrs. Eddy wrote to Mrs. Longyear:

> God is moving on the face of the waters of your thoughts and His creations will appear.
>
> I propose that the institution you found be called Sanatorium ... that it be a resort for invalids without homes or relatives available in time of need; where they can go and recruit ...
>
> Our cause demands a wider circle of means for the ends of philanthropy and charity and better qualifications for *practical* purposes. This latter

[7] *Mary Baker Eddy, A Life Size Portrait,* Lyman P. Powell. Copyright, 1930, 1950, The Christian Science Publishing Society.

lack in Students of Christian Science is a great hindrance to our Cause and it must be met and mastered. The Students need to be qualified so that under the fire of mortal mind they can stand, "and having done all, to stand." (St. Paul).

Through the next twelve months the two women were in frequent correspondence, with Mrs. Eddy writing to Mrs. Longyear on January 21, 1906:

> Since reading your letters, pondering the subject of an institute or Sanatorium and studying our Manual, I see it is not best for you to take the initiative in this matter. It properly belongs to the Christian Science Board of Directors to do that, for thereby we shall avoid much confusion in the future. So please drop the matter.

The way was open although nearly three and a half years were to pass before Mrs. Eddy again acted.

Meantime, there were other matters that required her attention. In the late years of the nineteenth century and the very early years of the twentieth, the criticism of Mrs. Eddy and of her teachings was violent and widespread; it was led by New York newspapers such as *The Times,* which wondered editorially how long people would be "victims of Christian Science," and was blown up into magazine importance by Mark Twain, the eminent American author.

Having lost much of his savings by backing a defunct typewriter company, Twain used this means to make some quick money. In successive issues of the *Cosmopolitan Magazine,* Twain denounced Mrs. Eddy as a charlatan, a crook, and a woman who regarded herself "a second Christ," or, if not that, "a second Virgin Mother."

Feeling impelled to respond, Mrs. Eddy wrote two letters. One was to the Editor of the *New York Herald;* the other was to the Editor of the *Boston Herald.* In her letter to the *New York Herald,* she said, in part:

> ... I have not the inspiration nor the aspiration to be a first or second Virgin-mother—her duplicate, antecedent, or subsequent. What I am remains to be proved by the good I do . . .[8]

Her letter to the *Boston Herald* was brief:

> I even hope that those who are kind enough to speak well of me may do so honestly and not too earnestly, and this seldom, until mankind learn more of my meaning and can speak justly of my living.

In 1897, Mrs. Augusta E. Stetson tried to combine three or more Christian Science churches in New York City into one church and assume its leadership. Mrs. Eddy put a stop to Mrs. Stetson's efforts by publishing a letter in the January, 1898, issue of the *Journal* in which she advised all students of Christian Science:

> ... The Empire City is large, and there should be more than one church in it.
>
> The Readers of The Church of Christ, Scientist, hold important, responsible offices, and two individuals would meet meagrely the duties of half a dozen or more of the present incumbents. I have not yet had the privilege of knowing two students who are adequate to take charge of three or more churches. The students in New York and else-

8 For full text see *Miscellany,* pp. 302–303.

where will see that it is wise to remain in their own fields of labor and give all possible time and attention to caring for their own flocks.[9]

In her seventies and early eighties, Mrs. Eddy initiated the setting up of the first Christian Science hymnal, supervised the selection of its contents, and suggested additions when revisions were made. Up to the time (1892) of the appearance of their own hymnal, Christian Scientists used the *Social Hymn and Tune Book* published by the American Unitarian Society.

At the same time she watched over the introduction and the spreading of her teachings to the British Isles and to Europe, recalling her own prediction made in 1868 to early students that she could "introduce Christian Science in England more readily than I can in America." In 1898 and 1899 she gave serious thought to making a trip to London that she might "teach two or more classes" and said of London that it was "the most important field outside of the United States."

A book of poetry published late in 1893 brought so much criticism and misunderstanding that in early 1894 Mrs. Eddy withdrew the small volume from sale. The book was entitled *Christ and Christmas*. The criticism was centered largely about one illustration. It was a drawing of a man and a woman, the head of each being encircled by a halo. In one hand, the woman held a scroll on which was written "Christian Science," while her other hand clasped the hand of the man. As Mrs. Eddy explained, the illustration was intended to "foretell the typical appearing of the womanhood, as well as the manhood of God, our divine Father and Mother."

The clergy would not have it that way. Instead, it ac-

[9] *Miscellany*, p. 243.

cused Mrs. Eddy of instructing the artist to use her as a
model and the rightful recipient of a halo of equal size to
that which was about the head of a man intended to represent Jesus.

The accusations were not true but, rallying to her side,
a good many followers fell into the morass of adulation. She
rebuked both the clergy and her followers not only by
withdrawing the small book from sale but also by informing them:

> . . . This little messenger has done its work, ful-
> filled its mission, retired with honor (and mayhap
> taught me more than it has others) , only to reap-
> pear in due season. The knowledge that I have
> gleaned from its fruitage is, that intensely contem-
> plating personality impedes spiritual growth; even
> as holding in mind the consciousness of disease
> prevents the recovery of the sick. . . .[10]

Accompanied by Judge and Mrs. Septimus J. Hanna,
Mrs. Eddy went to Tremont Temple in Boston in the
early afternoon of June 6, 1899, to address the annual meeting of The Mother Church. Rather than press through the
thousands who were crowding the front entrance, Mrs.
Eddy and her companions were driven to a side door.
Entering the Temple, they learned that the elevator was
not in running order. Without hesitation she walked up
the two long flights of stairs that led to the stage.

As she walked out on the stage, the audience, which completely filled the auditorium, the balconies, the foyer, and
the entrances, arose as one person and stood in silence
as, escorted by Judge Hanna, she took her place on the
platform.

[10] *Miscellaneous Writings,* p. 308.

To Mrs. Eddy, even if but momentarily, must have come the memory of a day more than fourteen years previously, when from this same platform another overflow audience had listened to her in cold hostility—and regarded her leaving with an equal coldness. Then it was an assembly of New England clergymen who, in response to her request to be heard, decided that "the best way of meeting the evil was to let it show itself" and offered her ten minutes to speak of teachings that knew God as did the disciple James:

> Let no man say when he is tempted, I am tempted of God: for God cannot be tempted with evil, neither tempteth he any man. . . . Every good gift and every perfect gift is from above, and cometh down from the Father of lights, with whom is no variableness, neither shadow of turning.

Now, on June 6, 1899, her followers had multiplied many times. They were in many countries, and some were in Boston and were listening. Wearing a gray satin dress covered with black lace, she was standing before them and was saying:

> . . . The Christian Scientist knows that spiritual faith and understanding pass through the waters of Meribah here—bitter waters; but he also knows they embark for infinity and anchor in omnipotence.[11]

About two years after moving from Boston to Concord, Mrs. Eddy was driving one afternoon and stopped her carriage at the crest of a hill to look southward down a narrow valley, seeing, in remembrance, the farmhouse in Bow where she was born. Returning to Concord, she made in-

[11] *Miscellany,* p. 132.

quiries regarding the small farm at the crest of the hill where she had lingered, learned it was for sale and bought it, transformed it, and called it Pleasant View.

Without orderliness within herself and within her household she could not have accomplished all these things, as well as the many other duties that attended her work.

She arose at six o'clock in summer (seven o'clock in winter) and except for the interruption of breakfast at seven o'clock, the morning hours from six until nine o'clock were devoted to meditation and prayer. From nine until twelve o'clock correspondence had her attention. Often she wrote by hand as many as forty or fifty letters to the Directors of The Mother Church, to Boards of branch churches, to the Trustees of the Publishing Society, to students, and sometimes in reply to questions from editors.

Dinner was served at twelve o'clock. At one o'clock, with Calvin Frye holding the reins, she was in her carriage taking her daily drive along the country roads or through the streets of Concord. Returning to Pleasant View after an hour, she gave over the remainder of the afternoon to studying and revising her textbook, making frequent contributions to the literature of the Movement. She supervised her household. At three o'clock she received callers—officers of the Church and visitors. She inspected the plans and watched over the building of First Church of Christ, Scientist, in Concord, which was her gift to the members. She also contributed the greater part of ten thousand dollars that was used to pave a street in Concord, transforming a strip of unattractive farmland, an equally unattractive farmhouse, a scattering of spindly pine trees into a place of beauty.

The small dwelling on the property was in the valley. She had it moved to the crest of the hill, added wide verandahs, bow windows, a porte-cochere in front, and behind she built a tower from whose four sides she could look out on her native state. From these windows she could see no confusion. Listening, she heard the whisper that is prophetic of that which is to come—knew that life remains and, always, under the deep snows of winter, there is Resurrection. Where the farm dwelling once stood, she built a small pond [12] and ringed it with footpaths. She surrounded her home with flower gardens, low hedges, sloping lawns, and shade trees; to these she added fruit trees, shrubs, lilac bushes, honeysuckle.

After supper at six o'clock (a meal which, as with all meals, was served promptly) she sometimes gathered with members of her household around the piano in the parlor, singing hymns; more often, she sat on the verandah in the gathering summer dusk, listening to the sleepy conversation of nesting robins, watching as the lights of Concord silhouetted the homes; but most of all her thoughts were joined in friendship with the unutterable truths that lie too deep for words.

William Elmer Crofut, a Syracuse newspaperman, was visiting in Concord in 1896. He requested an interview with Mrs. Eddy. Recalling his impressions, he wrote:
"I knew then and I know now that I was in the presence of an extraordinary person. It was as though here was one who had fasted—had been in long periods of prayer and solitary communion with her God and her Christ and that something of the heavenly, something of the great spiritual life eternal, had settled upon her." [13]

Frank E. Irwin, a lumber salesman, was in Concord in 1903 and was in a customer's office when Mrs. Eddy called.

[12] This pond, the gift of students, inspired one of her shorter compositions, "Pond and Purpose." For full text see *Miscellaneous Writings*, pp. 203–207.

[13] *Historical Sketches*, Clifford P. Smith.

She was seeking information concerning the contract for the building of First Church of Christ, Scientist, in Concord. Irwin did not see her at close range, but he heard what she said and was impressed by her questions, her manner, and the intelligence she displayed, in contradiction to his previous attitude of criticism of Christian Scientists in general and her in particular.

An hour later, on a Concord Street, he saw her face to face. In his book, *Historical Sketches*, Clifford P. Smith quoted from a letter received from Irwin:

"I heard a voice behind me, I looked around quickly, and looked into Mrs. Eddy's face. I never want to, and know I never shall, forget the look on her face. Any ideas derogatory to Mrs. Eddy or Christian Science vanished into thin air, and I know from that moment on I was a better man. It seemed a turning point in my life when I was thrown into contact for the first time with absolute purity."

Mrs. Mary Henderson Toms, of Knoxville, Tennessee, was one of thousands of Christian Scientists who gathered at Pleasant View in 1903 and heard Mrs. Eddy speak from a balcony of her home. She recalled the event.

"At the appointed hour, Mrs. Eddy appeared on the upper verandah and walked slowly out on the balcony, where she stood silently for a few minutes looking into the upturned faces. Her expression was one of great tenderness and yearning love. . . . She must have been about eighty-two years of age. To me, she did not look sixty. . . . There was nothing rigid or feeble about her posture; she had a buoyant step. Her eyes looked dark and luminous. I wish I could describe her expression that day. To me, it was one of victory over the material world. . . ."

In the following year, Mrs. Mary Lloyd McConnel, of Ilkley, England, heard Mrs. Eddy speak in First Church of

Christ, Scientist, in Concord, saw her at close hand, and described her appearance:

"She was lovely, old and yet so very young. Indeed, ageless seems the best word to employ. Her hair was white, her complexion as fair and smooth as that of a young child. Her eyes were marvelous. You could not possibly tell what color they were. They were just full of light."

The letters from Mrs. Toms and Mrs. McConnel are in the archives of The Mother Church and were published in Clifford P. Smith's book, *Historical Sketches*.

Having succeeded John Wilson as head of University Press, William Dana Orcutt was planning his first trip to Europe and had written several clients asking them to advise him if they anticipated the arising of manufacturing problems in his absence. In response, he received a letter from Mrs. Eddy requesting his appearance, at his convenience. The year was 1901. Almost ten years had passed since he had seen her.

As he was ushered into her study at Pleasant View, he was impressed by the few changes that had been made in his absence, but "the most extraordinary fact" as he wrote in *Mary Baker Eddy and Her Books,* "was the lack of change in Mrs. Eddy herself.

"When she entered the room, just as she had done on that first visit of mine, she seemed just as she had always seemed: the same bright smile of welcome, the same penetrating, assessing eyes, the same alertness of manner, the same clear, musical voice, the same physical vigor I had always remembered—yet the ten years that had been added to the history of the world had added the same number of years to this slight little woman—years of conflict and triumph, years of disappointment and gratification, years of consecration and of arduous labor, years of achievement and accomplishment—and had left no visible mark. Mrs. Eddy was eighty years old at the time, and had summoned me to discuss with her not some trivial detail associated with her business, but to make definite arrangements for the consummation of her long-determined plan to place the finishing touch on her textbook as her bequest to the world, and further plans to make the volume more available. During that concentrated, detailed discussion there was never the slightest evidence of uncertainty or of fatigue."

Early in the discussion, she had inquired about the date of his expected return and upon being told "in three months . . . she was thoughtful for a moment" before saying:

"That will fit in perfectly with my plans. When you return I shall need your assistance. I have been working on what will be my final revision of *Science and Health,* except perhaps for later verbal changes, and this means resetting the entire book. There will be new problems in the typography, for I want the lines to be numbered. . . .

"The simplicity of this announcement did not blind me to the vastness of her project. A short half-hour before I had thought that this calm little woman sitting in front of me was settling back to watch the fulfillment of her plans, when as a matter of fact she was at that moment involved in elaborate preparations for the coming year which would demand of her actual spiritual and physical labor—in concentration and writing, to say nothing of her meticulous supervision—even beyond what she had given in years gone by!

"I left Pleasant View with wonder and admiration in my heart, and with her best wishes for a happy voyage and a productive European trip."

The real testimony of her mission is found in her eyes. In them is gentleness, patience, compassion, insight. It was not in her to draw advantage out of others; she desired only to do what she believed was her great privilege to do—God's work on earth.

Mary Baker Eddy knew that spiritual cause, far more than all other causes, leads to human progress. In the physical universe the earth has its own motion but always on its own axis; and always repetitiously revolving around the sun. In the universe of Spirit, the movement is always true to its Center, but always closer to its goal.

It heralds the time—less distant now than in 1866—when to believe, as Mrs. Eddy believed, that God is the ever-present Healer shall no longer be regarded as heresy, or hypocrisy, or weakness.

CHAPTER FIFTEEN

"Earmarks of Hostile Action"

THROUGH the windows of her sitting room on the second floor of her home at Pleasant View, Mary Baker Eddy watched the seasons come and go—the Merrimack Valley she knew so well white with snow; the bright green urgency of spring; fireflies dancing in the summer dusk; the silver threads of milkweed seeds riding the autumn winds.

In the southeasterly corner of this large room was an easy chair between a desk and table. Here she did most of her writing, here in this room she met people who came to see her, and from this room she directed the affairs of her church and of her household. On this morning of the twelfth of February, 1907, she was talking with Laura Sargent and was saying:

"Laura, I am going to put business out of my mind. I cannot go on being pulled one way and the other by material and spiritual matters. I am going with God."

Since the day twenty-five years before when he had responded to Mrs. Eddy's telegram to meet her train at Plymouth, New Hampshire, and ride with her to Boston, Calvin A. Frye [1] had kept bookkeeping watch over all of her business affairs. He was not a bookkeeper. But he was honest, which to her was all that mattered. He told her of his lack of training. It did not disturb her. As he recalled years

[1] For list of Mrs. Eddy's secretaries see Appendix IV.

later, her only instruction was to keep such information to himself.

Setting up his own system, Frye went to work. His salary was ten dollars a week, plus room and board. Early in 1898, accompanied by Mrs. Eddy, Frye went to the Loan and Trust Savings Bank of Concord, where Mrs. Eddy kept her general account, and asked Fred N. Ladd, treasurer of the bank, to look over his books and accounts. Explaining, Frye said he wanted to be sure he had made no mistakes; also, he needed some help on how best to keep the books.

Sitting with Frye at Ladd's desk and listening, Mrs. Eddy told the bank official, who was the son of Mrs. Eddy's second cousin, that she did not care anything about having the accounts audited, such was her confidence in her secretary, but because he wanted it done, "I would like to have you do it."

In May 1907, Harvey Chase, of the firm of Harvey Chase & Company, public accountants and auditors, with principal offices at 27 State Street in Boston, Massachusetts, was employed to make an "expert examination covering every detail of Mrs. Eddy's business transactions for a number of years." He reported to the Trustees: "Mr. Frye has made more errors against himself than against Mrs. Eddy, so that the latter . . . will have to pay over a balance of cash to Mr. Frye when the time for final adjustment of these accounts arrives. From the examination . . . it appears that the balance due . . . to Mr. Frye will amount to $677.41."

In the same general report, Ladd certified that as of the same date, the amount of bonds turned over to the Trustees (Mrs. Eddy having already divested herself of the management of her property) was $788,770 (par value). There was also turned over a promissory note on which was due a balance of $50,000 and some interest, also some savings bank books, on which was due $8,614.64; and cash items amounting to $24,476.82—making a total of $871,861.46.

The bonds consisted entirely of United States, state, and municipal bonds. There were no shares of stock in any corporation. Ladd also reported that "Every bond was accounted for, and every coupon or other interest which should have been deposited was in fact deposited. We further find from the books and accounts that Mrs. Eddy's income from March 10, 1893 has been derived almost entirely from the monthly remittances of her publishers, from interest on her bond investments and from rents of her Commonwealth Avenue houses. Receipts from sources other than these were relatively small in amount."

On deposit on March 10, 1893, were $100,000 in bonds representing Mrs. Eddy's savings from the time Frye set up his books in 1883. In the years immediately preceding 1900, Frye's salary was $12 a week with room and board; and, as he recalled, "From October, 1900, to April, 1903, I was paid $1,000 per year and board; and from April, 1903 to March 1, 1907, I have received $100 a month and board (as a member of the household "board" included room). During the twenty-five years I had been in her employ, Mrs. Eddy has made unsolicited presents to me of money and jewelry, in all to the amount of not exceeding seventy-three hundred dollars. I have never received anything else from her."

When compared with today's salary standards the figures recited by Frye are small. In 1907 they were generous. Seven years later, in 1914, Henry Ford electrified the world by announcing a wage rate of five dollars a day for the sixteen thousand men working in the Ford factories and a work week of five eight-hour days.[2]

---

[2] Actually, when the five-dollar-a-day wage was put into effect in April, 1914, about two hundred Ford factory employees were getting seven dollars

The reaction of *The Wall Street Journal* was typical of business in general. It accused Ford of injecting "Biblical or spiritual principles into a field where they do not belong" that he might "get advertising and get riddance to Henry Ford of his troublesome millions."

Over and above the $871,861.46 that was on deposit in two banks in Concord—as well as a trust fund of $100,000 that Mrs. Eddy had donated to First Church of Christ, Scientist, in Concord—were deposits in banks elsewhere approximating $166,000. The records were as meticulously kept as were the records in the Concord bank, so that on the morning of that day in February, 1907, when she told Laura Sargent, "I am going to get business out of my mind," Mrs. Eddy was planning to divest herself from ownership of more than a million dollars.

In her mind were two things she must do. One was to establish a trust deed for the care of her son and his family; the other was to establish a trust deed for the "advancement of the cause and doctrines of Christian Science."

A few days later she called in Frank Sherwin Streeter of Concord, her personal counsel, and told him of her wishes. There is no record of their conversation, but it is probable that in discussing the matter, the careful and thorough Streeter recalled the year 1899, when she built and furnished a home for her son and his family in Lead, South Dakota, and reminded her that "it is better than the house you live in here at Pleasant View"; besides, "from time to time you have been sending him money." However, whatever their conversation, she informed the lawyer what provisions she wanted contained in a trust deed for her son and his family.

---

a day; about one thousand were getting six dollars a day and the remainder, or about fifteen thousand, were getting or soon would get five dollars a day.

Salient paragraphs in the document, which Streeter prepared and Mrs. Eddy approved, follow:

1. I direct my trustees to pay to my son George W. Glover, or for the benefit of my son George and his wife (as in the discretion of my trustees may seem best), the sum of fifteen hundred dollars annually during the lifetime of said George; and, upon his decease, to pay to his said wife, or for her benefit, such an amount annually during the balance of her life as, in the discretion of my said trustees, may seem reasonable for her comfortable support and maintenance; also to pay the taxes and insurance on their homestead in Lead, South Dakota, and keep the buildings thereon in reasonable repair.

2. I direct my trustees to pay to my granddaughter, Mary B. Glover, the sum of five hundred dollars annually until the termination of the trust hereby created or until her decease, if that event shall happen before the termination of the trust.

3. I direct my trustees to pay to my grandson Gershon Glover the sum of five hundred dollars annually during my earthly life.

4. I direct my trustees to pay the reasonable and proper expenses of my grandson George W. Glover in obtaining a liberal college education under the care and supervision of Rev. Irving C. Tomlinson, who shall receive from said trustees a reasonable and proper allowance for his services and expenses in the exercise of such care and supervision; also that my said grandson George W. Glover shall receive from the trustees such an annual allowance as, in their discretion, may seem

best, until the termination of the trust hereby created or until his decease if that event shall happen
before the termination of the trust.

5. I also direct that my said trustees shall pay the
reasonable and proper expenses of my grandson
Andrew Jackson Glover in obtaining a thorough
school education, not including a college course;
also that my said grandson Andrew Jackson Glover
shall receive from the trustees such an allowance
as, in their discretion, may seem best, until the
termination of the trust hereby created or until
his decease, if that event shall happen before the
termination of the trust. . . .

Second: I hereby authorize my said trustees, by
their unanimous action, to expend such further
sums from time to time as, in their judgment,
may seem best, for the benefit of my son George
W. Glover, and his wife and their children (my
grandchildren), my purpose in making this provision being to provide against unforeseen con-
tingencies and necessities of my son and his wife
and my grandchildren which may arise during the
continuance of this trust.

Third: This trust shall continue during the life
of my son George W. Glover and his wife and at
least until my youngest grandchild reaches the age
of twenty-one years. Upon the death of my son and
his wife and the arrival of the youngest grandchild at the age of twenty-one years, this trust shall
terminate and the balance of the trust property
then remaining in the hands of my said trustees
shall then be paid over to and become the property of my grandchildren, in equal shares, namely,
the children of my son George W. Glover and his

present wife; *provided,* however, that if any one
or more of the beneficiaries under this trust shall
directly or indirectly make any contest or opposition to my last will or to the disposition of other
property by me, all right and interest of such
beneficiary or beneficiaries in this trust fund shall
thereupon and thereby terminate, and all their interest in this fund shall become a part of my estate
and pass to the residuary legatee in my will.

Fourth: I give unto my trustees full power to
manage, care for, control, and reinvest said trust
property and securities and the income thereof,
with all powers necessary or convenient for such
purposes, desiring, however, that investments of
income and reinvestments of principal shall always
be made in bonds or other securities of a conserva-
tive character, having regard for the safety of the
principal. It is my wish that in the making of investments preference shall be given to state, government, city, and municipal bonds, but I leave
this to the judgment and discretion of said trustees, relying on said discretion being conserva-
tively exercised.

The Trust Deed became effective February 25, 1907
when, in the presence of Hermann S. Hering and Josiah E.
Fernald, witnesses, Mrs. Eddy attached her signature.

With the completion of the first step toward divesting
herself from all property holdings, Mrs. Eddy turned her
attention to the important task of establishing a trust deed
for the "advancement of the cause and doctrine of Christian Science." This matter, particularly this matter, had
long been in her prayers. Again, in the sitting room on the
second floor of her home at Pleasant View, she conferred

with her personal counsel, Frank Sherwin Streeter. This time she acquainted him with specific clauses she wanted included in the document. Especially did she emphasize the time and the conditions under which the trust should terminate.

As trustees she named Josiah E. Fernald, Henry M. Baker, Archibald McLellan. Fernald was President of the National State Capital Bank of Concord. He was fifty years old, and she had known him since May 16, 1890, when she opened an account in the bank. At the time he was cashier. Henry M. Baker was sixty-one years old. His father was Mrs. Eddy's cousin. Henry M. Baker was a lawyer and was born in the same house in Bow, New Hampshire, in which Mrs. Eddy was born. Archibald McLellan, forty-nine years old, had met Mrs. Eddy in Chicago in 1888 and was editor of *The Christian Science Journal, The Christian Science Sentinel,* and *Der Herold der Christian Science.*

In the early afternoon of March 6, 1907, the three trustees, along with Fred N. Ladd and Streeter, all gathered at Pleasant View and with Calvin A. Frye, who was present part of the time, met with Mrs. Eddy for a reading of the trust deed Streeter had prepared. Mrs. Eddy was sitting at her desk when the six men came into the room. Getting to her feet, she greeted them by name, and when they were all seated she joined in a few minutes of personal conversation.

As the conversation subsided, Streeter handed her one original copy of the deed and gave the other to her cousin, Henry M. Baker. Mrs. Eddy inquired of Streeter if she should read her copy. He said she should. She then asked if she should read it aloud. He shook his head and after a minute or two changed his mind, saying, "Perhaps you had better read it aloud."

She did so, often pausing at the end of a paragraph to say, "That is all right," "That is what I wish," and to speak of her great confidence in Calvin A. Frye. After reading paragraph four, which concerned the conditions under which the Trust should terminate, she said, "That is just what I want."

As she finished reading (and from start to finish she read without visual aid of any kind) she turned to Streeter, saying, "Where do I sign?" He indicated the place and she signed the originals. As she did so, she apologized for a slight trembling in her hand and, turning to Baker, laughed as she said, "Now, cousin, you are a young man; your hand should not tremble," and laughed with the others when Baker's signature came out quite illegible.

Following the meeting the trustees elected Baker as chairman, Fernald as treasurer, and Ladd as secretary. In its complete form, the Trust Deed reads:

DEED OF TRUST

Mary Baker G. Eddy to Henry M. Baker,
Archibald McLellan,
Josiah E. Fernald.

Know all Men by these Presents:

That I, Mary Baker G. Eddy of Concord, New Hampshire, in consideration of one dollar to me paid by Henry M. Baker of Bow, New Hampshire, Archibald McLellan of Boston, Massachusetts, and Josiah E. Fernald of Concord, New Hampshire, who are hereby constituted trustees and attorneys in fact for the purposes hereinafter set forth, do hereby grant, convey, assign, and transfer unto the said Henry M. Baker, Archibald McLellan, and Josiah E. Fernald, their heirs, successors, and assigns, all my interest of every kind and description in and to any real estate wherever situated; also all my interest of every kind and description in and to any estate, personal or mixed, which I now own or possess, including stocks, bonds, interests in copyrights, contracts, actions, and causes of action at law or in equity against any person.

To HAVE AND TO HOLD the above granted and assigned premises, with all the privileges and appurtenances thereto belonging, unto said Henry M. Baker, Archibald McLellan, and Josiah E. Fernald, trustees, to them and their heirs, successors, and assigns; *but, in trust, nevertheless,* for the following purposes and upon the following conditions, viz.:

First: To manage, care for, and control all the above granted real estate and interest therein during my earthly life and, at the termination thereof, to dispose of the same in accordance with the provisions of my last will and the codicils thereto; but I hereby reserve for myself the right of occupancy and use of my homestead, "Pleasant View," in Concord, New Hampshire. I hereby also reserve all household furniture, my printed library, and all horses, carriages, tools, and other articles of use or adornment now being or in use in or about my home premises at "Pleasant View." I hereby also reserve the right to occupy and to rent for my own benefit my two houses at 385 and 387 Commonwealth Avenue, Boston, Mass.

Second: I give unto my trustees full power to manage, care for, control, invest, and reinvest all said trust property and the income thereof with all powers necessary or convenient for such purpose, desiring, however, that investments of income and reinvestments of principal shall always

be made in bonds or other securities of a conserva-
tive character, having regard for the safety of the
principal. It is my wish that, in the making of investments, preference shall be given to the state,
government, city, and municipal bonds; but I
leave this to the judgment and discretion of said
trustees, relying upon said discretion being conser-
vatively exercised.

Third: Said trustees shall pay to me, from time
to time, out of the net income of said trust property, (1) such sums as I may need or desire for the
purpose of keeping up the homestead "Pleasant
View," and paying the expenses thereof and of
my household, in the same general way as heretofore; (2) such sums as I may desire for my own
personal expenses and for charitable purposes; and
(3) such sums as I may personally desire to use
for the advancement of the cause and doctrines of
Christian Science as taught by me. Said trustees
shall also pay and discharge whatever claims and
accounts may be outstanding against me at this
date.

Fourth: At the termination of my earthly life,
this trust shall terminate, and all the personal estate then held by my said trustees shall pass to the
executor of my last will and the codicils thereto, to
be disposed of in accordance with the provisions
thereof.

Fifth: Said trustees are hereby appointed my
attorneys in fact and, as such, are hereby vested
with full power and authority for me and in my
behalf and in behalf of the trust estate hereby created, either in their own names as trustees or in
my name, as they shall decide, to bring, appear in,

prosecute, defend, and dispose of as in their judgment shall seem best for the protection and preservation of the trust estate, any actions, causes of action, suits at law or in equity, whether now pending or hereafter brought with reference to any matter in which I may be personally interested or the trust estate hereby created in any way affected. And I hereby give to my trustees and attorneys in fact full power and authority to employ attorneys-at-law and other agents in such matters and in all other matters pertaining to the trust estate.

Sixth: In case of a vacancy in said board of trustees, caused by death, refusal to act, or resignation of any of them, or for any reason, a new trustee or trustees shall be appointed by me and, in case I fail to act, said new trustee shall be appointed by the chief justice of the Supreme Court of New Hampshire for the time being, preference being given to the nomination of the remaining trustee or trustees.

Seventh: I direct that my trustees shall be liable only for their own acts in the management of this trust and that no trustee shall be answerable for loss or damage which may happen to the trust property without his own wilful fault or misfeasance.

Eighth: I desire said trustees and their successors to furnish a surety bond or bonds to the amount of five hundred thousand dollars, and the expense thereof shall be paid from the trust funds.

Ninth: The trustees shall receive a reasonable payment from the trust fund for their personal services as such, and shall also be reimbursed for all expenses incurred by them in the management of the trust estate.

Tenth: The trustees shall render to me personally, semi-annual accounts of the trust property and the income and expense thereof.

IN WITNESS WHEREOF, I have hereunto set my hand and seal this sixth day of March, A.D. 1907.

MARY BAKER G. EDDY [*seal*]

Signed and sealed, and delivered in the presence of:

FRANK S. STREETER.
FRED N. LADD.

State of New Hampshire, ⎱ *ss.*
    MERRIMACK ⎰

On this sixth day of March, personally appeared the above named Mary Baker G. Eddy and acknowledged the foregoing instrument to be her free act and deed.

Before me: FRANK S. STREETER,
[*Notarial seal*]   *Notary Public.*
        CONCORD, N.H. *March 6, 1907.*

We, Henry M. Baker, Archibald McLellan and Josiah E. Fernald, severally accept the foregoing trust and agree to perform the same according to the conditions and terms thereof; but we severally reserve the right to resign said trust.

HENRY M. BAKER,
ARCHIBALD MCLELLAN,
JOSIAH E. FERNALD,
Trustees.

THE BOND

KNOW ALL MEN BY THESE PRESENTS,

That we, Henry M. Baker of Bow, New Hampshire, Archibald McLellan of Boston, Massachusetts, and Josiah E. Fernald of Concord, New Hampshire, as principals, and the United States Fidelity & Guaranty Company of Baltimore, Maryland, as surety, are held and firmly bound to Mary Baker G. Eddy of Concord, New Hampshire, and her executors in the sum of five hundred thousand dollars to be paid to said Mary Baker G. Eddy or her executors, to the payment whereof we bind ourselves and our heirs, firmly by these presents.

Sealed with our seals and dated the eighteenth day of March, A.D. 1907.

THE CONDITION OF THIS OBLIGATION IS, that

WHEREAS, the said Mary Baker G. Eddy, by deed duly executed and delivered on the sixth day of March, 1907, subject to certain reservations therein named, granted, conveyed, assigned and transferred unto the said Henry M. Baker, Archibald McLellan and Josiah E. Fernald, their heirs, successors and assigns, all the grantor's interest of every kind and description in and to any real estate wherever situated, also all the grantor's interest of every kind and description in and to any estate, personal or mixed, which the grantor then owned or possessed, including stocks, bonds, interest in copyrights, contracts, actions, and causes of action at law or in equity against any person, but, in trust, nevertheless, for the purposes and upon the conditions fully set forth in said trust deed;

now, if said Henry M. Baker, Archibald McLellan
and Josiah E. Fernald, as such trustees, shall well
and truly carry out and perform all the obligations
imposed upon them and each of them by and according to the terms, conditions and stipulations
set forth in said trust deed, then this obligation
shall be void.

HENRY M. BAKER.
ARCHIBALD McLELLAN.
JOSIAH E. FERNALD.

The United States Fidelity
& Guaranty Co.
By Arthur P. Morrill,
Its Attorney-in-Fact.

Signed, sealed, and delivered in the
presence of:
FRED N. LADD.
FRANK S. STREETER.

But even while Streeter was preparing the trust deed for
her signature, Henry M. Baker was studying the contents of
a letter received by Mrs. Eddy a few days after she had
executed the trust deed providing for the care of her son
and his family. On March 1 Mrs. Eddy sent for her cousin,
who for a number of years had served her as a consultant in
legal matters of a special nature. The letter was from Washington, D. C., and carried the signature of her son.

Handing the communication to the lawyer, Mrs. Eddy
inquired as to its meaning and remarked (as Baker recalled), "George could not write that letter. That letter was
written by an educated man who is skilled in the use of
language."

Reading slowly and measuring each word, the lawyer observed that as for its meaning the letter carried the "ear-marks of contemplated hostile action," and advised Mrs. Eddy to "await whatever proceedings are intended."

She did not have long to wait. On the same day a document signed by her son, George W. Glover, his daughter, Mary B. Glover, and Mrs. Eddy's nephew, George W. Baker, living in Bangor, Maine, was filed in a Concord court. The document was identified as The Petition of "Next Friends." The petition stated "that being unable to guard and manage her own property, Mrs. Eddy was under the influence, control, and fraud of others." Named as defendants were four members of The Christian Science Board of Directors, Ira O. Knapp, William B. Johnson, Stephen A. Chase, and Joseph Armstrong, as well as Calvin A. Frye, Alfred Farlow, Irving C. Tomlinson, Edward A. Kimball, Hermann S. Hering, and Lewis C. Strang. Among other things the petition asked:

"That a receiver or receivers be appointed to take possession of all the property of the said Mary Baker G. Eddy now in the hands or under the control of the defendants or otherwise wrongfully withheld from her control by any person or persons and to take charge of and manage all her business affairs; and to make such ultimate disposition of all her estate as this court may hereafter decide to be wise and prudent; and for such further relief as to the court may seem requisite and just."

The court action was the closing episode of a conspiracy to destroy Mary Baker Eddy, her person, and her teachings. Months before, in 1906, a magazine (*McClure's*) and a newspaper (*The New York World*) began publishing a series of articles. In the newspaper on October 28, 1906, Mrs. Eddy was described as "a skeleton, her hollow cheeks thick with red paint . . . fleshless, hairless, bones about the sunken eyes pencilled a jet black, the features thick with powder, above them a big white wig. . . . She reeled as she stood clinging to a table. Her sunken eyes gazed helplessly, almost pleadingly at her visitors. . . . It was clear the old woman had been doped."

In the magazine there was a recital of early years in Bow, New Hampshire. Mark Baker was described as "an ignorant, dominating, passionate, fearless old man tromping doggedly along a highway breaking the ground with a huge walking stick"; quarrels between Mary, "a child ten years old and her father . . . frequently set the house in an uproar"; all the children except Albert were without education; all the family except Albert "died from cancer." [3]

In the newspaper it was charged that aside from being physically and mentally incapacitated and under the constant care of medical doctors, Mrs. Eddy was under the control of "a cabinet" that was looting "treasure estimated at $15,000,000 and an annual income of an estimated $1,000,000" and that on her daily drives she was impersonated by a student. There were other charges. They drew an immediate denial in the form of a statement signed by Calvin A. Frye:

THE ANSWER OF CALVIN A. FRYE

Filed April 17, 1907

"1. The said defendant admits that said Mary Baker G. Eddy is a resident of Concord in said County of Merrimack, and, so far as he knows, the names and places of residence of the other persons named in paragraph 1 of said bill are correctly stated.

[3] Mark Baker was not an ignorant man. In fact, he was well educated. In a law suit between neighboring communities of Bow and Louden, he represented Bow and Franklin Pierce represented Louden. Mark Baker won the suit. There were no quarrels between Mary Baker and her father. All the children were given good educations. None of the family suffered from cancer.

"2. The said defendant is informed that said Mary Baker G. Eddy is 86 years of age; but he denies that her mind is or ever was so impaired by the infirmities of age and otherwise as to render her in her circumstances incapable of managing her affairs and protecting her property rights as to be able to exercise her full and unbiased will with respect thereto; and he denies that she is, or ever has been, incapable of managing her affairs and protecting her property with prudence and discretion against the undue influence, control, or fraud of others; and he denies that she is incapable of managing the present legal proceedings.

"3. The defendant says that he has been in the employ of the said Mary Baker G. Eddy for about twenty-five years, and for a considerable part of said time he has acted as private secretary for her; that during all the time of his said employment her said house at Concord, and all other houses in which the said Mary Baker G. Eddy has resided during the period aforesaid, together with all persons employed and residing therein or connected therewith, has always been, at all times, under the absolute control and direction of the said Mary Baker G. Eddy; he denies that he alone or in conjunction with the said defendant Strang or others of said defendants kept the said Mary Baker G. Eddy carefully or otherwise surrounded and secluded, either by themselves or by household servants selected for that purpose by himself and the said Strang or other of the said defendants.

"The said defendant cannot state how many persons see the said Mary Baker G. Eddy at her said house or elsewhere, nor does he know the exact length of time by her allowed to them when calling upon her, but he says that the said Mary Baker G. Eddy is and for a long time has been engaged in important religious and literary work, which, together with the transaction of her business affairs, consumes her entire time, and that, by her express direction and the rules adopted by her in the allotment of her time, only such persons as have the most important matters concerning which they wish to consult her are at any time seen by her; that the said Mary Baker G. Eddy determines for herself whom she will see, and the length of time that will be given for that purpose.

"He denies that he ever personally or in conjunction with the said Strang or other of said defendants refused to allow any person or persons to see the said Mary Baker G. Eddy or that he has prescribed or limited the time to be allowed to persons desiring to confer with her except in accordance with the rules prescribed by the said Mary Baker G. Eddy for the conduct of her household and business.

"4. Respecting the matters alleged in paragraph 4 of the said bill of complaint, the said defendant says that he is advised that the greater part, if not all of the same, is wholly immaterial, and upon this question the said defendant asks the judgment of the court. But as to such of said allegations as shall be found to be material, the defendant does not admit the same, but demands proof thereof.

"5. The said defendant denies so much of paragraph 5 of said plaintiff's bill as apparently alleges that said Mary Baker G. Eddy is mentally and physically unable properly to care for her person and estate, and that she is surrounded by designing persons who are using her and her condition for their own selfish ends. As to all other allegations therein set forth the defendant is advised that the same are immaterial; but if any of said allegations shall be found by the court to be material, the defendant does not admit the same, but demands proof thereof.

"6. The defendant denies so much of paragraph 6 in said bill as apparently alleges that the said Mary Baker G. Eddy has been and is transacting business either in her name by others, or by herself while unfitted for the transaction thereof, and as to all other allegations in said paragraph set forth the defendant is advised that the same are immaterial, but if the court shall find that the same are material, the defendant does not admit such allegations, but demands proof thereof.

"7. The said defendant denies that he now is or ever has been engaged in a combination with the other defendants, or any of them, or with any other persons, either to surround and seclude the person of the said Mary Baker G. Eddy or to take charge, possession, and control of all her property and business affairs and manage the same solely according to his or their own will and pleasure; he denies that any such combination has ever been effected or ever was attempted or contemplated by himself or with the other defendants, or either or any of them; and he denies that any act by the said Mary Baker G. Eddy, conveying property during many late years, has been controlled and directed by himself, nor, as he is informed and believes, by any other of the said defendants; and the defendant denies that the said Mary Baker G. Eddy is and has been for many late years not legally responsible for the acts done by her, and unfit to manage and control her business and property, but, on the contrary thereof, he avers that the said Mary Baker G. Eddy always has, as he is informed and believes, most intelligently directed and managed her business affairs.

"8.   The defendant says that he is advised that the matters set forth in paragraph 8 of said bill in respect to copyrights, the Metaphysical College, the Mother Church, and the real estate are immaterial, but, if any part thereof shall be found by the court to be material, so far as relates to this defendant, he does not admit the same, but demands proof thereof.

"9. And the said defendant answering further says that he denies that either he alone or with the other defendants and their associates acting with him have ever wrongfully converted to his or their own use or have otherwise misappropriated or unlawfully diverted large sums of money and large amounts of property of the said Mary Baker G. Eddy, or any sum or amount whatsoever; and he denies there is "abundant" or any reason whatever to believe that such acts ever were committed by himself alone or in conjunction with the other said defendants, or any of them; and he hereby demands the proof of these and all like allegations against him in the said bill of complaint set forth."

CHAPTER SIXTEEN

The Purpose Was to Destroy
Mrs. Eddy and Her Teachings

THE "legal proceedings" decided as necessary by *The New York World* were instituted by Attorney Chandler on March 1, 1907. Named as "next friends" were George W. Glover, his daughter, Mary B. Glover, and Mrs. Eddy's nephew, George W. Baker, of Bangor, Maine. The three plaintiffs were joined by two recruits on March 11. They were Mrs. Eddy's adopted son, Ebenezer J. Foster-Eddy, who was living in Waterbury, Vermont, and Fred W. Baker, of Epsom, New Hampshire.

Through several succeeding weeks there was an exchange of legal maneuvers. Acting for the "next friends," Attorney Chandler employed delaying tactics; acting for Mrs. Eddy and her supporters, Attorney Streeter strove for immediate hearings.

On June 15, Attorney Chandler filed a motion denying "statements made by Streeter (in a previous motion) reflecting upon the good faith of the 'next friends' "; and stating "that the 'next friends' are and always have been proceeding in good faith in this action; that no other persons or parties whatsoever having any interest in, control over, or direction of this action whatsoever and never had; that this action is none other than what it purports to

be, namely, an action brought exclusively by the next of
kin in good faith and from honest motives against the several defendants. . . .

"Wherefore, the 'next friends' pray:

(a) That said motion . . . filed June 5, 1907, be stricken
from the record, or

(b) That a hearing be ordered thereon in so far as the
good faith of the 'next friends' is questioned therein and
proofs ordered submitted, or

(c) That said motion be denied by this court.

(d) And that whichever of the orders prayed for is made
be made and the hearing concluded (if one is ordered) before any other order or decree is made in this case by this
court."

Scarcely was the motion filed when George W. Baker, one
of the "next friends," requested permission to withdraw
from the case and have his name stricken from the records.

Looking upon the withdrawal of Baker as a warning of
the possible collapse of their case, attorneys representing the
"next friends" filed a petition requesting a trial by jury and
stating:

"3. If a Master is appointed we believe that the only
instructions to him should be to investigate the question of
Mrs. Eddy's incompetency as averred in the bill in equity.
If any limitations upon these instructions are contemplated
we desire a hearing before a decision is reached.

"4. If any limitations upon the character, amount or extent of the evidence are to be prescribed we desire a hearing
before any decision is made. As the pleadings are not yet
completed, nor issue joined, we desire that this may be
done before any decision by the court in reference to any
mode of trial.

"5. Inasmuch as the defendant Frye has acknowledged
the wisdom and necessity of this suit begun on March first,

by causing Mrs. Eddy on the sixth of March to put all of her property out of her own hands, and as the 'next friends' are destitute of means, it is proper that an order should be made by the court for an allowance to the plaintiffs from Mrs. Eddy's estate to be used for the purpose of taking testimony.

"6. We will attend your Honor's pleasure in reference to a hearing upon the above suggestions at any convenient place and at any time after June 26."

The motion for trial by jury was denied. The motion for payment by Mrs. Eddy's estate of costs to the "next friends" was denied. The motion requesting a hearing of arguments was denied.

On June 27 Robert N. Chamberlain, member of the New Hampshire Superior Court, named Edgar Aldrich, a jurist of wide experience, as Master and as co-Masters, Dr. George F. Jelly of Boston and Dr. G. Alden Blumer of Providence, Rhode Island. At the same time, Judge Chamberlain defined the issue as being:

". . . Whether on the first day of March, 1907, and for such period of time before that date as may seem reasonable, to inquire if said Mary Baker G. Eddy was capable of intelligently managing, controlling and conducting her financial affairs and property interests. . . ."

On July 12 Judge Chamberlain revoked the appointment of Dr. Blumer, who had refused to serve, and in his stead appointed Hosea W. Parker of Claremont, New Hampshire. At the same time, the court "ordered that all objections to the Master or co-Masters be filed with the clerk of court on or before July 20, and stated that all objections not so filed would be regarded as waived."

In replying to the order on July 19, 1907, Attorney Streeter and his associates made it clear that in acting for Mrs. Eddy they neither withdrew, nor waived, "any objections or exceptions heretofore taken by her, (but requested) that the court may speedily act, so that whatever hearings the court determines shall be had before the Masters, may be begun immediately and concluded without delay."

Hearings were begun before the Masters on August 13, 1907, Judge Edgar Aldrich having announced that the single question before the Masters for decision was Mrs. Eddy's competence on or about March 1, 1907, to manage her own affairs.

Sitting as Masters were Judge Edgar Aldrich, Hosea W. Parker, and Dr. George F. Jelly.

Representing the "next friends" were William Eaton Chandler of Waterloo; Martin & Howe of Concord; John W. Kelley of Portsmouth; and W. C. Harriman of Nashua, all of New Hampshire; and Fred W. Peabody of Boston.

Representing Mrs. Eddy were Frank S. Streeter and Allen Hollis of Concord, and Attorney General Eastman of Exeter; representing the Massachusetts, New Hampshire, and Chicago defendants were Samuel J. Elder and William M. Morse, both of Boston, and Oliver E. Branch of Manchester, New Hampshire.

Because of the great public interest in the case, the courtroom was crowded, and press tables were filled by newspaper correspondents. Almost the entire opening day was taken up by Attorney Chandler in recounting the difficulties under which he and his associates had labored in preparing their case.

He dwelt on the lack of funds available to the "next friends" and emphasized his disappointment over the court's refusal to allow them compensation from Mrs. Eddy's estate. He contended that the "next friends" had been unfairly dealt with because of the court's denial of their request for a jury trial although under their own charges of "incompetence" such a trial would have been unconstitutional. He insisted that the "next friends" were placed at a disadvantage because they were denied access to Mrs. Eddy's presence for the taking of depositions—not one, but four or five depositions. He noted that he considered it unreasonable that a proposal should be made to the court requesting that the "next friends" file a bond to cover the costs of the litigation.

As the Masters were preparing to adjourn for the day, Judge Aldrich said to Attorney Streeter: "I do not ask that the question shall be answered now, Mr. Streeter, but sometime I shall ask you whether we are to be permitted to hear the statement of Mrs. Eddy in respect to her business affairs. I do not ask you to answer that now."

"May I not answer it now?"

"You may, yes. Let me say one thing further: the answers to this question, we think, will have a very prominent and useful bearing upon the scope of the inquiry in respect to time."

"I shall be very glad to answer it at this first opportunity," returned Streeter. "Mrs. Eddy's life is so occupied and her daily work so organized that if the appointment could be set for a particular hour it would be a kindness. Mrs. Eddy will be very glad to see you, will be pleased to have you come to her home—if the Masters, under the circumstances, will do so—she will be very glad to confer with you touching these matters as fully as may be, and it was because of her attitude of mind on that question that her counsel were so persistent in asking for an early hearing. I do not know that I can answer any more fully or frankly than I have. She very much desires it, and her counsel very much desire it, and at the earliest moment possible. And then if the Masters will consent, you can see her; you can talk with her and you can then decide how much time may be taken with her without unnecessarily inconveniencing her."

Attorney Chandler objected to Attorney Streeter's use of the word "confer," explaining that in the interest of not only the "next friends," and in the interest of truth, more than a single meeting should be held with Mrs. Eddy, following which he began discussing various subjects, some of which had little or no bearing on the case. Finally he was interrupted by Judge Aldrich:

"I stopped Mr. Streeter's general discussion of the question in order to see if we could have an opportunity of properly examining Mrs. Eddy. Mr. Streeter stated his position, which we think we understand. Of course, it is no disrespect to say to any woman of Mrs. Eddy's years that she is entitled to every court clemency."

Attorney Streeter explained his use of the word "confer," saying he used it only because it best illustrates what he had in mind. His thought was that the Masters should go to Pleasant View, sit down with Mrs. Eddy, talk with her, and be talked to by her, and that after they had seen and talked with her they would be better qualified to do the thing most likely to solve the difficulties, and afterwards, if it seemed right and best, an extended examination might be had.

Judge Aldrich agreed "that it could not be determined in advance and that it would have to be determined by circumstances, as they developed. Now, dissociating this case entirely from any talk about Mrs. Eddy's ability to come here, we think it entirely reasonable, out of deference to her, to go there if desired. I do not think it would be wise to examine with more than one counsel on a side. Counsel might confer about that. We did not bring up this question for the purpose of forcing it at this early stage, but for the purpose of knowing what scope we should give to the investigation. It may be unnecessary after certain things have happened to prolong this hearing very much, and, on the other hand, we cannot tell."

Attorney Streeter responded: "May I make a further suggestion to your Honors. I saw Mrs. Eddy yesterday and . . . I have no doubt, if it was agreeable to you, that the talk should be had tomorrow. But I would ask you to consider making the appointment to get there, say, at two o'clock in the afternoon. The reason I ask that is because her daily life is ordered with such regularity; I ask your Honors, if you can with convenience, to go up there at, say, two o'clock in the afternoon."

After listening to Attorney Chandler's objections to interviewing Mrs. Eddy at Pleasant View on the following day, Judge Aldrich commented:

"You may or not, as you please, confer as to the time, Mr. Chandler, but we desire, of course, to meet the suggestion conveniently to both sides, and you have been protesting pretty vigorously that you have not had an opportunity to see how things are done at Mrs. Eddy's. If we are to meet this question, and if we may hope to have an opportunity of going there under reasonable conditions, and you do not see fit to go, why, that is a pretty good answer to your protest. I do not say tomorrow or next day."

"I did not say it should not be tomorrow," returned Attorney Chandler. "I said I should not be prepared to go."

On the following morning when the court convened, Attorney Chandler proposed that the *first* meeting with Mrs. Eddy should be a preliminary visit only, and:

"2. There should be present, in behalf of 'next friends,' William E. Chandler, with right to examine, George W. Glover and daughter, for identification, and a court stenographer, for a full report."

"3. It should be agreed there should be five other examinations of Mrs. Eddy."

"4. As a result of the preliminary examination, if the Masters conclude that Mrs. Eddy physically cannot sustain other and thorough examinations, counsel for 'next friends' should be afforded necessary opportunity to have her observed by persons of their selection."

"5. If, as the result of the preliminary examination, it appears to the Masters that Mrs. Eddy is unable mentally to sustain further examination, they should announce that the plaintiffs have established a *prima facie* case."

"6. The hours for the examinations should be at varying times during the day, without notice, and no member of the household should be present."

Suspecting what was in the opposing lawyer's mind, Attorney Streeter was on his feet as Attorney Chandler completed his proposal.

"If your Honors please, this brings us to the preliminary question that ought to be settled. This is an investigation into the competency of Mrs. Eddy to manage her business affairs. It has been stated that this is not an investigation of the doctrines of Christian Science; it is a property matter. The question is, whether Mrs. Eddy's condition on the first day of March, 1907, required the aid of the court in administrating her business affairs. Now, in the opening yesterday there was not a syllable of a suggestion that Mrs. Eddy's business affairs had not been managed properly; no fact was stated, no suggestion was made, that any business transaction would be inquired of.

"We apprehend that the counsel on the other side have misconceived the purpose of this hearing. This is not, as we understand, a trial or an examination of the soundness of any particular religion. We ask your Honors now, at the outset, to investigate the question which is submitted to the Masters—the question whether Mrs. Eddy on the first day of March was competent to manage her business transactions.

"We are ready to show the entire management of her business affairs for the last twenty years, and the results thereof, and should your Honors see that, you will know the fact that there is absolutely nothing to the charges that have been made."

Led by Chandler, attorneys for the "next friends" protested the pertinency of the remarks, but the court permitted Mrs. Eddy's chief counsel to proceed:

"As a matter of law, these suggestions of delusions—which simply mean that Mrs. Eddy believes in some things that Mr. Chandler and others don't believe—unless those are in some way connected with the transaction of her business affairs, are absolutely incompetent.... The question is, was this woman capable of managing her business affairs? not that she believes in a particular doctrine upon that point or this point...."

In rebuttal, Attorney Chandler argued:

"This bill is a bill for an accounting to find out things we do not know and as preliminary to the accounting which would disclose the facts and show whether any wrong has been done or not, this question of capacity, mental capacity, arises, and these delusions are all pertinent as bearing upon that ... our case is that this woman has been possessed, for all these past years, of systematized delusions that make a part of her life, therefore are unfitting her for doing any kind of business."

Continuing his argument, Attorney Chandler sought to show that everything Mrs. Eddy had written or said or did belonged in the testimony as evidence of her incompetence to manage her own business affairs.

Instead of Attorney Streeter, Attorney General Eastman replied, saying, "I hope you will pardon me if I make a suggestion or two. I want to say that I do not understand that this proceeding is one for an accounting. The question now is as to the rights of these parties to appear as 'next friends.' If Mrs. Eddy is competent to manage her business affairs, then they have no standing in court. Now, that is the question which we are to pass upon, not the matter of the accounts; that is, is or was Mrs. Eddy on the first day of March competent to manage her business affairs? That is the question. If she was, why, then, there is no occasion for the interposition of 'next friends,' or anybody else. She is competent and has a right to manage her affairs the same as every other citizen of this country.

"... If it turns out that the property has not been well managed, then it is to be accounted for in some way, and if it is to be accounted for by showing that Mrs. Eddy has been under the influence of systematized delusions and is in a situation to-day bordering on senile dementia, or any other sort of dementia which may be named, why, then, that might be a cause for it.

"But if the property is well managed, if you should find on investigation that here is a property which amounts practically to one million dollars, and in that whole estate to-day there are not, as the saying is, any yellow dogs, but the securities are of the highest kind and of the best kind that can be selected, why, it is pretty good evidence that there has been good management of that property; and if, in addition to that, that every one of these securities has been selected by Mrs. Eddy herself, that would be pretty good evidence of her ability to manage the property and show that there has been no mismanagement of it.

"Now, then, if that question is settled one way or the other as I suggest—if it is settled that it has been well managed, and it is well managed, there is no occasion then to inquire what religious notions he may entertain, whether they are absurd or otherwise."

Attorney Chandler argued that with proper management

there might have been two million dollars rather than one million in the estate—and it was not possible to determine whether her property had been well managed without an inquiry into the delusions themselves.

Attorney General Eastman met this argument:

"I want to suggest one thing that I did not suggest before, that is this. That this court—not this tribunal, but the court sitting as a Court of Chancery—has no jurisdiction whatever in a case of this kind except in cases where property rights are invaded. If it were a proceeding which related solely to the person of the party, it must be with another court and before another tribunal; so that it is only where property rights are in danger that the court has jurisdiction.

"That is the first thing really to be inquired about. If the property has been well handled here, I say then that is the best evidence, provided we show that it has been managed by the party whose competency is in question. That is the best evidence of ability to manage it. As has been suggested, if it has been well managed, then that is the end of the case, as it seems to us."

Speaking as attorney for the "next friends," John W. Kelley asked Eastman "to explain the manner in which he would have an examination of Mrs. Eddy's business affairs made"; but Kelley was interrupted by Judge Aldrich:

"I don't think we will allow counsel to continue the controversy among themselves. . . . Perhaps counsel may as well understand now as later that this hearing is not for the purpose of disestablishing the Christian Science faith, treating it as a primary proposition. Neither is this hearing had for the purpose of laying any foundation for an accounting. . . .

"The theory of the opening statement is that Mrs. Eddy, who is a lady of eighty-seven years, is under delusions. Now, as a legal proposition, so far as it relates to property, it is of no consequence whether the delusions are in respect to religion, or politics, or other things. . . .

"If we understand Mr. Chandler's opening statement, it was that there were two kinds of delusions: one that there was a mental or spiritual force operating upon her 'next friends'—some force not seen or heard, but some occult force that was operating to prejudice her against her relatives—and that that delusion, if it exists, might operate upon her property management. This theory of the plaintiffs addresses itself to the question of relevancy. I entirely agree with the position of Mr. Eastman, that a delusion, however palpable and whatever its nature, is of no significance upon an issue of this kind unless it is connected in some way so as to be likely to operate upon her business management. . . .

"It seems to be fair enough to say that we are to have some sort of examination of Mrs. Eddy. We are unanimous in the idea that we should not make any hard and fast rule about it. We are inclined, not arbitrarily, but on equitable and humanitarian lines, to hold this examination entirely in our own hands. It strikes us that the presence of the 'next friends' would be more injurious to the situation than beneficial. We think we can see that it might, especially if there is a misunderstanding between Mrs. Eddy and the 'next friends.' On a public occasion it might be inappropriate that they should be present. We might think the examination of Mrs. Eddy should be entirely conducted by Dr. Jelly or by Mr. Parker or by myself, not permitting counsel on either side to ask any questions."

At a conference between counsel for both sides it was agreed that Chandler and Streeter should accompany the Masters to Pleasant View at two o'clock on that same afternoon and that a stenographer should go with them.

Before closing Judge Aldrich made it clear that the hear-

ing was not adjourned, nor was a recess taken, by saying
to the contending lawyers:

"We do not take a recess really. The hearing is going on,
but going on at another place. I do not see any occasion to
say anything about it." [1]

Upon returning to the courtroom, the Masters continued
the hearing and listened while Attorney Kelley introduced
a deposition given by Arthur T. Buswell, an early student,
on happenings and conversations that had taken place, according to Buswell, twenty-three years previously.

Attorney Streeter objected to the introduction of the
deposition as being testimony that had no bearing on the
case. Attorney Howe entered the argument on the side of
his associate (Chandler), saying that "anything in Mrs.
Eddy's life that went to show delusions was admissible."
The argument continued throughout the remainder of the
afternoon of the second day of the hearings, and through
the third day, with Howe charging Mrs. Eddy with "general
insanity" and with Chandler getting to his feet to inquire
of the court:

"Is a system of teaching the curing of diseases necessarily
a religion because it has the name 'Christian' put upon
it? I discriminate between Mrs. Eddy's so-called religion
and Mrs. Eddy's method of curing disease, and I put Mrs.
Eddy's various notions together and I say they are systematized delusions. . . ."

Judge Aldrich expressed the view that "we think that we
should not rule upon this question until we hear the parties, if they desire to be heard."

Speaking as Mrs. Eddy's counsel, Streeter said "We shall
be very glad to have a discussion of this question, because

---

[1] The full testimony given by Mary Baker Eddy before the Masters on
the occasion of their visit to Pleasant View on the afternoon of August 14,
1907, see Appendix V.

it is apparently a vital question, and the proposition is put up plainly now without reserve, that the Christian Science religion, as taught by Mrs. Eddy twenty-three years ago, was by an insane person, and the five hundred thousand or a million followers of her since are all insane, and we are prepared to meet the question."

As the third day of hearings neared its close, there came this exchange between the court and Attorney Howe:

> ALDRICH: If we were to assume that what you propose to show is a delusion, yet it is not necessarily the test, and I am looking at Mr. Chandler because that was the theory of his opening— it must be connected with the thing which you complain about, namely, want of business capacity by reason of delusions.
>
> HOWE: It is my understanding that before we can make that connection we must first get the evidence of the delusions into the case. Of course, a simple isolated delusion similar to the one I have mentioned—
>
> ALDRICH: You must get it into the case, of course, but if it is so general, or if its nature is such as not to tend to show the connection, it is too remote, is it not?
>
> HOWE: Certainly. If it is too general, so general that it has no bearing, it would be inadmissible, of course.
>
> ALDRICH: Then, in the sense which I have illustrated, if you should introduce something about Christian Science, which, you say, is a delusion, what bearing has that, as an abstract proposition, on the question of business management?
>
> HOWE: I do not understand that we are attempt-

ing to introduce anything of that kind. What we
are attempting to introduce are specific instances
of insane delusions, and for the purpose of arguing from them and asking your Honors to
find—

ALDRICH: Now, Mr. Howe, that is not the proposition which you put up to us yesterday. It
came upon the specific question in the deposition of Mr. Buswell, if that is the name, whether
Mrs. Eddy twenty-three years ago to his knowledge was practising the system known as Christian Science.

Much discomforted, Howe agreed that the question which
began the whole discussion was of little or no moment.
With this admission, the suit of the "next friends" was in
a state of collapse, although the voices of Chandler and
Howe continued to be raised through three more days, when
the case collapsed completely.

With the convening of court on the morning of the sixth
day, Attorney Chandler arose:

"May it please the court, it will doubtless be a relief to
the Masters to be informed that the counsel for the 'next
friends' have this day filed with the clerk of the court a
motion for the dismissal of the pending suit, and that they
hereby withdraw their appearance before the Masters without asking from them any finding upon the questions submitted to them by Judge Chamberlin."

Immediately, Attorney Streeter was on his feet:

"If your Honors please, in behalf of Mrs. Eddy, my associates, the Attorney-General, Mr. Eastman, and Allen Hollis, join me in presenting the following motion: That the
Masters proceed with the hearing, to determine the ques-

tion submitted, namely, Mrs. Eddy's competency to manage her business affairs. . . .

"Upon this motion I desire to speak briefly, and perhaps more temperately than the circumstances would justify me in speaking. . . .

"Now, your Honors, neither Mrs. Eddy nor her counsel have the power to prevent her so-called 'next friends' from trying to persuade Judge Chamberlin to let them dismiss the bill and get out of court. Neither have we the power to prevent their unconditional surrender in the middle of this hearing before the Masters.

"They volunteered to begin this wretched assault upon the person, property and religious faith of an aged citizen of New Hampshire and now . . . when their charges have utterly collapsed, they run to cover. This is their legal right, but I speak of the legal rights of Mrs. Eddy. . . .

"You were appointed Masters to pass on the question submitted in your commission.

"Knowing that upon the evidence there could be but one outcome. . . . She [Mrs. Eddy] has assented to every suggestion made by the Masters to enable them to arrive at a just decision. She has submitted herself to your personal examination in the presence of counsel for the alleged 'next friends.' . . . She has been asked to submit herself to the examination of hostile alienists, and, for the purpose of enabling you to reach a just conclusion in your own way, she has assented to that.[2] Nothing that your Honors thought would aid in the ascertainment of the truth has been objected to by her or her counsel. . . .

"Under these circumstances, we submit that Mrs. Eddy

[2] Dr. Allan McLane Hamilton, an alienist with thirty-five years of experience, was selected by Attorney Chandler to investigate the mental condition of Mrs. Eddy. Recognized as the leading alienist in the United States, Dr. Hamilton had been publicly critical of Mrs. Eddy's teachings. Following a long study, he released his findings for publication. See Appendix VI.

has a legal right to a finding of her competency—to such a finding on the case as it now stands. If you think otherwise, then to a finding upon such further evidence as she may produce....

"I speak, your Honors, not only for Mrs. Eddy, but for every other citizen of this state whose person, property, and religious convictions are now endangered...."

On September 30, 1907, the report of the Masters and co-Masters was filed with the clerk of the court, and on the same day Judge Chamberlin dismissed the case, but not without an exchange of opinions with Attorney Chandler.

Chandler requested a delay, saying he needed time to prepare in final form a record of his exceptions to ruling by the Masters that he might explain his request for dismissal of the suit.

Judge Chamberlin: "This is a motion to dismiss, is it not?"

Mr. Chandler: "Yes."

Judge Chamberlin: "What necessity is there for argument?"

Mr. Chandler: "In order that the court may note the reasons for the motion to dismiss."

Judge Chamberlin: "Mr. Streeter, do you oppose the motion to dismiss?"

Mr. Streeter: "No."

Chandler returned to his wish to submit a brief containing his objections to the rulings of the Masters. Streeter reminded the opposing counsel that having requested dismissal of the suit, he had no standing in court, hence was not in a position to demand the filing of any papers.

Judge Chamberlin then rendered his verdict:

1. Chandler was denied permission to file his brief.
2. The motion to dismiss the suit was granted.
3. The report of the Masters was affirmed.

4. Permission was given to the Trustees to be heard by the court on the subject of costs.

5. (a) The "next friends" were given until October 10, 1907, to file their brief on the subject of costs; (b) counsel for the Trustees was given until October 15, 1907, to reply; (c) both sides were given until October 15, 1907, to submit arguments.

On November 12, 1907, the court ordered:

1. The Trustees, by agreement, will pay the Masters' fees received as compensation, a judgment against the "next friends" for $3,000.

2. Judgments were given against the "next friends" in favor of the defendants for all legal costs.

3. The "next friends" were ordered to pay the regular court costs.

In this year of 1907—on June 8, it was—Arthur Brisbane, one of the best known of American editors, visited Mrs. Eddy and wrote of her in the *Cosmopolitan Magazine:*

"It is hopeless to try to describe a face made very beautiful by age, deep thought, and many years' exercise of great power. The light blue eyes are strong and concentrated in expression. And the sight, as was soon proved, is that of a woman one-half Mrs. Eddy's age.

"Mrs. Eddy's face is almost entirely free from wrinkles— the skin is very clear, many a young woman would be proud to have it. The forehead is high and full, and the whole expression of the face combines benevolence with great strength of will. Mrs. Eddy has accumulated power in this world. She possesses it, she exercises it, and she knows it. But it is a gentle power, and it is possessed by a gentle, diffident, and modest woman." [3]

[3] *What Mrs. Eddy Said to Arthur Brisbane,* M. E. Paige, Publisher. Copyright, 1930.

CHAPTER SEVENTEEN

Mary Baker Eddy Was Never Old

A T eighty-nine, Michelangelo was wearing, as Emerson
said, "the four crowns of architecture, sculpture, paint-
ing and poetry"; and, though wearing them, was found
walking alone within the ruins of the Coliseum.

"I go yet to school that I may continue to learn," was
his reply to a question. One of his last sketches was of an
old man, with an hourglass and a motto, "I still learn."

Of him, Emerson also wrote:

"Here was a man who lived to demonstrate, that to the
human faculties, on every hand, worlds of grandeur and
grace are opened, which no profane eye, and no indolent
eye, can behold, but which to see and enjoy, demands the
severest discipline of all the physical, intellectual, and normal faculties of the individual."

Goethe expressed it this way: "The beautiful is a manifestation of secret laws of nature, which, but for this appearance, has been forever concealed from us."

There have been many men and many women who have
found in the arithmetic of the years a continuing unfoldment, as the mind disentangles itself from illusions and
realization comes that work, all work, is cumulative; and
life, being eternal, is the same *for all.*

There have been many men and many women who did
not believe the arithmetic of the years put any limit on the

ability to serve, on the strength to work, on the capacity to learn—or that somewhere along the line is a place to stop and say, "There is nothing I can do."

And of them, there was one who understood that the "worlds of grandeur and grace" in the work of Michelangelo do no more than suggest the perfection in the universe of the Infinite.

Her name was Mary Baker Eddy, and it was in her acknowledgment of God as perfect and eternal that she found her life and her work. It was a conception of God that did not make prayer an occasional thing, and an acknowledgment that to live in God is to understand not one truth but all truth.

Recognizing her eternal duty as one of serving God, Mary Baker Eddy was never old.

Nor did she ever think she was.

Nor did it occur to her at seventy-one years, or at eighty-seven years, that she was too old to begin what was new.

When she was eighty-seven she founded *The Christian Science Monitor,* one of the world's great newspapers.

The idea of a newspaper had long been in Mrs. Eddy's thought, and it came to realization after the usual careful preparation. While in her twenties she was a contributor to New England weeklies, and in the second edition of *Science and Health* (1878) she expressed this thought:

"We have not a newspaper at our command through which to right the wrongs and answer the untruths being circulated about the teachings." On June 2, 1882, at a meeting of her own Christian Scientist Association, she declared, "If I have to give up other work I will have a paper."

Thirty-one years had elapsed since the second printing of *Science and Health;* more than sixty years had elapsed since the appearance of her first contribution in New England newspapers. Meanwhile, in 1883 she established *The*

Christian Science Journal, a monthly publication, and in 1898 the *Christian Science Sentinel,* a weekly publication.

Five years afterwards, with thought of a newspaper strong in her mind, she wrote, "Until I start a widespread press, we should have in Boston a born editor." In preparation, she named Archibald McLellan as successor to Septimus J. Hanna as editor of the *Journal* and *Sentinel.*

But before then, on January 25, 1898, she executed a deed of trust "for the purpose of more effectively promoting and extending the religion of Christian Science." Under this deed of trust she gave to three Trustees, the building and real estate occupied by The Christian Science Publishing Society at 95 and 97 Falmouth Street.

Having reached the conclusion in her eighty-eighth year that the time for a daily newspaper was near at hand, she began confidential discussions within her household, with the Directors and with the Trustees of the Publishing Society. On July 28, 1908, she informed the Directors:

> *Notice:* So soon as the Pub. House debt is paid I request The C. S. Board of Directors to start a daily newspaper called *Christian Science Monitor.* This must be *done* without fail.

And, on August 8, 1908, she sent an official message to The Christian Science Board of Trustees.

> Beloved Students:
>
> It is my request that you start a daily newspaper at once, and call it the Christian Science Monitor. Let there be no delay. The Cause demands that it be issued now.
>
> You may consult with the Board of Directors, I have notified them of my intention.
>
> Mary B. G. Eddy

There were many who disagreed with her because of her insistence on the words "Christian Science" in the name, saying the inclusion of the two words would handicap the newspaper beyond any hope of success. Mrs. Eddy was equally certain that the use of the words would protect the newspaper. The years have proved her right.

On November 25, 1908, the day before Thanksgiving, the first issue was on sale in Boston, and copies were in the mails to subscribers in Canada, England, and the United States.

In the introduction to his book, *Commitment to Freedom*,[1] Erwin D. Canham, editor of the newspaper, told the story of *The Christian Science Monitor*, which circulates throughout the North American continent and in 120 other countries:

"The Christian Science Church does not publish a newspaper for the purpose of maintaining contact with its members, or for stimulating them to deeper religious zeal or greater church activities. The paper is not published to advertise Christian Science. It is published as a public service, in the words of Mrs. Eddy in its first editorial 'to injure no man, but to bless all mankind.' This public service does in fact serve to promote and extend the religion of Christian Science, which is the basic obligation of The Christian Science Publishing Society, set forth in its Deed of Trust.

"The *Monitor* is a 'religious newspaper' in the sense that its fundamental obligation is to a religious purpose, its net revenues are turned over to The Christian Science Board of Directors, and many of its decisions and actions are motivated by profoundly religious criteria. By law and

[1] *Commitment to Freedom*, Erwin D. Canham. Copyright, 1958, by Houghton Mifflin Company. Reprinted by permission of Houghton Mifflin Company.

public authority, under the federal postal regulations and taxation rules of city, state, and federal governments it is defined as a religious newspaper.

"In a broad, nontechnical and nonlegal sense, the *Monitor* is not a religious newspaper. Down through the years, from the very outset, the *Monitor* was designed to be a 'real newspaper,' as its first editor, Archibald McLellan, defined it before it was ever issued."

With the *Monitor* safely launched, Mrs. Eddy turned her thoughts beyond the horizon of the moment to the years when she would not be available in person for guidance.

Already, she had written Archibald McLellan, one of the Trustees under the deed of trust, expressing her wishes regarding the institution [2] discussed with Mrs. Mary Beecher Longyear. Mrs. Eddy wrote to Mrs. Longyear on January 21, 1906, saying the subject "properly belongs to The Christian Science Board of Directors . . . for thereby we shall avoid much confusion in the future." In a letter dated December 12, 1907, she wrote to McLellan:

> *My Dear Trustee:*—I desire to commence immediately to found a Christian Science institution for the special benefit of the poor and the general good of all mankind. The founding and endowment of this institution will cost at least one million of dollars.
>
> Please come to me at your earliest opportunity, and I will give you further details.
>
> Most truly yours,
>
> Mary Baker Eddy.

[2] The Christian Science Benevolent Associations at Chestnut Hill, Massachusetts, and San Francisco, California, represent the fruition today of Mrs. Eddy's wish to establish a sanatorium.

The letter was published in the *Sentinel* (December 21, 1907) and in the following week, in the same publication. McLellan disclosed the founding of the institution, saying it would be known as "Mary Baker G. Eddy's Charitable Fund."

More than eighteen months passed during which Mrs. Eddy moved from Concord back to Boston. They were months in which the Fund was never out of her prayers. On July 27, 1909, she sent a new By-law for inclusion in the *Church Manual* to The Christian Science Board of Directors and attached to the suggested By-law a brief letter:

The Christian Science Board of Directors.

Beloved Brethren:

Please vote on the adoption of the following by-law, and if adopted publish it in our periodicals and in the Church Manual.

Mary Baker Eddy

The By-law read:

The Mother Church shall establish and maintain a Christian Science resort for the so-called sick.

The By-law was adopted, and there followed correspondence between Mrs. Eddy and the Directors over the ability of the members of The Mother Church to assume the responsibilities attendant upon the building and maintenance of such an institution. On August 11, through her secretary, Mrs. Eddy notified the Directors of her willingness "to let this matter rest for the present and suggests that you vote on the repeal of the by-law providing for the same."

By her request that the by-law be repealed, Mrs. Eddy disclosed her complete confidence in the Directors to choose the right time and the right way to "establish and maintain a Christian Science resort for the so-called sick," it being understood that the identification, "Mary Baker G. Eddy's Charitable Fund" was but temporary. The right time for the announcement came almost six years after Mrs. Eddy's passing.

In a statement published in the *Sentinel* on October 7, 1916, the Directors said "that preliminary steps have just been taken toward the formation of a new and important department . . . to be known as The Christian Science Benevolent Association." In the statement, the Directors told of their acceptance of "a gift," by Mrs. Longyear, "of a valuable tract of over twenty acres of land, beautifully situated in the suburb of Brookline, as a site for the first Christian Science home or sanatorium to be established and conducted by The Mother Church."

Chartered in 1916, the Sanatorium was opened in 1919. Yet, although fourteen years had elapsed since the first discussions between Mrs. Eddy and Mrs. Longyear, there was never delay. As Mrs. Eddy indicated in her letter to Mrs. Longyear on January 15, 1905, a great deal of preliminary work remained to be done before students of Christian Science would "be qualified so that under the fire of mortal mind they can stand, and 'having done all, to stand.' "

The years since have proved the wisdom of what appeared to be delay. Once students were ready "to stand" undismayed before the battering winds of materialism, she knew her church would continue. She was sure the truths she taught needed not Mary Baker Eddy to save them because they were eternal; but, standing beside them, she knew these truths would save her students and her church.

In the evening of a long life during which she did no one any harm and many people much good, Mary Baker Eddy's thought never left the ministry. As Clifford P. Smith wrote in *Historical Sketches,* "Christian Science had to have a Discoverer and a Founder." Doubt never entered Mary Baker Eddy's mind that she was chosen by the Eternal Father for the task. Humbly she accepted.

Believing that the stream of life always flows upward, she drew her inspiration and her strength from what she also believes is the source of all inspiration, and all strength— God. Finding God in prayer, a world of difference separates ritualism and the higher law her teachings represent.

She accepted completely the words of Jesus to the woman of Samaria: "God is a Spirit: and they that worship him must worship him in spirit and in truth." To her, the manifestation of the prayer of understanding is a great fact, a great assurance, and a great prophecy. In the perspective of the years, her discovery of the lost element of Christianity —healing—may well take rank as the chief event of the world's history of the past fifteen hundred years—take precedence over wars and national boundaries, great works of art, flights into remote distances, the scrutiny by man of the smallest detail of the electron.

Obscurity could not have been the lot of Mary Baker Eddy. Having caught a glimpse of the eternal life which testifies of the Christ, she could not do less than share her discovery with all mankind. All mankind was not willing to listen. Nor could she have remained obscure—because the Christianity she taught accepted the words of Jesus as meaning what they said. In *Science and Health* (p. 52) she instructed her followers:

> The highest earthly representative of God, speaking of human ability to reflect divine power, prophetically said to his disciples, speaking not for their day only but for all time: "He that believeth on me, the works that I do shall he do also."

Her teachings aroused the indignation of the clergy.

By practicing Jesus' commandment to his disciples, "Heal the sick," as being a commandment to all Christians, she could not avoid the hostility of the medical profession. By teaching "there is no death," she confirmed her acceptance of Jesus' statement in the temple in Jerusalem: "If a man keep my saying, he shall never see death." For saying the same thing, she was boisterously laughed at by the public and in the press.

It seemed not to be understood by the clergy, by the medical profession, by the public and by the press that in accepting his words to the woman of Samaria: "God is a Spirit: and they that worship him must worship him in spirit and in truth," she interpreted Jesus' teachings in their spiritual import. She did not, nor could she, belittle God with human conceptions or with human limitations.

Deep, deep in her heart was the conviction that "God will heal the sick through man, whenever man is governed by God." And with that conviction as expressed in *Science and Health* (p. 495) is another: "Truth casts out error now as surely as it did nineteen centuries ago. All of Truth is not understood; hence its healing power is not fully demonstrated."

In the *Manual of The Mother Church* (Art. xxx, Sec. 7) Mrs. Eddy expressed this hope: "I recommend that each member of this Church shall strive to demonstrate by his or her practice, that Christian Science heals the sick quickly and wholly, thus proving this Science to be all that we claim for it."

Time after time Mrs. Eddy proved her own words, and in an address to the members of her church in Concord in February, 1899, she called upon them to:

> Remember, thou canst be brought into no con-
> dition, be it ever so severe, where Love has not

been before thee and where its tender lesson is not awaiting thee. Therefore despair not nor murmur, for that which seeketh to save, to heal, and to deliver, will guide thee, if thou seekest this guidance.[3]

Through the years she continually emphasized healing. Here are a few illustrative excerpts from letters, only a few:

To know there is but *one* God, one Cause, one effect, one Mind, heals instantly. Have but One God, and your reflection of Him does the healing.

The power to heal is gained through peace, wisdom, love, dominion over ourselves, and good will toward men. You possess these graces of Spirit, or Christ power, only by loving God, Good, supremely. After this cometh the recognition of but one Mind which enables you to know there is no power or presence that can resist Good, or can prevent your prayers being effectual. While you remain in this attitude of mind you are obedient to the Principle of your being, and naught can hinder your healing the sick and the sinner.

You say "when shall we learn the way?" I reply, when you have *all faith in Truth* and no faith in error.

Healing is the best sermon, healing is the best lecture, and the entire demonstration of *Christian Science*. The sinner and the sick healed are our best witnesses.

Demonstration is the whole of Christian Science, nothing else proves it, nothing else will save it and continue it with us.

[3] *Miscellany,* pp. 149, 150.

As I understand it, God has His cause demonstrated in healing the sinner, and the sick. Jesus
taught this.

In the ten years that had passed since 1898, when Mrs.
Eddy formally organized The Christian Science Board of
Lectureship, these missionaries of her teachings were traveling as far from Boston as Hong Kong and, within four more
years, would be traveling the world. Whereas, ten years
before, a small hall was large enough to accommodate the
few who wished to attend Christian Science services in London, England, in 1908 throngs of latecomers were not able
to gain entrance to large halls where a Christian Science lecturer was speaking.

Upon these lecturers, as upon all members of her church,
Mrs. Eddy imposed one rule: "Be charitable towards all
men."

One of the early members of The Christian Science
Board of Lectureship was an educator, Professor Hermann
S. Hering, of Johns Hopkins University, in Baltimore,
Maryland. He became a member of the Board in 1905,
which was seven years after its inception.

Professor Hering's father was Dr. Constantine Hering,
who often was called the "father of homoeopathy in the
United States." He founded the first homoeopathic hospital in America, the Hahnemann Hospital in Philadelphia, naming it after Dr. Samuel Hahnemann, a German
physician who was the founder of homoeopathy. Hermann
was Dr. Hering's youngest son.

Hermann S. Hering entered the Department of Science
in the University of Pennsylvania in 1881, graduated in
1886, and in 1887 was made Professor of Mechanics and
Electrical Engineering by the Philadelphia Board of Education. In 1891, he was called to Johns Hopkins University
as Associate in Electrical Engineering.

In 1893, as a result of the healing of his wife after medical efforts had failed, he became interested in Mrs. Eddy's teachings. After three years of careful study he became a member of the Christian Science Church in Baltimore. In 1899 he gave up his profession to engage in the public practice of Christian Science.

Professor Hering brought to his studies of Christian Science the curiosity of one who had dealt with material phenomena and the curiosity of a physical scientist. He came to see and to say, as early as 1914, "through mechanical and chemical processes a material object may be reduced to its ultimate mechanical limits ... a form of energy ... in which every vestige of the characteristics of matter, or the object has disappeared."

Now accepted by physical scientists, these were unusual ideas in 1914. What they said was what Mrs. Eddy had been saying since 1866: "There is no such thing as matter." In the same year of 1914, Professor Hering also said:

"Those who question Christian Science healing should ask themselves whether they really believe in the healing work done by Christ Jesus and his disciples. If they do not believe in the spiritual power exercised over material conditions and its possible availability for all time, as declared in the Bible, then their opposition is not to Christian Science, but to the Christianity Jesus taught and practiced.

"Christian Science stands ready to come to their rescue and to bring an elucidation of Jesus' teachings which will result in blessings such as they have never before believed possible. Those who have not read the New Testament recently will do well to do so. Let me ask them to read at least one of the Gospels, also the book of the Acts of the Apostles, which record the healing done by Christ Jesus and his followers of that day which are verified by the works of Christian Science today.

"The fact that Christian Scientists do not yet do all the

wonderful works that Jesus did is a cause for regret, but not for discouragement or criticism. We are glad that Jesus' work proves Christian Science to be true and that Mrs. Eddy rediscovered the Science of Christian Healing and has given it to the world. This healing is possible in proportion to our spiritual understanding."

Among the medical doctors who became followers of Mrs. Eddy while she was watching over the affairs of her church was John M. Tutt, of Kansas City, Missouri.

After graduating from the college at Liberty, Missouri, which was one of the first colleges west of the Mississippi River, Tutt attended and graduated from the University Medical College, Kansas City. Here he studied under Dr. John Allen, both in the University and in Dr. Allen's office under his personal direction. Besides being President of the University Medical College, Dr. Allen was President of the American Medical Association.

After graduating from the University Medical College in 1900, Dr. Tutt attended the St. Louis Medical College in St. Louis, Missouri, following which he moved to Oklahoma, not yet a state, but a territory whose people preferred the name Sequoyah, in honor of the creator of the Cherokee alphabet. In 1906 the Congress of the United States voted statehood for the territory but rejected the name Sequoyah in favor of Oklahoma.

In 1905 Dr. Tutt was healed in Christian Science of severe stomach and other physical disorders after medical treatment and skill had failed. In 1906 he joined The Mother Church, became a teacher in 1916, and in 1917 was appointed to The Christian Science Board of Lectureship. He served on that board thirty years.

After pointing out that Christian Science makes no war on other systems of religion and medicine, nor upon the individuals subscribing to them, Dr. Tutt wrote:

"The natural oneness of religion and medicine is indicated by the early efforts of humanity to express that essential unity in speech. The root word for health and holiness in the Anglo-Saxon, and in the more primitive tongues is the same, and it means wholeness, completeness. Again, the Scriptures sustain the essential unity of religion and medicine.

"Prophets and psalmists and preachers, kings and commoners throughout the Bible, when they turned to God as a very present help in all sorts of trouble, were healed and saved from sin and disease. Christ Jesus earned the appellation, The Great Physician, not because he was a product of some medical college, or versed in the material medicine of his day, but because he was literally a healer of body and mind, a healer that never failed.

". . . Whatever it was that divorced the healing and saving arts, and whenever that calamity befell the human race and the hospital and the doctor took up their abode on the opposite side of the street from the church and its ministers, certain it is that Jesus, by his purely spiritual precepts and practice, reunited these great ministries as one in his theology and medicine. . . .

"In both theology and medicine Jesus utterly disregarded material theories and methods. Christ Jesus' medicine and theology were one with Spirit, not matter.

"This he illustrated when he said to his orthodox critics: 'Whether it is easier, to say, Thy sins be forgiven thee; or to say, Arise, and walk?' indicating the common origin of sin and sickness, and showing that he healed both by the same spiritual power and process."

Quietly, Mrs. Eddy watched over her Church. She chose to give The Christian Science Board of Directors jurisdiction, as authorized in the *Church Manual,* in the management of the affairs of The Mother Church, even withdrawing herself from frequent personal contact with members of the Board. There was an occasion when she counseled a straying student to obey the *Manual*.

In New York, on November 30, 1908, Mrs. Augusta E. Stetson used the news columns of the *New York American* to announce plans for the building of an edifice "rivaling in beauty of architecture any other religious structure in America"; and which, like The Mother Church, would have branches. Clearly, this plan to build a branch church, which, in turn, would have branches of its own, was a violation of the *Manual*. As Archibald McLellan wrote in the *Sentinel* on December 5, 1908: ". . . No branch church, however large, is privileged to oversee or supervise another branch. Such action would violate a fundamental rule in Christian Science."

In an effort to help the student to extricate herself from a difficult position, Mrs. Eddy invited Mrs. Stetson to visit her at Chestnut Hill. Upon returning to New York, Mrs. Stetson announced the abandonment of her plan to build a new edifice which would have branches, but persisted in practices so contrary to Christian Science teachings that the Board of Directors of The Mother Church finally was compelled to erase her name "from the roll of membership of said church." A few days later (on November 22, 1909) Mrs. Stetson resigned her membership in First Church of Christ, Scientist, in New York City.

In addition to trying to rescue a drifting pupil and establishing a daily newspaper, Mrs. Eddy used these quiet years to make quite extensive revisions in *Science and Health* and, in the same year of making these clarifications (1907), read her textbook consecutively from beginning to end for the first time. She continued her daily carriage rides and must have been amused many times, within herself, over public speculation concerning her successor.

On May 1, 1901, at Pleasant View, she had received a reporter for the *New York Herald* and, during the course of the interview, had been asked and had answered questions. To one question regarding the future of her church, she replied:

"The continuity of The Church of Christ, Scientist, is assured. It is growing wonderfully. It will embrace all the churches, one by one, because in it alone is the simplicity of the oneness of God; the oneness of Christ and the perfecting of man stated scientifically."

"How will it be governed after all now concerned in its government shall have passed on?"

"It will evolve scientifically. Its essence is evangelical. Its government will develop as it progresses."

"Will there be a hierarchy, or will it be directed by a single earthly ruler?"

"In time its present rules of service and present rulership will advance nearer perfection. . . . You would ask, perhaps, whether my successor will be a woman or a man. I can answer that. It will be a man."

"Can you name the man?"

"I cannot answer that now." [4]

On May 16, 1901, in response to many inquiries, the Associated Press carried a brief interview over its news wires:

"I did say that a man would be my future successor. By this I did not mean any man to-day on earth.

"Science and Health makes it plain to all Christian Scientists that the manhood and womanhood of God have already been revealed in a degree through Christ Jesus and Christian Science, His two witnesses. What remains to lead on the centuries and reveal my successor, is man in the

[4] *Miscellany,* pp. 342, 343.

image and likeness of the Father-Mother God, man the generic term for mankind." [5]

Speculation as to a successor had not lessened in the ten years that had elapsed since publication of the *New York Herald* interview. Mrs. Eddy now was approaching her eighty-ninth birthday. So, within herself, she must have smiled a good many times over the speculation. She had provided the answer years before the *Herald* reporter asked the question.

Soon after the dedication of The Mother Church, in January, 1895, there was a new order of services. In a letter to all Christian Science churches in April, 1897, Mrs. Eddy named the Bible and the Christian Science textbook, *Science and Health, With Key to the Scriptures,* as the only preachers of the Christian Science Church, thus eliminating for all time any personal pastor.

The first and second editions of *The Manual of The Mother Church* were published in 1895. On page four of the second edition the name of Mary Baker Eddy, Pastor Emeritus, headed the list of church officers.

Thus it will always be. In perpetuity, she remains the Pastor Emeritus of The Mother Church and the Leader of all Christian Scientists—but, in perpetuity, not the human person known to the world as Mary Baker Eddy, but her eternal self, the spiritual self as found in her writings. As she herself wrote: "Those who look for me in person, or elsewhere than in my writings, lose me instead of find me." [6]

As with her textbook, the *Church Manual,* and her other writings, so with her mission; each was completed.

[5] *Miscellany,* pp. 346, 347.
[6] *Miscellany,* p. 120.

CHAPTER EIGHTEEN

Journey Toward the Light

ONE day when she was living in Lynn, Mrs. Eddy was asked to help a sick baby. She responded, and found in the small home not only a sick baby, but two sick children and one sick adult. The adult was the baby's father, the other child her sister. The children were healed, and while the parents were still rejoicing, the father discovered that he, too, was healed.

Returning to her own home, Mrs. Eddy was recalling the experience when she heard the anxious voice of a student:

"Oh, Mrs. Eddy, when will we be able to do such work?"

The answer was forthcoming—as one who was present remembered—almost before the question was completed. In substance, according to this student, Mrs. Eddy said, "When you believe what you say!"

There was another who used not the same words, but who said the same thing. After failure to heal, his disciples sought the reason, and heard him say: "That whosoever shall say unto this mountain, Be thou removed, and be thou cast into the sea; and shall not doubt in his heart, but shall believe that those things which he saith shall come to pass; he shall have whatsoever he saith."

In her explanation, *When you believe what you say,* Mary Baker Eddy gave the complete testimony of her own faith.

Yet, even when using the words, she knew that while they were easy to say, they first had to be understood.

Understanding is a word of frequent appearance and specific meaning in her teachings. As she wrote in *Science and Health* (p. 297), "Until belief becomes faith, and faith becomes spiritual understanding, human thought has little relation to the actual or divine."

Mrs. Eddy often stressed the importance of healing in the practice of Christian Science. In the first volume of *We Knew Mary Baker Eddy*,[1] Abigail Dyer Thompson, a member of Mrs. Eddy's last class, wrote:

"At one time when our leader was talking with me of the importance of more and better healing work in our movement, she asked if I had been careful to keep a record of my own cases of healing for future reference. I said it had never occurred to me to take any particular note of them.

"To this Mrs. Eddy replied with earnestness, as near as I can recall her words, You should, dear, be faithful to keep an exact record of your demonstrations, for you never know when they might prove of value to the Cause in meeting attacks on Christian Science. Then she added, sadly, I regret to say that in the rush of a crowded life it is easy to forget even important experiences, and I am sorry that this has been true of much of my best healing work."

There were healings Mrs. Eddy recorded; also there were healings she did not record, but students did. There must also have been a good many that went unrecorded because the recipients did not recognize their benefactor. One such healing was related in an article written by Judge Septimus J. Hanna in the October, 1896, issue of the *New Hampshire Granite Monthly:*

"About the year 1879, before Charles Slade's door in Chelsea, Massachusetts, there stopped an emaciated pale-

---

[1] Copyright, 1943, The Christian Science Publishing Society.

faced cripple, strapped to crutches. His elbows were stiff and lower limbs so contracted his feet touched not the ground. (Mrs. Eddy was present in the Slade residence and saw the man.)

"A few weeks later, sitting in her carriage, Mrs. Slade noticed a smart looking man having that same face, vending some wares on the grounds where General Butler held parade. She drove to where he (the man) stood. Their gaze met, and simultaneously they exclaimed: 'Are you that man?' 'Where is that woman?'

"Then followed an explanation, he narrating that after leaving her house he hobbled to the next door, and was given permission to enter and lie down. In about an hour he revived and found his arms and limbs loosed—he next could stand erect and walk naturally. All pain, stiffness and contraction was gone; and he added, 'I am now a well man.'

"Mrs. Slade then answered his question as to 'that woman,' and afterwards narrated to Mrs. Eddy the circumstances." Mrs. Eddy recalled the case but told students who questioned her that believing the man "was restored to health" he passed out of her thought "until being informed by Mrs. Slade of his sudden restoration."

In one of her classes at the Massachusetts Metaphysical College a clergyman asked Mrs. Eddy if he could be healed of "a partial blindness." "Yes," she replied, "if you will only touch the hem of His garment." The healing was instantaneous.

Mrs. Laura Lathrop was invited to spend a Sunday with Mrs. Eddy. After dinner, Mrs. Eddy ran upstairs, with Mrs. Lathrop following as fast as she could because she had been told she was a victim of heart disease. At the top of the stairs, she collapsed. Turning quickly, Mrs. Eddy rebuked the error. Mrs. Lathrop was healed and afterwards learned that, knowing of the difficulty, Mrs. Eddy purposely had run up the stairs.

In the book *We Knew Mary Baker Eddy* Abigail Dyer Thompson recalled her own healing from hip trouble. The pain became so acute that her mother went to Chestnut Hill at five o'clock one morning, rang the bell and talked with Calvin Frye.

"Mrs. Eddy heard them talking," wrote the student, "and, recognizing my mother's voice, stepped to the head of the stairs and listened to the conversation. When mother entered my room a few moments later, even before reaching the bedside, she was greeted with the cheery ring of my voice calling to her the welcome message, 'Mother, I am better!' "

"Returning to our Leader's home at the appointed hour, my mother bore the joyful news of the sudden change in my condition, to which Mrs. Eddy smilingly replied, in substance: I overheard your conversation this morning and said to myself, It is time for me to step in on this case and save that child. Hurrying to my room, I dropped into a chair and immediately reached out to God for the healing."

The healing was complete.

In childhood, Mary Baker Eddy read and reread, and read again, the words of Jesus, and seeking spiritual understanding, took the words with her in her prayers. Years went by before she began to understand; when she was able to hear them the answers came.

The years went by, thirty-three years more—with the Bible always at her side.

At the end of those thirty-three years, Mary Baker Eddy was forty-five years old. The year itself was 1866. On February 1, of that year, she had fallen on an icy street in Lynn, Massachusetts, and, as stated in the *Lynn Reporter* on February 3, 1866, "she was removed to her home in Swampscott in a very critical condition." On Sunday, February 4, while reading her Bible, she was instantaneously healed.

For three years after her healing in 1866 she did little else but search the Scriptures for what, in *Science and Health* (p. 109), she called "a positive rule" by which she would be able to heal, to heal again, and to teach others to heal. She often remembered her mother's assurance when she was a little girl confined to a bed in the farmhouse in Bow, "God is able to raise you up from sickness," [2] and recalled her own experiments in homoeopathy and how they led to her own conviction that God is the healer.

Thus it was that in searching the Scriptures for the way to healing, she went with Jesus and his disciples as they walked together over the hills, through the valleys, and into the towns and villages of the fragrant land of his birth, and when they were in Jerusalem she went with them into the temple and in the evening into the garden that was just beyond the brook of Cedron, where he talked of his Father and of his Sonship—even as he turned the pages of the disciples' doubts, seeking to persuade them that the things they saw him do were not miracles at all.

They were the fruits of prayer, the prayer of spiritual understanding that has its roots deep in the eternal verities —the prayer that knows "the Father that dwelleth in me, he doeth the works." The disciples still did not understand.

Many times his disciples saw him bring sight to the blind, health to the leper, strength to the sick, life to the dead. They listened as he preached in the temple, and heard him say to the Pharisee, "The kingdom of God is within you." Twelve disciples were with him on that day when coming to the coasts of Caesarea Philippi, he asked, "Whom do men say that I the Son of man am?

[2] *Science and Health,* p. 359.

"... And Simon Peter answered and said, Thou art the Christ, the Son of the living God.

"And Jesus answered and said unto him, Blessed art thou, Simon Bar-jona: for flesh and blood hath not revealed it unto thee, but my Father which is in heaven."

Having told them who he was, there was the time, when he had questioned them after he had fed the multitude: "When I brake the five loaves among the five thousand, how many baskets full of fragments took ye up? They say unto him, Twelve.

"And when the seven among four thousand, how many baskets full of fragments took ye up? And they said, Seven. And he said unto them, How is it that ye do not understand?"

There was the time Peter questioned him about what appeared to Peter a miracle, and he explained: "Have faith in God.... Therefore I say unto you, What things soever ye desire, when ye pray, believe that ye receive them, and ye shall have them."

He had many disciples, but of the many only twelve remained on the night of Gethsemane, and while he was yet at the Supper Table, there were eleven. There were many times when he spoke of their unbelief, and knowing they continued in this unbelief, he gave them a last instruction on this night of betrayal.

"A new commandment I give unto you, That ye love one another; as I have loved you, that ye also love one another." And giving this instruction dwelt upon it: "By this shall all men know that ye are my disciples, if ye have love one to another."

Searching the doubts of his disciples and pondering the prayers of the Master, Mary Baker Eddy came into many truths. Theirs was a faltering belief that in him was the Christ; his was the steadfast awareness of the constant presence of God. His prayers were testimonies of complete surrender of self to the Eternal Father:

"I can of mine own self do nothing." "My doctrine is not mine, but his that sent me." "Return to thine own house and shew how great things God hath done unto thee. . . ." There was his prayer in the Garden before Judas came with the High Priest:

"Father, all things are possible unto thee; take away this cup from me: nevertheless not what I will, but what thou wilt."

There in three words is the full acknowledgment: "What thou wilt"—and by this acknowledgment he possessed his full heritage as a Son of God.

Three days later he left the tomb wherein Joseph of Arimathaea had laid him and appeared first to Mary Magdalene. Afterwards, on the shore of Galilee, Jesus asked three quite similarly worded questions, saying to Peter a third time, "Simon, son of Jonas, lovest thou me? Peter was grieved because he said unto him the third time, Lovest thou me? And he said unto him, Lord, thou knowest all things; thou knowest that I love thee. Jesus saith unto him, Feed my sheep."

Did Peter's thoughts go back to the night in the palace of the priest when he heard the cock crow—and hearing, wept bitterly?

Or did his thoughts return to the uplifted moment on the coast of Caesarea Philippi when, in answer to Jesus' question: "But whom say ye that I am?" Peter, still known as Simon, replied: "Thou art the Christ, the Son of the living God." And Jesus answered and said unto him, "Blessed art thou, Simon Bar-jona; for flesh and blood hath not revealed it unto thee, but my Father which is in heaven. And I say also unto thee, That thou art Peter, and upon this rock I will build my church."

And Peter came to know that the healings which seemed to be miracles were not miracles at all but "the divine Spirit, casting out the errors of mortal mind." [3] *This* was the rock on which he built his church.

In the forty days of his stay on earth after the crucifixion, "he was seen of above five hundred brethren at once; of whom the greater part remain unto this present, but some are fallen asleep. After that, he was seen of James; then of all the apostles.

"And last of all he was seen of me also, as of one born out of due time." [4]

One of the great religious statements of history is Abraham Lincoln's Thanksgiving Proclamation of 1863, part of which reads:

"Whereas it is the duty of nations as well as of men to own their dependence upon the overruling power of God, to confess their sins and transgressions in humble sorrow, yet with assured hope that genuine repentance will lead to mercy and pardon, and to recognize the sublime truth, announced in the Holy Scriptures and proven by all history, that those nations only are blessed whose God is the Lord....

"... We have been the recipients of the choicest bounties of Heaven; we have been preserved these many years in peace and prosperity; we have grown in numbers, wealth, and power as no other nation has ever grown. But we have forgotten God. We have forgotten the gracious hands which preserved us in peace and multiplied and enriched and strengthened us, and we have vainly imagined, in the de-

[3] *Science and Health*, p. 138.
[4] Chapter 15, I Cor., verses 6–8. Written about 58 A.D.

ceitfulness of our hearts, that all these blessings were produced by some superior wisdom and virtue of our own.
Intoxicated with unbroken success, we have become too
self-sufficient to feel the necessity of redeeming and preserv-
ing grace, too proud to pray to the God that made us."

There have been many times when men have forgotten
God. As Anson Phelps Stokes said when speaking of the
emerging nation in his work *Church and State in the
United States,* the conviction of the people was that "God
was their Father and that they were His children and there
was in them all a spark of the divine life which would make
them capable of great things if they would live worthy of
their birthright."

There have been many times in history when mankind
has sold eternal values for a mess of pottage; many times
when in the troubled climate of the mind the music of
Easter and Christmas and Sunday has not been heard;
many times when it seemed not to be understood that no
material possession is lost by keeping it subservient to its
chief purpose; many times when superficial cleverness has
left mankind wandering in a wilderness of confusion and
fear.

These things, confusion and fear, do not appear when
men know what is right. That which is right is chosen in-
stinctively. Truth always makes itself known to those who
unselfishly seek it.

Mrs. Eddy found in the troubled climate of the mind
Christmas and Easter and Sunday—all three. She heard
again the canticle of "Peace on earth, good will toward
men"; she understood why a manger more than a thousand
thrones had power to stir the hearts of men.

She saw that Easter represents the liberation of mankind
from the bondage of fear of death; she knew that Sunday is

the weekly acknowledgment of the event of which Easter is the yearly affirmation.

Mary Baker Eddy did not seek the path of comfort which could have been hers had she accepted the bounty of her sister; instead, she chose a most difficult path.

She chose to deal with the things of the spirit rather than with the things of the flesh. She sought to create in the hearts of men love of God and understanding of His ways. Conscious of the eternal freshness of the deep springs of life, her hope was to persuade people to claim their birthright as sons and daughters of God.

This birthright is stated in the Book of Genesis:

"So God created man in his own image, in the image of God created he him; male and female created he them."

And, being created in the image of God, life, for male and for female, is eternal—as Jesus said and proved.

It may be that Abigail, on that day in 1866, in Tilton, New Hampshire, looked at her sister in disbelief upon hearing the words of refusal. If so, it was because she did not understand that the younger Mary could not have done anything else. The younger Mary could not have abandoned her principles any more than she could have abandoned her love for God. Principle held her as much as she held it. There she was, herself and what she believed so vitally one that she could do no else than stand.

Mrs. Eddy distinguished between the human Jesus, the son of Mary, and the spiritual Christ, the son of God.

"This accounts," as she said in *Science and Health* (p. 30), "for his struggles in Gethsemane and on Calvary, and this enabled him to be the mediator, or *way-shower,* between God and men. Had his origin and birth been wholly apart from mortal usage, Jesus would not have been appreciable to mortal mind as 'the way.' "

Remembering that her teachings state that "the demands of God appeal to thought only," [5] so did the words of the Christ.

* * *

The young stranger came to Jesus asking, "What shall I do that I may have eternal life?" and heard the instruction: "Go and sell all that thou hast, and give to the poor." Sorrowing, the young stranger left, "for he had great possessions." Then said Jesus unto his disciples, "It is easier for a camel to go through the eye of a needle, than for a rich man to enter into the kingdom of God."

And, as the words of Jesus call for thought, so do Mary Baker Eddy's words of explanation. "It is 'easier for a camel to go through the eye of a needle,' than for sinful beliefs to enter the kingdom of heaven, eternal harmony." [6]

* * *

The opening sentence in the Gospel according to St. John reads:

"In the beginning was the Word, and the Word was with God, and the Word was God."

And a little further on in this paragraph: "And the Word was made flesh, and dwelt among us, (and we beheld his glory, the glory as of the only begotten of the Father,) full of grace and truth."

The words of explanation:

" 'The Word was made flesh.' Divine Truth must be known by its effects on the body as well as on the mind, before the Science of being can be demonstrated. Hence its embodiment in the incarnate Jesus,—that life-link form-

---

[5] *Science and Health*, p. 182.
[6] *Science and Health*, pp. 241, 242.

ing the connection through which the real reaches the unreal, Soul rebukes sense, and Truth destroys error." [7]

* * *

Having departed Dalmanutha, and having no bread but
a single loaf, the disciples were talking among themselves
of their oversight when they heard Jesus saying:

> Why reason ye, because ye have no bread? per-
> ceive ye not yet, neither understand? have ye your
> heart yet hardened?
> Having eyes, see ye not? and having ears, hear
> ye not? and do ye not remember?

The words of explanation:
"EYES. Spiritual discernment,—not material but mental.[8]
"EARS. Not organs of the so-called corporeal senses, but
spiritual understanding."
"Jesus said, referring to spiritual perception, 'Having
ears, hear ye not?' (Mark VIII. 18.)" [9]

* * *

Jesus was in the temple in Jerusalem, and after long
questioning as to his relationship with God, he answered:
"I and my Father are one." Not understanding, they who
surrounded him "took up stones again to stone him."
The words of explanation:

> ... Abraham, Jacob, Moses, and the prophets
> caught glorious glimpses of the Messiah, or Christ,
> which baptized these seers in the divine nature, the

[7] *Science and Health,* p. 350.
[8] *Science and Health,* p. 586.
[9] *Science and Health,* p. 585.

essence of Love. The divine image, idea, or Christ was, is, and ever will be inseparable from the divine Principle, God. Jesus referred to this unity of his spiritual identity thus: "Before Abraham was, I am;" "I and my Father are one;" "My Father is greater than I." The one Spirit includes all identities.[10]

* * *

On the night of treachery, and as the remaining eleven were eating, "Jesus took bread, and blessed it, and brake it, and gave it to the disciples, and said, Take, eat; this is my body.

"And he took the cup, and gave thanks, and gave it to them, saying, Drink ye all of it;

"For this is my blood of the new testament, which is shed for many for the remission of sins."

The words of explanation:

Our baptism is a purification from all error. Our church is built on the divine Principle, Love. We can unite with this church only as we are newborn of Spirit, as we reach the Life which is Truth and the Truth which is Life by bringing forth the fruits of Love,—casting out error and healing the sick. Our Eucharist is spiritual communion with the one God. Our bread, "which cometh down from heaven," is Truth. Our cup is the cross. Our wine the inspiration of Love, the draught our Master drank and commended to his followers.[11]

In perceiving the Christ, Mary Baker Eddy beheld the very presence of God. Whether preaching to the multitudes

[10] *Science and Health,* pp. 333–334.
[11] *Science and Health,* p. 35.

on a hillside by the Sea of Galilee, or surrounded in the temple in Jerusalem by those who sought to trap him in his teachings, or imprisoned in the palace of the chief priest on the night before Calvary, or walking unrecognized with two disciples on the road to Emmaus, the voice Mrs. Eddy heard was the voice of Jesus, but the words were to her the words of the Christ.

"Blessed are the pure in heart: for they shall see God.

"Render to Caesar the things that are Caesar's, and to God the things that are God's.

"Ye shall see the Son of man sitting on the right hand of power, and coming in the clouds of heaven.

"And beginning at Moses and all the prophets, he expounded unto them in all the scriptures the things concerning himself."

From Spain and Gaul on the west to Galatia on the east, and almost encircling the Mediterranean, Caesar's legions were on watch over the Roman empire. Tiberius was Emperor of Rome and Pontius Pilate was procurator of Judea. On this day within the far borders of the empire of the Caesars scarcely anyone was troubled over whether this man who was crucified was alive or not.

They did not know, but history was taking on a special character, a special brightness. It would be history very unlike that in which a Caesar was born, ruled, and died.

Where once his birth carried the year of a Caesar's glory, now almost all of civilization's calendars date from the year of birth of the one who was crucified. As Ernest Renan said in his *Life of Jesus,* "All history is incomprehensible without him."

Today, nearly two thousand years afterwards, the truths he spoke are repeated in more than one hundred languages; one day in every seven is set aside in observance of him;

there have come the festival days of Christmas and Easter and a host of other days of commemoration.

Yet, as has happened in some parts of the world, all idea of right and all responsibility to God is thrown to the winds. Substituted is denial of God and responsibility to the state, with its accompanying compulsion by all the people to do the will of one man. In areas such as these, justice and goodness are stamped out as signs of weakness.

Nevertheless, the force that was loosened through Christ is a force that will not cease until all its promises are fulfilled. And not even then will it cease. It will keep going on and on until *all* people grow into the understanding that in eternity there is no beginning and no end—only growth in spiritual power. God has not deserted His people.

Mary Baker Eddy lived practically half her lifetime with the distressing realization that human slavery was an accepted practice in the land of her birth. She early knew that man was given "dominion over the fish of the sea, and over the fowl of the air, and over the cattle, and over all the earth, and over every creeping thing that creepeth upon the earth"—*but was not given* dominion over his fellow man.

This authority God kept for Himself; and they who attempt to usurp this power will meet the fate of all whose acts are at variance with eternal law. They will be recorded among the failures of human history. Truth, deep-rooted in the eternal verities, makes men free because it bestows freedom.

Is not this why the Master said to those who believed in him: "Ye shall know the truth, and the truth shall make you free." Being inseparable from the eternal verities, freedom is a Gift that is wholly spiritual. Without this acknowledgment, it is useless to speak of or seek or hope for any other kind of freedom.

The Christ of Easter said, "In my Father's house are many mansions: if it were not so, I would have told you." We are scarcely beginning to realize that when he is free man is already living in one of those mansions. Spiritual in nature, freedom is a shaft of the dawn that proclaims the Light—the Light that is life eternal for all.

Preoccupied with the material world, there are those, and there always have been, who are so impressed by the acquisition of material knowledge that they cry "no" a million times to the question of eternal life, forgetting that it is not in time the wonder is. It is in life.

Having given nearly half a century of work and thought to persuading humanity to claim its heritage, even as Jesus claimed his on that night in the garden, Mary Baker Eddy was claiming what belonged to her. Her task was finished, although her hope of immediate acceptance was not fulfilled. Nor after the first flush of hope did she believe it quickly would be.

Nevertheless the lines of her teachings ascend higher and higher toward fulfillment. Converging upon the Highest, they are teachings that are prophetic of the future. Everywhere men are asking for spiritual reality. Everywhere conviction is arising that life has a deeper meaning than chaos and fear—that, in the words of Karl Barth, the Swiss theologian, "We must simply accept the fact that humanity is loved by God. . . . We must tell man that he is 'a loved one.' "

This Mrs. Eddy did from her childhood, first in the hope, then in the knowledge that in God's Kingdom there is no chaos and no fear, only spiritual reality and love. In her long quest for spiritual reality she knew that to think or act in fear and confusion was to aid what is evil because it suited the purposes of her adversary, "the evil one."

This is a religion which teaches that Spirit, not matter,

is the eternal element; a religion which declares that Christianity is not a sentiment but a power let loose; a religion which insists that everything that is not of God is destined to oblivion—a religion which speaks of "a Throne never vacant, a glory never departed."

The unbelievers say they are only words. Yet nearly two thousand years ago they healed the sick and destroyed evil as they did in the "ancient of days," as they do today, when it is understood that, as words, they do not stand alone. Standing alone, they are what the unbelievers say they are, *only words.*

Written not on leaves of memory, but written on the heart, they will move mountains as Jesus said they will. There is nothing new in them. They are words that are in the rhythm of eternity.

There is nothing new about Christian Science. It is the affirmation of truths that are everlasting. In her teachings Mrs. Eddy confirmed this continuity and gave it meaning. It is all the continuity there ever was.

In keeping with this same continuity, and on December 3, 1910, Mary Baker Eddy continued her journey toward the Light.

* * *

The closing hymn had been sung, and the congregation in The Mother Church, The First Church of Christ, Scientist, remained standing, waiting the pronouncing of the benediction by the First Reader. Instead they first heard:

My Beloved Students:—You may be looking to see me in my accustomed place with you, but this you must no longer expect. When I retired from the field of labor, it was a departure, socially, publicly, and finally, from the routine of such material modes as society and our societies demand. Rumors are rumors,—nothing more. I am still with you on the field of battle, taking forward marches, broader and higher views, and with the hope that you will follow. . . .

A hushed silence fell over the congregation and kept it standing as realization came that being repeated on this Sabbath of December 4, 1910, was the message Mrs. Eddy had sent in June, 1891, to the meeting of the Christian Scientists Association of the Massachusetts Metaphysical College to explain her absence in person—but now it was an absence that had a deep significance.

First to a few, then to all, came realization that their Leader was reaching out from eternity to take their hands, to steady, if need be, a faltering step.

Captain John Lovewell's Last Expedition

Published in 1831 and edited by John Farmer, Belknap's *History of New Hampshire* gives the following account of Captain John Lovewell's last expedition against the Indians. It was a company that was greatly distinguished, first by its success and afterwards by its misfortunes.

"Encouraged by ... success, Lovewell marched ... intending to attack the villages of Pequawket, on the upper part of the river Saco, which had been the residence of a formidable tribe, and which they still occasionally inhabited. His company at this time consisted of forty-six, including a chaplain and surgeon. Two of them proving lame, returned; another falling sick, they halted and built a stockade fort on the west side of great Ossipee pond; partly for the accommodation of the sick man, and partly for a place of retreat in case of any misfortune. Here the surgeon was left with the sick man, and eight of the company for a guard. The number was now reduced to thirty-four.

"Pursuing their march to the northward, they came to a pond, about twenty-two[1] miles distant from the fort, and encamped by the side of it. Early the next morning, while at their devotions, they heard the report of a gun, and discovered a

[1] The printed accounts say forty; it is probable that the march was circuitous.

single Indian, standing on a point of land, which runs into the pond, more than a mile distant. . . .

"They suspected that the Indian was placed there to decoy them, and that a body of the enemy was in their front.[2] A consultation being held, they determined to march forward, and by encompassing the pond, to gain the place where the Indian stood; and that they might be ready for action, they disencumbered themselves of their packs and left them, without a guard, at the northeast end of the pond in a pitch-pine plain, where the trees were thin and the brakes, at that time of the year, small.

"It happened that Lovewell's march had crossed a carrying-place, by which two parties of Indians, who had been scouting down Saco river, were returning to the lower village of Pequawket, distant about a mile and a half from this pond. Having fallen on [the single Indian's] track, they followed it till they came to the packs, which they removed; and counting them, found the number of his men to be less than their own. They therefore placed themselves in ambush to attack them on their return. . . .

"Seeing no other enemy, they returned to the place where they had left their packs, and while they were looking for them, the Indians rose and ran toward them with a horrid yelling. A smart firing commenced on both sides, it being now about ten of the clock. Captain Lovewell and eight more were killed on the spot. Lieutenant Farwell and two others were wounded. Several of the Indians fell; but, being superior in number, they endeavored to surround the party, who, perceiving their intention, retreated; hoping to be sheltered by a point of rocks which ran into the pond, and a few large pine trees standing on a sandy beach. In this forlorn place, they took their station.

"The Indians invited them to surrender, by holding up ropes to them, and endeavored to intimidate them by their hideous yells; but they determined to die rather than yield; and by their well directed fire, the number of the savages was thinned,

[2] The Indian, who lived in a nearby village, was hunting ducks.

and their cries became fainter, till, just before night, they quitted their advantageous ground, carrying off their killed and wounded, and leaving the dead bodies of Lovewell and his men unscalped. . . .

"This was one of the most fierce and obstinate battles which had been fought with the Indians. They had not only the advantage of numbers, but of placing themselves in ambush, and waiting with deliberation the moment of attack. These circumstances gave them a degree of ardor and impetuosity. Lovewell and his men, though disappointed of meeting the enemy in their front, expected and determined to fight.

"The fall of their commander, and more than one quarter of their number, in the first onset, was greatly discouraging; but they knew that the situation to which they were reduced, and their distance from the frontiers, cut off all hope of safety from flight. In these circumstances, prudence as well as valor dictated a continuance of the engagement, and a refusal to surrender; until the enemy, awed by their brave resistance, and weakened by their own loss, yielded them the honor of the field. After this encounter, the Indians resided no more at Pequawket, till the peace."

Judge Hanna's Address to the World's Parliament of Religions, 1893

REVEREND Mary B. G. Eddy, the discoverer and founder of Christian Science, was born in the little town of Bow, among the hills of New Hampshire. Her family tree, taking root in illustrious ancestry, spread its branches from London and Edinburgh, Great Britain, to the United States. The family crest and coat of arms bear these mottoes: *Vincere aut mori,* "Victory or death," and *Tria juncta in uno,* "Three joined in one." In her work, *Science and Health with Key to the Scriptures,* the textbook of Christian Science, the author writes:

> In this revolutionary period the voice of God in behalf of the African slave was still echoing in our land, when this new Christian crusade sounded the keynote of universal freedom, asking a fuller acknowledgement of the rights of man as a Son of God, demanding that the fetters of sin, sickness, and death, be stricken from the human mind and body, and their freedom should be won, not through human warfare, not with bayonet and blood, but through Divine Science.
>
> God has built a higher platform of human rights and built it on diviner claims. These claims are not made through code or creed, but in demonstration of "peace on earth and good-will to men." Human codes of theology, medicine, and hygiene cramp the

mind, which needs freedom. Christ, Truth, rend asunder these fetters, and man's birthright and sole allegiance to his Maker go on undisturbed in Divine Science.

I saw before me the sick, wearing out years of servitude to an unreal master, in the belief that the body governed them, rather than the Divine Mind. The lame, the deaf, the dumb, the blind, the sick, the sensual, the sinner, I wished to save from the slavery of their own beliefs, and from the educational systems which to-day hold the children of Israel in bondage. I saw before me the awful conflict, the Red Sea, and the wilderness; but I pressed on, through faith in God, trusting Truth, the strong deliverer, to guide me into the land of Christian Science, where fetters fall, and the rights of man to freedom are fully known and acknowledged. Christian Science derives its sanction from the Bible; and its divine origin is demonstrated through the holy influence of its Truth, in healing sickness and sin. The healing power of Truth must have been far anterior to the period in which Jesus lived. It is as ancient as the Ancient of Days. It lives through all Life, and extends through all space. Science is not the shibboleth of a sect, or the cabalistic insignia of a philosophy. Science is Mind, not matter, and because Science is not human it must be Divine. In 1867 I commenced reducing this latent power to a system, in a form comprehensible by and adapted to the thought of the age in which we live. This system enables the devout learner to demonstrate anew in some degree the divine Principle upon which Jesus' healing was based, and the sacred rules for its present presentation and application to the cure of disease.

The Principle of Christian Science is God. Its practice is the power of Truth over error; its rules demonstrate Science. The first rule of this Science is, "Thou shalt have no other gods before Me." The second is like unto it, "Thou shalt love thy neighbor as thyself." To demonstrate these rules on any other than their divine Principle is impossible. Jesus' sermon on the Mount is the essence of the *morale* of this Science. In 1893, for more than a quarter of a century, these rules have been submitted to the broadest practical tests; and everywhere, when honestly applied, under circumstances which made demonstration possible, they have shown that Truth has lost none of its divine and healing efficacy, even though centuries have passed away since Jesus practised these rules on the hills of Judea and in the valleys of Galilee. Jesus said: "And these signs shall follow them that believe;... They shall take up serpents; and if they drink any deadly thing, it shall not hurt them; they shall lay hands on the sick, and they shall recover." This promise is *perpetual*. Had it been given only to his immediate disciples, the scriptural passage would read *you*, not *they*. The purpose of his great life-work extends through time, and touches universal humanity; its Principle is infinite, extending beyond the pale of a single period or a limited following. His miracles illustrate an ever-operative divine Principle, scientific order and continuity. Within one decade this Science has stopped the illicit clamor and advancing trend of "free love"; it has opened dungeon doors to the captives of sin, sickness and death; given impulse to honest inquiry and religious liberty; moderated the appetites and passions of men; reformed thousands of inebriates; healed over one million cases of disease considered hopeless, and advanced the race physically, morally and spiritually.

I learned that all real Being is in the immortal, divine Mind, whereas the five material senses evolve a subjective state of mortal mind, called mortality and matter, thereby shutting out the true sense of immortality and Spirit. Christian Science explains all cause and effect as mental and not physical. It lifts the veil from Soul, and silences the false testimony of sense. It shows the scientific relation of man to God, disentangles the interlaced ambiguities of Being, and sets free the imprisoned mind to master the body. The first commandment of the Hebrew decalogue unfolds the facts of universal brotherhood; since to have one God is to have one Mind and one Father, and this spiritually and scientifically establishes the brotherhood of man. Also, God being the only Mind, it is found impossible for God's children to have other minds, or to be antagonistic and war one with another. Mind is one, including noumena and phenomena, God and His thoughts. Mind is the center and circumference of all Being, the central sun of its own universe and infinite system of ideas. Therefore Mind is divine and not human. To reduce inflammation, dissolve a tumor, or cure organic disease, I have found Mind more potent than all lower remedies. And why not, since Mind is the source and condition of all existence?

Christian Science solves the problem of the relative rights and privileges of man and woman on their diviner claims. It finds in scriptural Genesis, that Eve recorded last is therefore first, she is a degree higher than Adam in the ascending intelligence of God's creation. Woman neither sprang from the dust of which *adamah* was formed nor from an ovum; she was the first discoverer of human weakness, and the first who acknowledged error to be error. Woman was the mother of Jesus, and the first to perceive a risen Saviour. Woman first apprehended divinely man's spiritual origin; and first relinquishes the belief in material conceptions. It is a woman that discovered and founded the Science of Christianity.

The Revelator had not passed the transitional stage in human experience called death, but he already saw in prophetic vision woman "crowned with twelve stars," types of the twelve tribes of Israel, and the spiritual enlightenment of primal religion.

If brain, blood, bones help constitute a man, when Adam parted with his rib he lost a portion of his manhood. Man is the generic term for God's children, made in his own image and likeness, and because they are thus made, reflected, the male and female of His creating are equipoised in the balances of God. So let it be. To the sore question "What are the workingmen's rights?" Science answers, justice and mercy, wherein the financial, civil, social, moral and religious aspect of all questions reflect the face of the Father. And this question will not rest till both employer and employe are actuated by the spirit of this saying of the meek and mighty Son of God: "Therefore all things whatsoever ye would that men should do to you, do ye even so to them."

The following are the tenets of the Christian Science Churches:

1. As adherents of Truth, we take the Scriptures for our guide to eternal Life.

2. We acknowledge and adore one Supreme God. We acknowledge his Son, and the Holy Ghost, and man in the Divine image and likeness.

3. We acknowledge God's forgiveness of sin, in the destruction of sin, and His punishment of "Whatsoever worketh abomination or maketh a lie." We acknowledge the atonement as the efficacy and evidence of Divine Love, of man's unity with God, and of the great merits of the Way-shower.

4. We acknowledge the way of salvation demonstrated by Jesus, as the power of Truth over all error, sin, sickness and

death, and the resurrection of human faith to seize the great possibilities and living energies of the Divine Life.

5. We solemnly promise to strive, watch and pray for that Mind to be in us which was also in Christ Jesus. To love one another, and, up to our highest understanding, to be meek, merciful and just.

Mrs. Eddy's Reply to Bishop Fallows

Christian Science

I HAVE waited for Bishop Fallows to resign his task of misstating my views, in each of your issues. If his design was to call out my fire, I can assure him I hold no masked battery to open upon my enemies, and shall offer no plea or apology for doing good.

Is the above gentleman quite sure that my statement of "God, man, soul, mortal mind, materia medica, science, metaphysics, the Holy Scriptures, etc., has not the slightest connection with the recovery of the sick?" Also, that "hitting upon a novel plan to cause a concentration of one mind upon another, for the well-being of the body, is *all* of metaphysics?" Then he has gained this knowledge through his ignorance of Christian Science. He tried to support his lame logic by this—that "numbers have read my books and gone into the healing business," and some who are healing by mind-cure repudiate the science. Here we ask, Does simply "going into the business" prove or disprove one's fitness to heal? And if one becomes a successful healer merely from reading my books, does it not prove that my statement of Christian Science *has* "connection with the recovery of the sick?" And "out of the mouth of babes and sucklings thou hast perfected praise."

The exorcists of old healed in the name of Christ, and their method might have accorded with Bishop Fallows' views, but not mine. The chief priests of that period said of Jesus' method of healing, that Christian Science would represent, "He casteth out devils by Beelzebub." If my religious system (as he is pleased to term it) exemplifies the teachings and demonstration of our Lord, it should be known by its fruits; and that system or its adherent, that designates this system unchristian, is at fault. Neither by his writings nor by healing, has the aforesaid gentleman furnished the first evidence, on the basis of my scientific statement, that he understands my works, principle or practice. It is a widely acknowledged fact that if he had a correct knowledge of my text-book, he could *prove* my statements true.

I challenge Bishop Fallows to this fair play and Christian consistency, namely: to demonstrate his knowledge of my system by healing the sick, or, failing to do this, and exposing his ignorance of the system that he condemns before understanding, he shall relinquish his vanity as a critic and prove his claim to a gentleman. As the founder, at this period, of Christian Science, I attest that he utterly fails to comprehend my statement of it. His explanation of one mind transferring its thoughts to another mind, thereby affecting the body, the human giving aid to the divine in its method of healing, is no more correct than to say a man assists the fall of an apple under the law of gravitation. It is virtually a denial of divine power to attribute all healing to mortals, implying it is done, either by mortal mind, or by a drug clad with more power than Deity.

His mental muddle confounding Christian Science with hypnotism, would make it the transference of mortal thought, or the grander secret of concentration! When to comprehend this science in the slightest sense, one must see beyond the rubbish of mortal thought, and be there to demonstrate the science.

To understand my use of the term *"God,"* one must exchange the evidence gained from the material senses, for spiritual evidence, namely, a true sense of divine power, the *omnis potens* of Spirit, the scientific sense in which I employ the term, and should find no fault with it begirt with additional power.

To learn my meaning of the term *"man,"* one must exchange the sense of man as sinning, sick and dying—that mortal sense "conceived in sin and brought forth in iniquity"—for the spirit-

ual sense of man, born not of the flesh, but of Spirit, made after
the image and likeness of God. Then would he improve more
rapidly the race, by transferring God's mind-pictures to mortals,
which correct their poor models, learn in part my definition of
man, and choose according to Christian Science, reason and
revelation, the divine model in thought, which helps to bring
out the true likeness.

To understand my use of the term *"Soul,"* he is to discern the
meaning of this scripture,—"the soul that sinneth shall die," and
see that Soul must be sinless to be immortal, the synonym of
Spirit, God. Man but reflects God, and it no more follows that
God, Soul, is in him, than that our earth contains the sun because it reflects his light.

To perceive the spiritual side and meaning of nature, one
should understand "metaphysics," as Paul expressed metaphysics
—"absent from the body and present with the Lord"—wherein
we learn the nothingness of matter, sensualisms, sickness, sin
and death, and the great somethingness of Spirit, through the
discipline, purification and sanctification whereby the facts of
Spirit are discerned, and the pure in heart see God. Proportion-
ately as the realities of Spirit appear, do the so-called pleasures
and pains of the body disappear; to admit the unreality of
matter tends to support the great facts of Spirit, eternal Life,
Truth, and Love.

To interpret to human thought the divine order of healing
and salvation is to discard the paganism of drugs, all idolatries
and false gods, since drugging originated in the loss of spiritual
power and the mythology of pagan priests. We should adopt the
"Materia Medica" and theology of the son of the Blessed, for
they are one and the same. When the devil was cast out the
dumb spake. To master the errors of the flesh with the divine
truths of Spirit, is the grand verity of Christian healing.

My definition of *"mortal mind,"* is a will opposed to the
Divine Mind; all that is sin, sickness and death; the transference
of mortal erring thought from one mind to another. Because of
the proof that Jesus gave healing the sick we should not ques-

tion in that it is the will of the Father to save man from sickness as well as sin. Christian Science is not scanned at a glance, summed up a lucky hit at concentration!

One human mind bringing its own supposed forces to concentrate upon another for the accomplishment of any object, is a mistaken kindness, the antipode of science or Christianity; it is a species of animal magnetism capable of all diabolism. The true method of Mind is so to concentrate with the lens of divine science the rays of immortal truth upon mortal error as to destroy it.

On March 15, during my sermon, a sick man was healed. This man had been assisted into the church by two men, a crutch and cane, but he walked out of it erect and strong, with cane and crutch under his arm. I was not acquainted with the gentleman, was not even aware of his presence, he having been helped to a seat before I entered. Other chronic cases of disease of which I was ignorant, were healed while I was preaching. Was that the effect of concentrating my mind upon the sick? Let us obey the divine command, "Render therefore unto Caesar the things which are Caesar's; and to God the things that are God's." [1]

[1] *Mind in Nature*, June, 1885.

Secretaries to Mrs. Eddy

Besides Calvin A. Frye, who was Mrs. Eddy's secretary from 1882 to 1910, the following Christian Scientists also served as secretaries to Mrs. Eddy at various periods from 1900 to 1910:

Gilbert C. Carpenter
Adam H. Dickey
Francis J. Fluno
Thomas W. Hatten
George H. Kinter
John Carroll Lathrop
Joseph G. Mann
Archibald McLellan
William R. Rathvon
Lewis C. Strang
Irving C. Tomlinson
Henry Cornell Wilson

Testimony of Mary Baker Eddy
Before the Masters at Pleasant View
on August 14, 1907

JUDGE ALDRICH: Mrs. Eddy, the gentlemen here wish to have an interview with you, and we desire to make this call as comfortable as possible for you, and we want you to let us know if we weary you.

MRS. EDDY: I am very glad to see you, and I thank you.

Q.: What is your native town?

A.: Bow, in New Hampshire. My father's farm lies on the banks of the Merrimack. He did much of his haying in Concord, but the house was in Bow.

Q.: How long have you lived in Concord?

A.: At this time, do you mean? About twenty years; between eighteen and twenty since I came here, after my marriage and residence in Boston.

Q.: Well, the gentlemen present want to ask you some questions, and we all want to make this interview as pleasant for you as possible...

A.: Thank you very much.

Q.: And to have regard all the time to your comfort and convenience, and if you feel at all fatigued, we want you to say so at any time.

A.: What?

Q.: If you feel fatigued, we want to have you speak of it and let us know.

A.: Thank you. I can work hours at my work, day and night, without the slightest fatigue when it is in the line of spiritual labor.

Q.: Did you acquire all this property here at the outset, or did you purchase it gradually?

A.: I purchased it at the outset and suggested every construction and arrangement of my grounds throughout, and I still attend to it.

Q.: How many acres have you?

A.: Really, I do not know the number of acres.

Q.: Well, that is something that women do not always carry in their minds.

A.: This little pond (indicating) was made for me by my friends. It is an artificial pond. I have a little boat down there, and the boathouse.

Q. (by Dr. Jelly): All this has been done under your direction, has it? The development of this place has all been under your direction, has it?

A.: It has. You can ask my foreman, August Mann. He resides in the cottage.

Q. (by Dr. Jelly): We shall be glad to take your word for it, Mrs. Eddy.

Q. (by Mr. Parker): Do you raise fruit here on the place? I see you have fruit trees.

A.: Yes, sir.

Q.: Oh, you do?

A.: And there were no trees here except pines when I came here. The rest of the trees I have planted, and when I suggested that a large tree be planted they laughed at me, but I said, "Try it and see if it will succeed." Every one of these trees around here (indicating) was planted by myself—that is, not by myself, but at my direction.

Q. (by Judge Aldrich): I have heard now and then that you have taken an interest in public affairs round about Concord and other places in New Hampshire. What about that? I have heard occasionally that you have given money to the city of Concord, and perhaps to other parts of the state, for highways, and other institutions. What about that?

A.: I have, with great pleasure. When I came here they had no State Fair grounds, and very little pavement. A one-horse car moved once an hour. There was very little being done in Concord then compared with what I anticipated when I came. It seemed to be going out, and I admire the apparent vigor and flourishing condition of this dear city now. I had great desire to build up my native place. . . . Am I talking too much?

Q.: No. We are all interested in what you say.

A.: They asked me in Boston to remain. Jordan & Marsh, White, and other firms requested me not to leave the city, and they said to me, "Have we not helped you to accumulate money since you have been here?" And I replied, "Have I not helped you?" And they said, "Yes, you have, and that is why we want to have you stay." Then I said, "I want to go home and help my native state a little."

Q. (by Dr. JELLY): And that was how long ago, Mrs. Eddy?

A.: Between eighteen and twenty years.

Q.: Did you go directly to this place then—to this spot?

A.: I did, and there was a hut here, a simple hut. I had it moved off and I made what is here. The house was not built by myself; it was moved from where my cottage is. I built the cottage and moved that house which was then in its place here.

Q.: (by Mr. PARKER): Did you come direct from Boston here?

A.: I did.

Q.: To this very place here?

A.: Yes sir. They laughed at me for taking this place, and I said, "You will see, it will be pretty, soon."

Q.: Did you live on State Street here in this town? Didn't you live on State Street at a time?

A.: I did not at this time, but I have resided on State Street.

Q.: When was that, Mrs. Eddy?

A.: It was when I—Well, I should think it was about seventeen years ago.

Q.: How long did you live there, Mrs. Eddy, on State Street?

A.: About two years.

Q.: And from State Street you came here?

A.: Yes.

Q.: Then, when you came from Boston you came and resided on State Street first, didn't you?

A.: I did. I had forgotten that.

Q.: And from State Street you moved here?

A.: Yes sir.

Q. (by JUDGE ALDRICH): Some one was telling me that you had given to the public streets—the improvement of streets in Concord—is that so?

A.: I have, $10,000 at one time.

Q.: Where was that expended?

A.: It has been expended on this street and on other streets, Main Street and State Street.

Q.: Was it done at the suggestion of anybody, or was it your own idea?

A.: It was mine. They consulted me with regard to it. My students contributed toward it also and left the decision to me. When I built this church here, I put into it one-half of my property. Mr. Whitcomb, the builder, an honest man, told me it cost over $200,000.

Q.: It is a beautiful structure.

A.: I think so.

Q.: Now about your investments; we will touch on those just a little today, not much. About your investments. You have some income, I suppose, now?

A.: Some income, yes.

Q.: My life insurance is coming due pretty soon, and I want to make good use of it. What do you consider good investments?

A.: I do not put it into life insurance. God insures my life.

Q.: I carry a little life insurance and it is coming due, so I am interested, you know. You wouldn't advise my throwing it away, would you? For instance, my life insurance comes due next year.

A.: Yes, I respect that. I respect the life insurance. I think it is very valuable to many, but I have not any need for it.

Q.: It was not really in that sense that I suggested it. I wanted to get your idea as to what would be a good investment.

A.: Yes.

Q.: What did you say?

A.: Shall I tell you my ideas?

Q.: Yes.

A.: Trust in God. God is infinite. Therefore, if we are the image and the likeness of Infinity, we have no beginning and no end, and are His image and likeness; that is my life insurance.

Q.: It is not a question of that at all—at least, my thoughts were not running in that particular direction, but, what would be a sound investment of money that comes from life insurance or anything else?

A.: Well, I should invest it in the hands, at my age, of trustees that I could vouch for and from my own knowledge. And why? Because, when I found my church was gaining over 40,000 members, and the field demanding me all over the world, I could not carry on the letters, make answers to inquiries that were made of me. Then I said, "Which shall I do, carry on this business that belongs to property, or shall I serve God?" And I said—and it came to me from the Bible—"Choose ye this day whom ye will serve. Ye cannot serve God and mammon." Then I chose, and I said, "So help me God," and I launched out, and gave my property—I gave $913,000 to the trusteeship, to others for the benefit of my son—no, not for the benefit of my son, but—$913,000 into the trusteeship for myself. For my son I have $125,000 into trusteeship for himself and for his family.

Q. (by JUDGE ALDRICH): Where did that idea of putting your property into the hands of trustees originate, with yourself or with someone else?

A.: Utterly with myself. It came to me in an hour in this

room, and I think the first one that I named it to was Laura Sargent, and I said to her, "Do not speak of it, but I feel impressed that it is my duty."

Q.: When was that?

A.: That was in February, 1907.

Q.: Last winter, you mean?

A.: I do.

Q.: Now this is all interesting and useful, but still I have not made myself understood. For instance, without regard to your trusteeship now, if you had a hundred thousand dollars to invest today, and we will lay aside for the purpose of this question the matter of trusteeship, what kind of investments would you consider sound, municipal bonds, or government bonds, or bank stock, or what?

A.: I prefer government bonds. I have invested largely in government bonds, and I prefer bonds to stocks. I have not entered into stocks.

Q.: Why?

A.: Because I did not think it was safe for me. I did not want the trouble of it, that was all. Perhaps I was mistaken, but that is my business sense of it, and the only time I took the advice of a student and went contrary, I lost ten thousand dollars by it.

Q.: What was that?

A.: That was in an investment that was made in property in the West, where the land, they said, was coming up and going to be a great advancement in value, and I lost it, and I never got caught again. I always selected my own investments.

Q.: How do you select them now?

A.: Now?

Q.: Yes.

A.: I leave them to my trustees.

Q.: Before that?

A.: I will tell you. I have books that give definitely the population of the states, and their money values, and I consult these, and when I see they are large enough in population and valuation to warrant an investment I make it.

Q.: Well, now, upon what philosophy do you base your calculations upon population? Why do you take population as the standard?

A.: Because I think they can sustain their debts and pay them.

Q.: Well, I should think that was pretty sound. Would you go West for municipal investments, or would you rather trust yourself in the East, in New England we will say?

A.: I would rather trust my trustees now. I do not take those things into consideration.

Q.: Dr. Jelly desires that I should ask you, laying aside for the present the matter of trusteeship, what would be your idea, whether there was greater security of investment in Eastern municipalities or Western?

A.: The East, I should say.

Q. (by DR. JELLY): Mrs. Eddy, are you willing to tell us something about the development of your special religion? Are you willing to tell us about how the matter came about, and how it has existed and developed? It would be interesting to us to know, if you are willing to tell us, about Christian Science. Tell us something about the development of that; are you willing to do it?

A.: I would love to do it.

Q.: Tell us as fully as you please. I think we would all like to hear about it.

A.: I was an invalid born in belief. I was always having doctors—

Q.: When you say "born in belief," I perhaps do not understand what you mean.

A.: I mean born according to human nature, born not of God, but of the flesh. That is what I mean. I was an invalid from my birth.

Q.: Can you tell us something about the way in which you were an invalid, if you can recollect it?

A.: No, I cannot recollect it, only I was considered weak and delicate.

Q.: I asked you to tell us something about the development of Christian Science. Will you go on, if you please?

A.: My father employed M.D.'s of the highest character, and they were estimable men, and they would say—Dr. Renton was one, and he said, and the others said: "Do not doctor your child, she has got too much brains for her body; keep her outdoors, keep her in exercise, and keep her away from school all you can, and do not give her much medicine." Then it was all allopathy, you know.

Q.: Can you tell us how long ago that was, please—about how long? I don't suppose you can tell exactly, but somewhere near.

A.: No. I should say I was eighteen years old, perhaps, and it came to me through Dr. Morrill, he was a homœopath, and I had never heard of it before; it was a new subject in New Hampshire, and father said: "I thought he was a fine fellow, but he must have gone mad to have taken up homœopathy." That was the general idea of things then. When Dr. Morrill came to Concord he healed cases that the other M. D.'s did not, and my father employed him, and I got well under his treatment. Then you asked me to tell my footsteps? I said, I will study homœopathy. I did. I was delighted with it. I took a case that a doctress considered hopeless, and I cured the case. It was dropsy; the patient looked like a barrel in the bed, and I cured her. I began to think something about what it was that cured, when the highest attenuation—

Q.: What did you say about the highest attenuation?

A.: I began with the highest attenuation in which the drug absolutely disappeared, and I sent that attenuation to Dr. Jackson of Boston and asked him if he could discover the origin of that? It was common table salt.

Q.: Was it Dr. Charles T. Jackson, the chemist?

A.: Yes sir, and he replied to me, "I cannot find a particle of salt in it."

Q.: I knew him personally.

A.: Did you?

Q.: Yes.

A.: Then I said, "I will be safe and see if I am deceived," and went to work on a patient. I gave her a high attenuation of medicine, and she took it and recovered quite rapidly. Then there were symptoms of relapse, and I had been quite interested in homœopathy and thought that by giving too much of this diluted, attenuated medicine there might be a crisis produced and difficulty, so I took away the medicine and gave her a single pellet unmedicated, nothing but a sugar pellet, and she gained just the same. At last I said to her, "Now you need no more medicine; go without it," and she said, "I will." In three days she came to me and said "I feel some of the old symptoms." I repeated my pellet, not one particle of medicine, and she began to gain again.

That was my first discovery of the Science of Mind. That was a falling apple to me—it made plain to me that mind governed the whole question of her recovery. I was always praying to be kept from sin, and I waited and prayed for God to direct me. The next that I encountered were spiritualist who were claiming to be mediums. I went into their seances to find out what they were doing. Shall I go on with this unnecessary detail?

DR. JELLY: I will not trouble you to go into that in any further particulars just now, but Mr. Parker would like to ask you a few questions.

MRS. EDDY: Yes. Shall I continue this subject to show how I entered into the understanding of Christian Science?

DR. JELLY: I will leave that to Mr. Parker.

Q. (by MR. PARKER) : I want to talk about everyday affairs. May I?

A.: Yes.

Q.: If we desire on some other occasion to have a talk with you, we will come again.

A.: Thank you.

Q.: Mrs. Eddy, you have not traveled much—you have not gone about the state much, have you?

A.: No, I have not.

Q.: Do you know where I live?

A.: No, I do not.

Q.: I live in Claremont.

A.: In Claremont?

Q.: Yes, over on the Connecticut River. We think it is a very beautiful town.

A.: Yes, it is, I am told.

Q.: In your drives, how far do you drive every day?

A.: I am out anywhere from half an hour to an hour.

Q.: Do you feel refreshed? Why do you go to drive?

A.: Yes, it is a pleasant recreation. It keeps me away from my desk.

Q.: Do you feel refreshed when you come back?

A.: Yes.

Q.: You don't leave your home here; at least you don't go out of town, or out of the city anywhere?

A.: No.

Q.: Would you have sufficient strength, do you think, to take the train for Boston? Could you do that?

A.: I could, but I should not wish to undertake it because I have so much resting upon me here to do.

Q.: I see. How many hours in the day do you work in an intellectual way? How many hours in the day do you keep your mind upon your work?

A.: Well, I rise in the morning early and have few hours during the day when I am not at work, and I have the care of the house as much as I ever did.

Q.: Now, your intellectual work, or your work in connection with your subject. Do you write? Are you writing? Do you write letters nowadays?

A.: I write them or dictate them. Others seldom write letters for me, save through dictation; then I look them over and see if they are right.

Q.: You look them over yourself?

A.: Yes, I do.

Q.: Is that invariable? Don't you ever let letters go away from you without that?

A.: I do not when they pertain to business of my own.

Q.: Is that so with regard to your property affairs, that you look over the letters before they are sent away?

A.: Yes, unless I know not when they are written.

Q.: My attention is called to your last answer. I asked you if you looked over your letters pertaining to your property matters and you said you did, unless they wrote letters when you didn't know about them.

A.: I am answering you there about my action before I constituted the trusteeship.

Q.: Yes, but I suppose you have more or less business now, don't you, of a financial character?

A.: Yes.

Q.: But the large responsibility you put upon your trustees?

A.: Yes. Mr. Fernald here is the Superintendent of the Old Folks' Home; he is a good man to take care of me, is he not?

Q.: Yes, I know him.

A.: And I know Henry M. Baker, my cousin, and I certainly know Archibald McLellan, and a better man we do not need to have. Now, I am thinking why cannot we have all this in love and unity and good will to man?

Q.: It is. Do you read more or less, Mrs. Eddy?

A.: Indeed I do.

Q.: You do?

A.: Every chance I get, for a rest.

Q.: Are you fond of music?

A.: I used to be exceedingly, and I have an artificial singer in my house. You know what I mean by that. I will have them show it to you in the vestibule. (*Ringing bell for attendant, who responds promptly.*)

MRS. EDDY *to the attendant:* Tell Mr. Frye to come to me.

A. (THE ATTENDANT): Yes.

MRS. EDDY: It will imitate a voice.

Q.: Were you musical in your younger days?

A.: Yes, I never was taught, but all the other members of the family were, and yet I would compose music.

(Mr. Frye came in at this point and was introduced to the Board of Masters.)

MRS. EDDY: Mr. Frye, I want you to show them my artificial singer.

MR. FRYE: Yes. It is a graphophone, gentlemen.

Q. (by JUDGE ALDRICH): I want to say before going that my mother is still living and she is eighty-seven years of age.

A.: Give my love to her.

Q.: I will.

A.: God bless her. She is not a day older for her eighty-seven years if she is growing in grace.

Q.: Well, she feels pretty happy.

A.: I have no doubt she is. I mean mere decaying when I say "older." She is rising higher. Decay belongs not to matter but to mortal mind. We do not lose our faculties through matter so much as through mind, do we? Now, my thought is, that if we keep our mind fixed on Truth, God, Life and Love, He will advance us in our years to a higher understanding; He will change our hope into faith, our faith into spiritual understanding, our words into works, and our ultimate into the fruition of entering into the Kingdom.

Q.: Well, I will have to say good afternoon.

A.: Pardon my mistakes, if I have made any.

DR. JELLY: Good afternoon, Mrs. Eddy.

MRS. EDDY: Excuse my sitting; come and see me again.

DR. JELLY: We do not want to tire you.

MRS. EDDY: Thank you.

MR. CHANDLER: Good-by, Mrs. Eddy.

MR. PARKER: Good afternoon, Mrs. Eddy. I am very glad to have met you.

MRS. EDDY: Thank you. *(To the stenographer)* We have kept you very busy. Thank you for your services.

(After they had listened to the graphophone, a message was brought to Judge Aldrich that Mrs. Eddy wanted to see the Board of Masters again, because she thought there was some-

thing she had omitted, and thereupon the Masters returned to her room.)

MRS. EDDY: I feel that I did not answer you fully; that I dropped my subject before I concluded it with regard to the footsteps in Christian Science. Now, allow me to complete that thought. I got to where I told you that I found it was mind instead of the drug that healed . . .

JUDGE ALDRICH: Let me make one remark. There were two reasons why we suggested we would not pursue that branch of the inquiry any further. One was, that we were a little afraid we might weary you, and the other was that in certain quarters it is suggested that this investigation is an attack on your doctrines, and we did not want to have it appear that we were requiring you to make any statements about it.

MRS. EDDY: Not at all. I shall regard it as a great favor if you will condescend to hear me on this.

JUDGE ALDRICH: If you desire it, we are bound to listen to you—if you desire to express yourself about it.

MRS. EDDY: When I came to the point that it was mind that did the healing, then I wanted to know what mind it was. Was it Mind which was in Christ Jesus, or was it the human mind and human will?

This led me to investigate spiritualism, mesmerism and hypnotism, and I failed to find God there; therefore, I returned to God in prayer and said, "Just guide me to that mind which is in Christ," and I took the Bible and opened to the words, "Now, go, write it in a book." I can show you where this Scripture is in the Bible.

I then commenced writing my consciousness of what I had seen, and I found that human will was the cause of disease instead of its cure; that neither hypnotism, mesmerism, nor human concepts did heal; they too were the origin of disease instead of its cure, and that the Divine Mind was the Healer; then I found through the Scripture that "He healed all our diseases." Also the command, Go ye into the field, preach the Gospel, heal the sick, and I felt there was my line of labor, and that God did the healing, and that I could no more heal a person by mortal mind, the mind of mortals, or will-power, than by cutting off his head. I do not know how to use will-power to hurt the sick.

When people began to talk mesmerism, I doubted it; and I said to a facetious student, "Hanover Smith, you go into another room and see if I can sit here and tell lies enough to make you suffer." He went into another room, and I commenced arguing what they said made folks sick, and I did my best talking it. When he returned to me, I said, "Hanover, do you feel ill?" He replied, "I never felt better in my life than I do now. I feel rested."

A Christian Scientist can no more make a person sick than he can at the same time be a sinner and be a Christian Scientist. He does not knowingly make people suffer or injure them in any way—he has not the power to do it. All the power that Christian Scientists have comes from on High. We have no other power, and no faith in any other power.

I thank you for your kindness and attention, very much.

Findings of
Dr. Allan McLane Hamilton
in "Next Friends" Suit

T HE alienist chosen to question Mrs. Eddy, to study the case, and to pass judgment upon her sanity was Dr. Allan Mc-Lane Hamilton, who probably was the most highly regarded alienist in the United States.

A critic of Christian Science and a medical man who had testified, in court, in his native state of New York, of his own disbelief in the teachings of Mrs. Eddy, Dr. Hamilton was a grandson of Alexander Hamilton, first Secretary of the Treasury of the United States.

Following the collapse of the suit by the "next friends," Dr. Hamilton released his official findings. They follow:

"I have informed myself in regard to the mental condition of Mrs. Mary Baker G. Eddy, and for this purpose have examined a large number of documents and letters, perhaps one hundred in all, and have examined her at her home, Pleasant View, in this city. I have also read the original bill filed by her 'next friends,' George W. Glover, *et als.,* and the affidavits presented by them in support of their contention that she is an incompetent.

"It will appear from the complaint of these people that she is 'incapable of so understanding her property rights as to be

unable to exercise her free and unbiased will with respect to
the same, or to manage her affairs and protect her property
with prudence and discretion against the undue influence, control and fraud of others, and to take charge of and manage the
present legal proceedings.'

"The inspection and examination of autographic letters written by her show inherent evidences of mental vigor. Her mode
of expression is logical and connected. Her construction is admirable, and these as well as the typewritten communications
emanating from her are the products of an unusually intelligent mind. Not only are their contents responsive, but they
show concentration and the exercise of a normal memory. In
several of them there are interlineations, corrections and additions, which convey more fully what she has already said.
In her letters to her counsel, which I have read with some
care, I find that she has returned to him certain ones with explanatory interlineations, and there has been a promptness and
vigor in her replies to his own letters. The handwriting itself is
remarkably firm for a person of her age, and there are no mistakes; neither are there omissions. Her words are well formed,
and although there is a slight tremor, not uncommon in old
people, and possibly because her mind travels faster than her
pen, I do not regard this in any way as pathological. From the
large number of letters appended which I have read, there is
no mental defect indicated. In those written to Mr. Farlow
there is a keen anxiety regarding her copyright, a desire to
avoid the violation of the copyright laws, an appreciation of
what has been done for her by him, certain directions in
regard to the preparation of the literature of the church, and
other matters connected with her daily life and her position as
the head of the Church. I find in the letters addressed to Mr.
McLellan the same kind of intellectual good order, and in fact
there is nowhere the remotest suggestion of mental feebleness.
My particular interest is with the papers written by her in
the period beginning March, 1906, and extending down almost
to the present time. These papers, which I understand have

been prepared or drafted by her, indicate, either alone or together, a good deal of intellectual strength and consistency, and
in this connection I will draw attention to the draft of a trust
deed prepared in March, 1906, and another in February, 1907,
one of which was the basis for the establishment of a trust for
the benefit of George W. Glover and his family.

"I have also read the instructions conveyed in the letter of
February 12, 1907, which were sent enclosed in a letter written
by Mrs. Eddy to her personal counsel, Mr. Streeter, and which
led to an extended correspondence. All these things prove that
she possessed a continuity of intention and much deliberation,
which is, of course, antagonistic to anything impulsive; that she
had good and sufficient reasons in the preparation of this trust
deed; that there was tenacious purpose in continuing to elaborate and carry out her original idea of providing for her next
of kin and in advancing the interests of the Christian Science
Church. She showed an ability to direct and criticise others, as to
her affairs, and in everything a normal amount of will power,
which was exercised in the proper direction. She had the capacity to appreciate details, to correct mistakes, and to see that others
were put right, which implied a power of attention that would
not exist in an individual of weak mind. She possessed a perfect knowledge of her surroundings and the duties and obligations of those who were serving her.

"My visit to her house was made on the afternoon of August
12, at two o'clock. I found her to be an elderly woman of delicate frame, and evidently somewhat affected by the heat. There
was, however, no visible indication of any motor symptoms of
insanity or nervous disease. Her expression was intelligent and
in consonance with what she said and did. She was dignified,
though cordial, and possessed a certain sense of humor which
led her to perpetrate a joke about the so-called 'next friends,'
to whom she referred as 'nexters.' There was no tremor, no
affectation of speech;—and besides a certain amount of slight
deafness, I found nothing the matter with her. She fully understood the nature and object of my visit, and was willing, as long

as she could, to answer my questions. In doing so she did not
manifest any excess of feeling, but responded quickly and
intelligently when she heard what was asked for.

"The interview was opened by her disavowal of any prejudice against physicians. In fact she said that her cousin was
a regular doctor who had become a homoeopath, and that
her father had believed he was getting crazy because he had
adopted this method of practice; but that he, however, had
taken care of Mrs. Eddy, who had gotten better, and then she
herself commenced a series of experiments, gradually giving
more and more feeble medicines, until she gave those with no
potency whatever, but her patients got well just the same.
She then referred to her exposures of spiritualism, which for
a time she became interested in. She said that she had afterwards investigated various religions, at different times criticis-
ing the older ministers, and finally adopted the idea that infinite love and salvation were universal; in other words, that
she adopted her present faith and that it was the evolution
from her earlier experiences.

"She referred to the fact that she had done and was per-
forming an enormous amount of work, which I knew to be
true. She said that she had no doubt she was going to win in
this matter; that her followers have done much to help her, and
that she would like to have me on her side. In answer to questions about her affairs, she said that she had put her property
into the hands of three trustees, Henry M. Baker, Archibald
McLellan and Mr. Fernald of Concord; that she did this because it was in conformity with her faith, and that no man
could serve two masters, God and mammon. She said that she
would do this to see that her money would eventually go where
she wanted it to go, that is, to the church she had established.
She declared that the trustees of the deed were Mr. Baker, Mr.
McLellan, and Mr. Fernald; that she had chosen Mr. Baker
because he was a good and successful man and to be trusted,
and that the others would dispose of her money conscientiously.

"She stated that she had taken care of her son, built him a

house and furnished it from top to bottom, and had done everything for him; that in February last she had put money in trust for him, and that she had made a trust of one hundred and twenty-five thousand dollars and put it in the hands of 'that honest man (pointing to Mr. Streeter) and two others.' She referred to the fact that many years before, when her husband died, she asked her son to come home, saying, 'You are all I have; come and stay with mother, and I will let you have all my property, all my real estate. Here is a home up here, and mother waiting for you, if you will come and live with me.' But he refused. She referred to the condition in her trust deed that George Washington Glover and Andrew Jackson were to have different forms of education.

"From my knowledge of the case and a careful study of all the letters and documents submitted to me, and from my examination of Mrs. Eddy, I am firmly of the opinion that she is competent to take care of herself and manage her affairs, and that she is not coerced in any way. In fact it would appear as if she takes the initiative upon all occasions. The allegations concerning Mrs. Eddy's belief in 'malicious animal magnetism' are ridiculous. I am convinced that the words are only used synonymously with 'malign influence,' 'malignant' or 'mendacious animal magnetism' and is therefore a *façon parler,* as the French say. She certainly has been subject to sufficient annoyance to entertain the fear that she is to be subjected to further disturbance. False reports that she was dead are among these, and her home has been broken into and valuable documents have disappeared. That she has delusions regarding her son is an absurdity, for only a few days before he brought the suit to have her declared incompetent, she had without suggestion made the trust deed to have him and his family provided for. Mrs. Eddy has no insane delusions, and in print and elsewhere simply enunciates the conventional part of her creed which she and eight hundred thousand believe in. No matter how improbable or unacceptable it may prove to be to the community generally, it is no more remarkable than others that have been before or that exist to-day, and her alleged delusion regarding mesmerism, the non-existence of matter, and the power of healing, form an integral part of very many religious beliefs.

"When asked, she said her property was mostly in bonds; she said that she could not be tempted to invest in stocks, not even in preferred stocks, and that upon one occasion she had taken the advice of one of her students and had lost ten thousand dollars, and that she has never bought stocks since. When asked if she had been interested in mining stocks, she said, 'No, I despise mining stocks.' When asked, 'Has any one ever tried to make you buy mining stocks?' she replied, 'Yes, indeed.' When asked who, she replied, 'My son.' She said that when she bought stocks she always picked out just those she wanted, government or municipal bonds, and that when she selected any, she had a book which she consulted in regard to the population of the chief cities, and that she would find out what the population was before she would take any interest in them, because it was safe to know if the community was responsible. When asked if it made any difference about the size of the cities, she said, 'Yes, I found it did,' and that she always formed an estimate of their wealth.

"Throughout the entire conversation she showed no evidence whatever of any mental disease. She did not manifest any delusions, which she probably would have done had she been a paranoiac, as it has been asserted she was, nor did she once refer to malicious animal magnetism, which I understand was alleged to be an evidence of her state of mind. In person she was neat and clean, I am informed is most careful about the condition of her house, quickly noting any changes that may be made in the arrangement of furniture, books, or decoration; that she gives her own orders, manages her own servants, and suggests the selection of food. During my visit I heard the sound of electric bells repeated two or three times, signals evidently being made, and I was informed that this was in accordance with a code she had established for summoning to her the different members of her household. She pays her own bills, sometimes questions the use of provisions, comments upon the change in menu, takes an intelligent interest in the affairs of her native town and the events of the day.

"Before leaving, she sent for a copy of her book, 'Science and Health,' and inscribed her autograph, apologizing for her nervousness in signing her name."

Index

G

H